SHE WHO DARES

SHE WHO DARES

ALANA STOTT, MBE

ARCHWAY
PUBLISHING

Archway Publishing books may be ordered
through booksellers or by contacting:

Archway Publishing
1663 Liberty Drive
Bloomington, IN 47403
www.archwaypublishing.com
844-669-3957

Because of the dynamic nature of the Internet, any web addresses or
links contained in this book may have changed since publication and
may no longer be valid. The views expressed in this work are solely those
of the author and do not necessarily reflect the views of the publisher,
and the publisher hereby disclaims any responsibility for them.

Any people depicted in stock imagery provided by Getty Images are models,
and such images are being used for illustrative purposes only.
Certain stock imagery © Getty Images.

ISBN: 978-1-6657-2422-7 (sc)
ISBN: 978-1-6657-2421-0 (hc)
ISBN: 978-1-6657-2420-3 (e)

Library of Congress Control Number: 2022909525

Print information available on the last page.

Archway Publishing rev. date: 4/11/2023

TO ALL THOSE GOING THROUGH STRUGGLES:
KEEP GOING, FIGHT HARD, PLAN HARD,
NEVER GIVE UP, AND
GRAB HOLD OF EVERY OPPORTUNITY.

CONTENTS

PROLOGUE

The sound of gunfire echoed through the receiver of the telephone.

As I stood there in the kitchen of the home we had created together, the past five years flashed before my eyes. Would our daughter remember him? Would she remember how he made her laugh, how they'd sang and played together, how they'd danced to "Magic Dance" by David Bowie in *Labyrinth* and mocked me for never quite getting the appeal?

"Dean, tell me what's happening." My heart was racing, and my blood was pumping. But to my husband on the other side of the world, I appeared as I always did—calm and together. You never show them how you really feel. You keep it to yourself. You have to hold it together, because when you fall apart, everything falls apart.

This was my life. I stayed home with the baby and managed our various businesses, including our security company we'd set up when he left his life as a Tier 1 operator with the UK Special Forces. He was away more than he was ever home. And on his return, I was usually cleaning blood off his shirts or hoovering sand and residue from his rolling thunder bags—residue that often transferred to all our own things, such as in an embarrassing episode traveling through airport security when my ten-month-old's push-chair tested positive for explosives, and I had to convince customs that I and my baby girl had no intention of blowing up the plane that day.

While he was on the ground with clients, I was home sorting logistics, typing up security proposals, writing evacuation plans, and keeping him updated with real-time data from various sources about wherever he happened to be in the world at that time. Wherever there was trouble in the world, Dean was usually not very far away.

But this call—it was different. He sounded different. Not scared; that wasn't a sound I would recognize anyway. It was worry, anxiousness, and disturbance in his voice. I had to stay calm and focused. I needed to get as much information as I could, as I had no idea how long the line was going to stay active. I needed his exact location, who he was with, and what the current situation was. Every little detail could prove to be crucial information.

It was 2014 in Libya, and I would actually be surprised if I didn't hear gunfire in the background. Over the summer of 2014, Libya descended into civil war between two opposing militia both with an aim of taking control of the government after Gaddafi was taken out. Arab Spring had brought a new way of life to Northern Africa and had given ISIS a fresh opening on the Mediterranean coastline. Dean had been there before, during and after it all, and the ringing sound of bullets and fireworks was never far away when he called. This time, however, the sound was different. The blasts sounded close by, multiple; and my sixth sense, my gut feeling or whatever you may call it, told me this time it was different.

I knew he was on the ground near the UK Special Forces troops; however, I was acutely aware they were there to observe only. If there was trouble on the ground, Dean would be on his own.

He had allies there though. Dean always made friends with the locals, and they were always drawn to him. If they were in trouble, he would protect them against anything. That was what worried me. The selfish part of me wanted him to walk away from trouble and put us to the front of his mind. But my heart knew different. That was why we fell in love—neither of us was the type to stand back and watch someone get hurt. We were both raised tough. We learned to look after ourselves and look after the vulnerable, and I knew neither of us could ever walk away from someone in danger.

The gunfire was getting louder and louder. I heard the phone drop to the ground as loud bangs pierced into my ear. The sound penetrated my ear so much I had to pull it away to stop my eardrums exploding.

These bangs were coming directly beside the phone. *Is he being fired upon or is Dean the one firing? I can't tell. In this situation, he must keep his focus. Do I hang up the phone? What if he needs me? What if I can't get back through?*

He had other colleagues and business partners who should have been helping him. But as usual when Dean was on the front line taking risks; they could often be found sipping wine and counting the profits.

Who could I call? There was no one. Dean was on his own, and I couldn't hang up.

As I sat there on the kitchen floor, another loud bang came, this time much closer to me. The kitchen door flew open, and a three-year-old came running in, saying, "Mummy, I'm hungry!"

Hungry. Wow, she picks her moments. Why doesn't she understand appropriate timing yet?

But up I got up from the floor, phone still in hand; painted on that big mum smile; placed my hand over the receiver; and asked her quietly what she would like. When you live this kind of life, you have to balance everything. She didn't understand what I did or what I was doing at any given moment in time any more than he understood what the other side was like. I had to keep the chaos as calm and normal as I could for both of them.

I was the mum, wife, businesswoman, housekeeper, peacekeeper, and family accountant. And I had to be all these things at the same time, while not allowing any role to influence the other. I gave Anthony Gatto a run for his money! Everything had to operate together while carrying its individual traits and skills. With Mollie's demands the most pressing priority, I quickly pulled together some snacks with questionable health benefits—though at this point, I genuinely didn't care. I turned on some back-to-back *Peppa Pig* in the lounge and got back to the call as quickly and calmly as I could.

I listened for a while and then heard his voice. "Babe, can you check with the embassy? The Zintanis are attacking the freeway. They have the civilians pinned down in their cars and are firing from the bridges. They have an elevation advantage, and these people have no way to get out. Our guys are not allowed to engage and can only observe."

I tried to gauge which bridge and where they could be, but the gun fire was getting louder, and I need more information. "Dean?"

"They are on their own, Alana." He paused. "I have weapons. I can't leave them."

"Dean?"

"Alana, I love you."

A hail of gunfire rang through my ears as the line went dead. *I'm not ready for this.*

CHAPTER ONE

GROWING UP

I remember vividly one Sunday morning in June. It was cold and misty—typical Scottish summer weather—the morning my early childhood life was about to change. Mum had told me Dad was coming to pick me up for the day, and he would no longer be staying with us.

Up to this point, I'd had a happy upbringing. Financially, we had nothing, but happiness and love were never far away. Our previous home had been repossessed due to the inflation of the eighties, and we now lived in social housing. But again, it wasn't something my mum ever allowed to be a negative in our life; she made every house she ever had a home. I had my parents and my brother. Friday evenings were spent at my beloved Great-Aunt Molly's house. And every Saturday, Molly, who was well into her sixties at this point, would go with me to the market and shop for all the local elderly people before going to Granny and Grandad's house. Grandad was Molly's younger brother. We would fill our tummies with warm, homemade soup and porridge. Money was in short supply, but I never felt underprivileged. How could I with that much love and warmth? I thought those feelings of love, safety, and warmth would never end.

Staring through that window that misty June morning, my little seven-year-old eyes filled with confusion. I looked up at my big brother for reassurance, and he looked down at me and said, "Dad's moved out; they are getting a divorce."

Just like that. He was never one for sugarcoating things. I held on tight to him that morning and wondered what we had ahead.

My father was the love of my life. I was—and in many ways still am—100 percent a daddy's girl. We grew up in an area where so many fathers were absent or unknown, and I saw every day the effects this had on kids. I was one of the lucky ones in a sense. Dad wanted to be in our lives, and Sundays became his day. My dad wasn't one for the deep and meaningful life lessons, survival crafts, or university plans. But what he did teach me—and in many ways, it was a much more valuable contribution to my life—was how to be a pool shark. Shooting pool with my dad on a Sunday was to become the new highlight of my week. Even when I was a small girl, he never let me win or took it easy on me. He knew, in real life, you don't get given chances or an easy ride. If I was going to learn, I was going to learn properly, with no quarters given. This would prove useful in later life.

My mum was a strong and beautiful woman, but she had a craving for love and a weakness for men—and usually the wrong men. Following the breakup of her marriage, she soon fell for a younger guy from work. The rebound relationship became a whirlwind romance, and before long, he had moved into our family home. That home was a three-bedroom apartment in a social housing area in Aberdeen, Scotland. To say my dad was furious was an understatement. This guy was thirteen years my mother's junior, and I think Dad had always thought there might be a chance one day they could give it another try. But Mum had moved on and was ready to live her new life with this guy, a guy she felt would give her the happiness she craved so badly.

Life began to get into a little routine. My brother and I went to school during the week. Finishing school on a Friday afternoon, I would head to Aunt Molly's house. Saturdays were for running errands and visiting my grandparents. And Sundays were all about shooting pool with my dad.

As always, money was tight at home. Dad was a bus driver and gave what he could by way of child support. Mum worked as a receptionist and cleaner, and her boyfriend, as a bartender. The absence of financial security in my life was never a negative to me. It was my earliest lessons in both working for the things you want and giving back. Even at that early age, I always had a side hustle—raising cash both for a treat and for helping others. I did my first sponsored famine around this time and raised almost $100 for kids in Africa. It was all over the news at the time—children starving in Ethiopia. It broke my heart, so I decided to raise funds to help them by putting myself in their shoes for forty-eight hours. It was a natural instinct for me even at seven; someone was in trouble, and I needed to help. This was something bred into me by both my mum and my aunt. No matter how little you had, if you had anything at all, then you had enough to help others.

Finding new ways to earn extra cash was one of my favorite things in life—still is really. One Sunday morning, we went to a car boot sale, similar to a swap meet in the United States. This was always an exciting thing for me. We would collect up all the things we no longer used or needed. My grandad would give us things he had made from old junk. I would spend Saturday evening cleaning them all up and making them presentable for selling. I was eight years old but already growing an independent streak. I made my own meals and looked after myself, for the most part.

Returning that evening, all of us were very tired. I drew the short straw to put the kettle on and make everyone a cup of tea. I issued the acceptable amount of complaints before conceding and headed through to the kitchen with everyone's order. I boiled a full kettle and poured it into our very large, very eighties metal teapot with the brown wooden handle.

Now, I was grown, but I was still only eight and wasn't quite at the right height to be comfortable pouring tea into the cups on our countertop. I looked around for something to give me more of a height advantage. I looked over at the pile of unsold items from the swap sale. There sat the old stool my grandad had made from the scraps of wood he'd found. No one had bought it that day, which surprised me. He was such a craftsman and was always making things, even before it was cool to upcycle. It was perfect to get me to the height I needed to pour the tea. I grabbed it and positioned it perfectly. I balanced myself on it and began to pour.

I poured the first cup barista style, perfectly. Then I stepped over to the left to pour the next cup. I hadn't checked my footing; the stool began to wobble and immediately gave way underneath me. The next few seconds went in slow motion—a few seconds that would dictate the course of the life ahead of me.

Losing my balance, I tumbled to the ground. There was a brief pause and then tremendous pain—pain that, even after having two children and multiple operations, I've never since experienced anything that compares. The whole pot had come flooding down on top of me, covering me in boiling water, as well as the steel boiling jug landing on me. For a brief moment, I was frozen. Call it shock, my body going into protective mode, who knows. I screamed out in pain, collected myself off the floor, and ran through to the sitting room. Mum, her boyfriend, and Thomas were sat watching TV. Mum told me later, the way I carried myself she thought I had been stabbed. They quickly realized I was burning; the pain was clear in my eyes, and the fear, mirrored in my mother's.

Scooping me up, they rushed me into the bathroom and began showering me in cold water, showering down my pink-and-white Minnie Mouse sweater. Mum's boyfriend decided to take it off. In his head, this was the right thing; the idea of getting the water onto the boiling skin was all that was running through his head. But my skin was boiling, secreting, and had already begun to stick to my clothes which had melted into my skin. When he ripped off my sweater, much of the skin from my chest came with it. Mum instinctively soaked large wet bath towels in cold water and wrapped me in them and, bundling me into the car, rushed me to the emergency room.

Arriving at the hospital, it was a bit of a circus. This was back when hospitals in the United Kingdom still had sisters in charge of the wards and a time when these ladies of God were not to be messed with. When I arrived at the hospital, the sister wasn't there—possibly on a break, who knows—but no one seemed to know what they were doing. They started covering me in wet towels; everyone was rushing around as my skin was bubbling in front of them.

It was then the sister entered. "Stop!" she bellowed.

Everyone stood at attention as if they were all trainee soldiers on exercise. She quickly took control and made fast assessments. She was firm and scary, but sometimes that is exactly the type of woman who is needed in a situation of crisis.

I was severely burned and placed into an incubation unit with no contact allowed. Burns are incredibly susceptible to infection, and the priority is always to avoid this by all means possible. My mum was given full protective clothing, and I was placed onto the bed naked in the middle of the room. All the staff looked like extras from *ET*, and I couldn't tell my mum from the nurses.

Sunday was usually the day with my dad. Due to the swap sale, I had missed the day with him. When the ER called him, he was at the snooker rooms and a fair few beers in at this point. I don't know how he felt receiving that call; having kids myself, I could never imagine the feeling of not being there when my kids were in pain. He ran straight out of the bar and jumped on the bus to get to me.

As he boarded the bus he looked down and saw a teddy in the gutter—a disgusting, old, one-eyed teddy. In his currently intoxicated head, he felt he was going to hospital; of course, he had to bring me a gift. He picked up the wet, filthy abandoned teddy; brushed it down; and popped it in his pocket to give to me on arrival. You can imagine his disappointment when the sister immediately removed and bagged the teddy, telling him his kind gift would most likely kill me. Thought that counts, I guess!

He did get the teddy back and we kept "Ugly" for several years after that before she got lost.

Dad was placed in protective clothing and could only stare at me through the window of the glass room.

A few days passed with round-the-clock care. But the doctors were becoming concerned. I had begun vomiting continuously. I was experiencing extreme pains and fevers. At first, these were symptoms the doctors had put down to shock from the injuries. But after a few days and more worrying symptoms, I was sent for tests.

That was when it was discovered I had appendicitis and required an emergency appendectomy. I was immediately booked in for surgery, put on nil by mouth, and preparations began. In very little time, they had me on the gurney on the way to the operating theater.

Unfortunately, on the way, my appendix burst, spreading poison throughout my body. Time was of the essence, and the doctors had to move fast. I was incredibly lucky to actually already be in hospital. If I hadn't been in, there's a high chance I wouldn't have made it on time.

I spent the next four to five months in hospital, receiving skin grafts, working on rehabilitation, and recovering. The main scarring was around the chest and arms. And after a few skin grafts, it was confirmed I would most likely be scarred for life.

Strangely enough, I loved my time in hospital. I was in for a number of months. And little did I know, my hospital schooling would prepare me for later in life. During the COVID-19 outbreak in 2020, there was a lot of concern over whether kids would cope with the aftermath of such a long period of homeschooling and social isolation. I remembered my time in the hospital and knew it would have pros and cons so put that into practice when managing 2020.

This is, by no means, saying the CV-19 situation was handled well or correctly. What I mean is you have to be able to not only adapt but also continue to thrive during any given situation. A bad time should not allow for complacency in life. That was as true with my hospital stays as it was with stay-at-home orders.

Although a lot of the time in hospital I was in pain (getting my dressings changed was the worst, and I avoided it like the plague), the majority of time I observed the nurses and helped them with things like bed changes and reading to the other kids. Every day, I would read to Gemma, a young girl my age who had been hit by a car and was in a coma. I formed a friendship with her even though she had never spoken to me. I would talk to her multiple times daily over the course of many months, and in many ways, I felt she understood me. She was there for me as much as I was there for her. It's strange to say, but I told her so much; I could literally tell her anything. I will always have a special place in my heart for that girl.

What may surprise many is that this was a happy time for me. From a young age, I always found the positives in any situation and learned to make the best of the environment I was in. This one was no different. After the year that had started with Mum and Dad separating, it was nice to have some routine and stability. The food was good, the nurses were amazing, and I got to play in the playroom and watch movies (*Return to Oz* was on repeat). It was, despite everything, a good time.

Mum and Dad would visit. But eventually they had to have separate visiting schedules, as arguments would generally erupt, with Dad feeling resentment toward Mum's partner for allowing me to be making tea at such a young age, Mum standing up for him, and then the two just bickering. Separate visits was definitely easier. My accident wasn't really anyone's fault. But often in stressful situations, people need to have someone to blame, as blame is a simple emotion that's easier to control than understanding and forgiveness. Sometimes, things just happen. It can't be controlled or changed. It just is. Learning to accept that is a tough lesson but an elevating one.

Every day at 2:00 p.m., I had to do a dressing change on my scars. I avoided this like the plague. I think this was the point of my life when I perfected the art of procrastination. I would go to the TV room around 1:15 p.m. and pop on *Return to Oz,* when the nurse came looking for me at 2:00 p.m., I would try (and fail) every day for an extension!

I also, however, perfected the art of stoicism at this point. This was due to one particular day when I was getting my dressings changed and my mum had come in to be with me. It hurt, oh yes it hurt, and I was happy to show it. My mum sat and held my hand; she gripped it tightly and looked into my eyes. Only now as a mum, I can really feel her pain. But her faced changed, and it wasn't pain anymore; she had gone white, and all of a sudden, she collapsed. The nurses immediately rushed to her and got her back up to the chair. The feeling of her little girl being in pain was enough to completely drop her blood pressure and faint—a mother's love. After that, I never cried out in pain in front of people again; even when I was having my babies, you would be hard-pressed to hear me scream.

The pain wasn't the only reason for Mum's collapse. This was around the final months of my time in hospital, and at this point, I was allowed home for weekends; it was like day release from prison for good behavior. That weekend, I went home, and early that Sunday morning, I woke to enjoy my day with the family before getting ready to head back to the hospital. During breakfast, Mum suddenly ran to the bathroom, and we could hear her being sick.

I was worried. What was wrong? But as I looked around the table, I saw everyone else was casually continuing to eat breakfast like nothing was out of the ordinary. "Is she OK?" I asked, concerned.

My brother, someone never known for his tact, said, "Yeah, she's fine. She's probably just throwing up the baby."

Mum's partner threw him a dagger with his eyes across the table.

I looked across to my brother. "Baby? What baby?"

Mum opened the door and came out of the bathroom right then, and everyone looked at each other.

"You're having a baby?" I questioned.

Mum looked at the boys with her unrivalled "mum stare." "Cheers, guys. Well done!" she scolded sarcastically. Mum sat down and told me, yes, she was having a baby, and it was due in January. There wasn't an upset moment for me. This was amazing; I was super excited. I'd always loved babies, and now we would have one. The thought of the new arrival kept me going during my recovery.

The recovery from a burn injury is long and, in all truthfulness, really can be never ending. It started with long summer months in full-body compression garments, which, as a kid, pretty much sucks. You can't do the things other kids are doing. You can't take part in sports, play in the park, or go swimming. You're restricted in these garments for twenty-three hours a day. It's horrendous but a necessary evil. The one hour a day you did get relief was to clean yourself and apply the cream.

Oh, the cream—that did it for me. Every time you took off the garment, you had to apply layers of specialized moisturizing cream. In Scotland, the cream you were given was called E45; it is meant to be odorless, but I am telling you it has a smell. The moist feeling between you and the garment; the smell; the cold feeling when applied, especially during the winter—all of it was the worst. Whenever I smell E45 moisturizer now, I am taken straight back there.

I was an eight-year-old just about to turn nine, a crucial age of development. Your body is changing, your personality is fully forming as you choose your peers, you are more active, and you're taking much more interest in grooming and your appearance. But for me, I was confined. I was in this garment all day. I wasn't allowed in the sun and wasn't allowed to take part in any sports. Instead of playing with friends, I was with my grandparents, who would choose food as a way to comfort you. In their defense, what else could they do? They didn't know any different.

Unfortunately, the food they chose and the portions were not so great. I began to put on weight—a lot of weight. My grandad lovingly referred to it as puppy fat. Soon the "puppy fat" became noticeable in school, and along with being burned and constantly sweating in the pressure garments, I was now teased about being fat.

I began searching for ways to lose weight. Mum and Grandma would leave magazines around. And every one of them had pages of articles about the importance of being thin—"How to Lose 10 Pounds in 10 Days"; "Ten Reasons You Can't Lose Weight"; and, a particular favorite, "Get the Man You Want by Getting the Body They Want." I would flick through these magazines obsessively and cut out anything that had a hint of wording about losing weight.

One day, my mum and I sat down to watch one of those Hallmark-style movies about one of her favorite singers, Karen Carpenter. It was a movie about the short life of this superstar, her childhood, the rise of her career, and her battle with anorexia. I didn't understand what that was at the time, but I got the theme. People had called her fat, and she'd believed them. She was conditioned to believe she needed to be thin to fit in in the industry, so she became obsessive about her weight. At one moment in the film, as it documented her descent into the horrific mental illness we know as anorexia, she started taking laxatives to help her lose weight.

Lacking in cognitive decision-making abilities, my little eight-year-old self was paying attention, and she was excited. She wanted to lose weight, and she'd taken laxatives to make it happen. I had seen laxatives in my mum's drawer and thought, *Yes, this will solve all my problems!*

CHAPTER TWO

ADAM

A few months down the line, one cold January morning, Mum gave birth to a beautiful baby boy. He was perfectly healthy and the most beautiful thing I had ever seen in my life. He was perfect, and this was my life's next curveball; this was when life was really going to change.

Adam, my baby brother, entered my life when I was nine years old, and in a moment, I went from being the youngest child, baby of the family, straight into discovering my first taste of maternal instincts. As soon as I set eyes on him, I fell in love. All new feelings came to me. I wanted to take care of him and protect him. I never wanted anyone to hurt him.

Adam's dad was still very young when he was born and was met with a sudden realization of what life with a baby was like. It was anything but easy. He worked, Mum worked, and Adam was very soon put into my room so they could get rest at night. It wasn't long until it was pretty much a given that he was my responsibility. Night feeds, meals, nursery, clothes washing, baby bathing, and storytelling quickly replaced any last remaining parts of that carefree childhood I'd once had. While my friends all played in the park and started hanging round with boys, I looked after this little bundle.

My big brother was always able to say no to my mum. He knew it wasn't his responsibility to look after our baby brother, and he wasn't afraid to say so. He was able to get on with his own life, growing up and becoming a teenager, but I could never do it. It wasn't that I was afraid to say no. I wanted to. I wanted to be sure Adam was safe and looked after. When this little guy was born, he had pretty much become part of me.

My dad would often get annoyed and argue with my mum. "He is your child," he would tell her. But it was all white noise to me. When I looked into Adam's beautiful brown eyes, he was all that mattered.

During this time, Mum and Adam's father struggled to hold their relationship together. They'd had a whirlwind romance; they'd fallen in love quickly, had to deal with struggling finances and a sick child, and then had a baby. It was a lot of pressure for anyone. So in one final attempt to save their relationship, they took a completely questionable step of buying a house together. They mortgaged themselves up to their eyeballs to move to a slightly improved neighborhood and a house with our own front door. We each had our own room, and I believe they were really excited to make it happen.

Their excitement was short-lived, and they soon found themselves struggling to pay the mortgage, fighting constantly, and eventually separating. After a few more fights, he eventually moved out. It wasn't long until, despite working three jobs, Mum couldn't keep up the repayments on the mortgage. Mum's little dream home was repossessed, and we moved in with our grandparents until we eventually got placed, once again, in social housing.

The house was in a location with a bad reputation; it was a three-bedroom, end-of-terrace, prefabricated concrete house, classing it as a defective home. The day we got the keys and opened the door for the first time, we were hit firstly by the smell and then by how cold it was and finally how it looked like something from a 1970's horror flick. We all looked up at Mum, and she just looked down and smiled. We knew what that meant—she had this.

One thing about my mum, she made the most of any situation and could make a cardboard box into a lovely, livable home if she set her mind to it. So, true to form, she quickly set upon transforming this shabby run-down property. She single-handedly stripped out the carpets; stripped the walls free of their "retro" chains; and sanded down, filled, painted, and wallpapered all the walls. She went to the carpet store for end cuts and sections ready for binning and made them fit perfectly. A clean, our own furniture, and some food in the oven, and just like that, she had the place looking, smelling, and feeling like it was our perfectly new family home.

She continued to juggle three jobs. But believe me when I say the house was always immaculate; she ran a tight ship. We all had our chores, and no one lived in her house rent free—well, except Adam; he was cute enough to get away with it. Pocket money was something my mum could neither afford; nor did she believe in it. She taught us, if we wanted something, we had to go out, we had to work, and we had to earn it.

At eleven years old, I got my first job working in a café at the railway station. I was off the books, so paid in cash; plus, they gave me free food. I always remember the ham and cheese croissant. At that time, this was exotic food to me; I loved it. I was getting paid one pound an hour (less than two dollars an hour), but on the plus side, the food was amazing!

Mum and I would manage childcare together. We worked around her work, my work, and my school. During the summer holidays, I was offered a few weeks' work near my dad's mum's place, which was a three- to four-hour drive from my house, up into the highlands of Scotland. Mum agreed I should take it—the money was the same as what she was getting at the time—and she would manage without me for a few weeks.

I headed up there and worked my little ass off during tourist season in Loch Ness. I saved every penny I earned, and on my return, I purchased my first ever pair of Levi jeans. It was a total indulgence and, as they were "designer," it was not the done thing where we lived. But Mum said, "It's your money. You earned it. You choose what you spend it on."

I firmly believe in Mum's statement here and adopt the same attitude with my daughter now. You can't tell people what they should and shouldn't do; they don't learn that way. The jeans were a good decision; many others since, not so much.

Apart from that trip, any time I wasn't at work or school, I was with my baby brother. Adam was growing fast, and it wasn't long before we entered the phase of the "terrible twos." If you are not familiar with the terrible twos, it is the stage of life when your little adorable bundle of joy switches from a delicate little angel to something replicating the spawn of Lucifer himself. Personally, I would say they are more aptly named the terrible two-to-fours. And if your baby also happens to be a boy, it extends to around the terrible forty-twos! Simply put, Adam was hard work that tested the very limit of your patience every day.

I still had my favorite times, and it was the hours just before bedtime and the moments just after he woke up. That's when the angel would reappear. I loved bath time, followed by getting him into his cozy pajamas and tucking him up into bed, his big, beautiful eyes staring at me. Those were great moments.

It was around this time I first remember Mum getting tired more often. It was very subtle at first, but it was becoming more and more obvious. She was still in her early thirties but would often get exhausted by small tasks. She still worked three jobs and still kept an immaculate home, but she was sad; she was sad and lonely. I would sometimes hear her crying alone in her room when she thought no one was listening. I didn't understand what made her sad at the time. But being alone tackling all of life's battles wasn't something she relished. She felt, just like she had been conditioned to feel, like she needed a man to make her happy, to complete her.

CHAPTER THREE

CROSSROAD

Growing up, I never had many friends. We had moved many times, and in my day-to-day life, I was usually working or looking after my brother. Friendship and fun weren't high priorities. I had one friend, though, my closest friend. She was a girl named Wendy. I met her when I was around seven, and we grew up together. She was as much a loner as I was, and we were tight. We were there for many of each other's firsts in life—first sleepover, first kiss, first time bunking school, the innocent things.

Soon, however, our firsts were not so innocent. I remember the day she "lost her virginity"; this was the term she used. Today, to the rest of the world, it would be called child abuse and rape. She was ten years old and had been invited to a party. At the party, a guy of eighteen years old encouraged her to smoke a joint. She was eager to impress, and when he offered her a beer, she took that too. He was nice to her. Wendy had a lot going on at home—much of the reason we bonded so much, as neither of our lives was easy. People like this guy can spot a girl like that a mile away, and they zone right in. She was particularly easy prey for him, and when she was just ten years old, he stole her innocence.

I remember vividly the following day when she told me what had happened. She wasn't upset, scared, or angry. She was excited.

She thought this eighteen-year-old guy was "the one." I was actually excited for her too, though I remember something always telling me it was wrong. I hold that memory firmly in my mind to this day. I recognize the innocence of children and the people willing to take advantage of that. And it's not an unusual occurrence; it's a common, everyday one.

Wendy and I were inseparable, but she always seemed so sad. The woman I am today would have spotted every sign she was exhibiting immediately. But the little girl I was wasn't equipped. She spiraled quite quickly after this.

I would often meet with Wendy after my work at the fast-food place, and we started smoking a bit of weed now and then. One particularly memorable time was when I had decided I play hooky with Wendy. We went for a walk to the park and lay on the grass smoking weed. This was very much illegal in the United Kingdom and, at the time of writing this, still is.

We moved around the back of the local mall and began rolling a spliff. Just as we rose our giggly little heads, we noticed a squad car sitting right next to us. I had no idea how long the officers had been sat there. They just shook their heads and told us to get in the car. Wendy put up a fight, but I was terrified. They sat us down and talked to us and removed everything we were carrying. They let us go with no charge and told us to go home. We got off pretty lucky there.

To be honest, it wasn't really for me, as I was much more about having energy. My life was too busy to be stoned.

On another occasion, we had both been smoking a bit of weed and chowing down on a lot of milk and cookies at Wendy's home when a friend of hers came around. She had a new drug and said it was amazing. She said we could have it for free.

It was heroin, and we were twelve years old.

This was one of the first major crossroads in my life. Wendy and I had a choice. That moment in life would define us both. I don't care who you are—every person, at some point in life, will be faced with such a moment. You'll come to a fork in the road, and you'll have a decision to make. These moments aren't always easy, and the right decision isn't always obvious, but you have a choice. The circumstances and moments aren't always defined, but the moments define us. I have experienced many of them, and I like to remember them and learn the lessons needed.

At this particular junction, this crossroad of my life, I made the decision to say no. Wendy made the decision to say yes. She made her choice; I made mine. Wendy was my best friend. She was funny, intelligent, kind, and an incredible athlete. But she said yes; this choice would define her life.

Years later, while I was working in a bank, I was serving a customer and immediately recognized the address on his account book. I told him my friend used to live next door to him. He asked her name, and when I said it, his expression immediately changed. I could tell right away this wasn't a positive expression change; it was very much the opposite. I learned in that moment that Wendy had fallen deep into addiction and turned to working in the sex trade in order to fund her habit. I heard she no longer had contact with her family, and she was pretty much on her own. I have always held a guilt there. Could I have forced her not to take that path on the crossroad? Could I have tried harder to save her?

But that's the thing about choices. You can encourage, you can persuade, but a person's choices are theirs and theirs alone—just like your choices are yours. You can't blame others for your choices, and you can't feel guilty about the choices others made.

CHAPTER FOUR

❧❧❧❧❧❧❧

CYCLE OF VIOLENCE

My older brother was now getting to the age where he wanted to earn money himself. I was already working twenty hours a week at the local chip shop for two pounds an hour and paid for all my "extras." Mum paid the rent and bills. Dad's child support paid for the weekly food shop, about thirty-five pounds a week for the four of us. But if we wanted extras like clothes, food treats, or a can of soda, we had to go earn the money to pay for them.

Thomas was now fifteen and wanted to hang out with his friends, have a burger, things like that. His friends all got pocket money, so it was no issue for them. But for us, the rules were if you wanted it, you worked for it. He spotted a job in the paper as a telemarketer. It was a great way for him to make the cash he needed. There was just one problem; he was incredibly shy, especially on the phone. He asked if I would call for him and find out more information about the position.

No problem. I rang the company up and pitched for my brother to get the job. I spoke with a woman, Yvonne. After a bit of talking, I convinced her enough that she said she'd think it over and call me back.

A few moments after I hung up, she called back. And to my surprise, she offered *me* the job!

"Oh, it wasn't for me. It was for my brother," I explained. "I already have a job, and I'm actually only thirteen."

Yvonne told me my age was no problem; the job paid in cash, so no one needed to know. She said I was a natural on the phone, and she wanted me on her team. She also explained the potential earnings, as it was commission plus salary. I was sold. I accepted the job but only with the condition that Thomas was also given a job. She agreed, and we both started the following week.

Back home, Mum, once again very lonely and still unable to see that she was an amazing woman who didn't need a partner to make her whole, fell for a new guy. Gary was a charismatic and confident guy who wined and dined her, making her feel special, and knew all her vulnerabilities. While we had become accustomed to hiding behind the sofa with the lights off when the "provie man" (a term used for the door-to-door money lender in Scotland) came knocking, this new guy had his own business, drove a BMW, and seemed to be from a world outside of our understanding. Mum felt special and enjoyed the attention. He would take her away on mini vacations, he lavished her with gifts, and he acted very much like he loved all her children.

The truth was anything but. He had no interest in any of us. We were an inconvenience, with Adam being his biggest problem. To solve this, he wanted to make sure I was always around to watch Adam. I often had to miss work or skip time with Dad, and he would take me out of school for extended periods so he could take Mum away and leave me with the baby. He was a guy with incredibly selfish needs. He fell for mum, and he wanted her; he wanted her exactly how he believed she should be, and he wanted to mold her into this perfect woman. She couldn't see beyond the feeling of being desired and forgot all the qualities that made her who she was. I know it would have gone against her every instinct to make me miss my education, skip earning, and make me feel the way I did. I already had a pretty lost childhood, and my teenage years were shaping up to be no different.

She would often return home from her trips away in a bad way. I never witnessed marks or bruises initially, but she was always pretty disheveled and upset. I always knew something had gone wrong, but she didn't talk to me about it, and I never really asked.

Upon return from one trip, Mum came back alone without Gary. She told me it was over; she told me they were finished for good and she would never go back to him. Within no time, however, he was at the door apologizing. I heard him begging and pleading, telling her it would never happen again, that it would be different this time. At the time, I didn't know what he had done, but I knew it wasn't good. Soon, he got his foot in the door and himself in her arms, and he was back in the game.

Over the following year, this pattern of breakup and apology continued. I couldn't say exactly how often, but if I had to guess, I would say it was in the dozens.

Saturdays were usually the night Gary took her away for a city break or took her out locally for wine and expensive food. One particular Saturday, they had gone out while I was home with Adam. I was expecting her home, but then she called to say she would be staying at his house. This was not highly unusual and not something I couldn't handle. I got Adam settled into bed, watched a movie, and headed to bed myself.

The next morning, she had not returned home by the time we got up. It was a Sunday, and as this was my day with my dad. I had to call Dad and explain that Mum had not come home the previous night. Dad never really took to Adam; he was the child of another man and wasn't his son. I don't know if it's a Glasgow thing or a man thing. Adam wasn't my son either, but that never stopped me completely adoring him and hurting when I wasn't with him.

Dad also had a new partner, and she was very precious and what you might call high maintenance. She tolerated time with me and Thomas, but Adam, absolutely not. It was a constant dilemma I had. I wanted to see my dad, had a duty to look after Adam, and needed to keep everyone happy. I told him I would just have to skip the day. But Dad wasn't having it. He asked his partner if we could both come round, and she reluctantly agreed.

When Adam and I arrived at the apartment, we were both met with icy hostility. She said hello and then went into the bedroom and closed the door. I couldn't really care at this point. I had still not heard from Mum. There was no answer on Gary's phone. I was worried about my dad. And I had Adam to take care of. Opinions of ignorance could not concern me.

Later that morning while I played with Adam at my dad's house, I got a call from my mum. She was very upset and struggling to articulate. She managed to tell me she was at Gary's house; that was as much as I could understand. She was in a bad way and sounded extremely distraught. I knew she needed me right then.

I was in a dilemma again. I couldn't take Adam with me, as I didn't know what situation I was about to be faced with. My only option was to ask my dad to help me out. I told him Mum was in trouble, and I had to go to her. Dad's girlfriend went into full-blown pouty teenager mode, huffed and puffed, and retreated to her room again. Dad was not happy, but he knew I needed his help and agreed to look after Adam for me.

At twelve years old, I wasn't worried about bake sales or playing with dolls; my worries were who would look after my baby brother while I went to deal with a violent man hurting my mum. I arrived at Gary's apartment within thirty minutes of the initial phone call. As I approached the stairs to his apartment, Mum was just coming out the door. She was rushing; her eyes were red and puffy; and, clearly, she was very upset. I stopped and looked at her, and she just pointed to the exit as she was running down the stairs. I put my arm around her and got her away from there as quickly as I could.

I never saw Gary that day; nor did I want to. She never told me what had happened, and I never really asked. Did I not want to know the answer? Or did I know the answer but not want to admit that these things happened? All I know is that it was the first time I had seen real pain and distress in this woman who I only really knew as being strong and together. She couldn't break because, when the matriarch broke, who would hold everything together?

What came after this was a series of lessons. I learned very early about domestic abuse and what I would call the gift cycle. Everyone who has experienced domestic violence, physical or mental abuse, whether living through it themselves or as a victim by proxy, will have a different experience. However, some things are guaranteed factors in every abuse cycle. This is commonly acknowledged as the three phases of the cycle of violence:

   1.   The tension-building phase

2. The acute/crisis phase
3. The honeymoon phase (gift cycle)

During the gift cycle, Gary would lavish Mum with gifts and loving sentiments, the most unusual of these gifts being a new front door for our three-bedroom social housing home. He explained to mum that, apparently, our solid oak door was not adequate enough to protect us, and he replaced it with a lovely white UPVC door. A few months previous to this during a particularly bad crisis phase, Gary had been on one of his heavy drinking and drugs binges, and he'd attempted to get to Mum by trying to break down our front door. The strong, solid oak door was not budging, and he was unsuccessful at getting to her.

I have often heard how abusive men "just see red," and they have no control over their actions. When the mist descends, they don't know what they're doing, and it's not premeditated. This incident is the reason I strongly disagree with this. Gary was very much sober and in the calm phase when he had that door replaced. Within a matter of weeks of replacing the door, he turned up again. This time, it took just one drug-fueled angry kick for our beautiful, new, expensive door to fall straight through, allowing him the perfect gap to enter the house.

I had not long turned thirteen. My baby brother was asleep upstairs, and my older brother and I had to react quickly. As soon as we saw Gary heading for the door, my big brother looked at me, and we both had a sixth sense; we each knew exactly what the other was thinking at that moment.

Thomas dashed to Mum's bedroom and hid her out of sight. Gary was coming through the broken door. I checked on Adam, who remained fast asleep in the bedroom he now shared with Thomas. It was close to midnight, and I was dressed in a little pink-and-white nightie with little piggies on it. I ran downstairs just as Gary was coming through the porch door. I saw the angry look on his face and knew I had to try and calm him down.

I have always had the ability to remain calm in a situation; even at this age, I knew the only way to defuse this was to work on calming him down. I was always good at this. Even in school fights, I could usually break the fight up by calmly talking and changing the atmosphere.

However, this night was different. No matter what I said, I couldn't seem to get Gary into the reality of the situation. The anger coming across his eyes was like nothing I had ever seen before.

I reached the bottom of the stairs but made sure I was still blocking the entrance to the staircase, my body positioned so he would not take that path. He brushed past me and stormed into the kitchen. He looked around, scanning eagerly for something. I could see he had something in mind, and it was then he spotted what he was looking for. He headed straight for the knife block, grabbing the biggest Michael Myers-style kitchen knife in the stack. He began demanding to know where Mum was.

I looked deep in his eyes. They were glazed over; they were dead. I looked down at the gleam of the knife. Fear and terror washed over me. *Stay calm. Stay calm*, I kept telling myself. This was 1996. We didn't have mobile phones, and our one home phone was in the lounge—way out of my reach. I had no way of calling for help. He held up the knife to me again; he demanded again, this time his voice even louder but almost with an eerie calmness, "Tell me where she is!"

I tell him where she is, and he will find her and kill her. I don't tell him; he could kill me and find her anyway. I thought of my baby brother upstairs, fast asleep. What could he wake up to?

Pull yourself together, Alana, and think.

"Gary, she's not home," I told him calmly.

He looked at me with disbelief.

I had to be quick and convincing here. "She went out with a friend. I don't think it was planned. They've gone into town. It's just me and the baby here." I asked him if he wouldn't mind keeping the noise low, as I had only just gotten Adam to sleep.

He still looked angry, but now the glazed dead eyes were softening; somehow, he actually believed me. I felt instant relief, but I stood firm in my position, firm on the stairs. He began to rant about how bad a mum she was, leaving me to look after the baby, saying that she should be home. I nodded in agreement, keen to get him onside.

He pulled himself together, knife still in hand, and went into the garden. He looked at the sky and began to circle round a hole in the ground where an old tree had once stood. Looking up at the sky, he began making inaudible sounds and shouting her name.

I was standing in the doorway where the door had once been. I wanted to secure the house and run to be with my family. But with no door there, I couldn't. I tried to encourage him to go home, to sleep it off. But he wanted her; that part I couldn't shift from him. I feared Mum would fear for my safety and come down. I feared he would come back into the house. I feared Adam would wake. All I could do was keep talking to him.

I kept this up for what felt like hours. In reality, it was probably ten to twenty minutes. But finally, it started to feel like I was talking him down; a slight air of calmness began to come over him. This was short-lived, however, as, unbeknownst to me and due to all of the shouting, one of our neighbors had called the police.

A police car came speeding up the street, lights flashing, siren blasting. The calmness I had been working so hard on instantly disappeared. The anger came back over his face, darker and deeper than before, the knife raised again. He looked straight at me staring deep into my eyes, his voice cold and ruthless, "You little bitch, you called the fucking police. I'm going to fucking kill you and her!"

I can't even describe my next emotions as pure fear. I would say it was a major mixture of emotions. Sure, fear was one of them. I also felt anger that my work had been undone and sadness at what I feared might be coming. But mostly, my fight mode kicked in, and determination was my strongest emotion. I was determined that this would not be the end, and he would not get to Mum. I remember looking at the police officers, who at this point seemed to be taking forever to get their asses out of the car and actually do something. It was after midnight. I was a child in my nightclothes. A grown man brandishing a ten-inch kitchen knife was ranting and raving on the lawn. And the officer in the front seat of the car was messing around with a notebook.

This was 1996, when victims of domestic violence were still fighting hard for rights and laws to protect them, and the police were still trying to play catch-up. Luckily, as soon as the policeman finally stepped out of the car, Gary's true self appeared, and he ran off like a coward, jumping over fences and running down the hills surrounding our neighborhood, our kitchen knife still in his hand. I will never forget the image of him running away; I can still see it now. He seemed like a frightened rabbit.

I never understood until later in life that for the perpetrators—from domestic violence to sexual assault to human trafficking—it's all about control, domination, manipulation, and power. But deep down, many of them are still stuck in arrested development. They were often bullied or a one-time victim themselves. They treat their victims like this to make themselves feel more important. They are using this situation to turn the tables on their childhood and be more powerful. But when that power is removed, and they are faced with a greater power, they will enter the fight-flight-or-freeze mode; many of them will eventually revert to type and run away in fear.

I never saw Gary again after this. But I later found out that, that evening, prior to him coming to terrorize us, he'd committed another attack. High on a concoction of alcohol and cocaine, he'd had an argument with a friend of his, and during the confrontation, he'd smashed a beer bottle and pushed the broken bottle in his friend's face, accusing him of having an affair with my mum. Once he'd left his friend on the ground, cut and bleeding, he'd grabbed his car keys and told others at the scene he was on his way to our house to kill my mum. The friend had to have over a hundred stitches, and the witness accounts from the evening say there was no reason for the suspicion; it was born purely from a drug-fueled paranoid psychosis.

The neighbor who had called the police came around to the house as the police took statements. It was then she told me the full extent of the abuse mum had suffered. Gary had been abusing my mum the whole time they were together, for years. In one particularly vicious assault, he'd hurt her so badly he'd damaged one of her kidneys. She had never told any of us about it, but I can't say we had never seen the signs.

She'd taken him back every single time. Was it low self-esteem? Need for security? Self-blame? Whatever the reason, when it was about protecting herself, she went back every time. But this time he had threatened and almost brought harm to her children. This was her limit, her breaking point. From that day onward, she cut all contact and never looked back. Gary had fled to another city due to the incident with his friend, and we never needed to see him again.

CHAPTER FIVE

❧❦❧❦❧❦❧❦❧

CANCER

M um was free, but her peacefulness was short-lived. Her health had begun to deteriorate. She was experiencing terrible pains constantly and spent most of her days exhausted. She was referred to a specialist a number of times by our family doctor, and each time the specialist would send her home, telling her there was nothing wrong. The truth was they didn't know what was wrong, and they couldn't clear her colon enough to find out the source of her issues. So rather than keeping her in and investigating further to find the problem, they would discharge her. I don't know if the hospital needed bed space, it was too complicated, or she just wasn't important enough to them. But every time, they would just send her home in pain. This continued for almost a year, with at least nine admissions to hospital.

One very vivid occasion, she had a day of unbelievable pain. My older brother and I tried everything to comfort her, but she was in agony. We got her to sleep, but in the middle of the night, she was screaming out in excruciating pain. We couldn't take it anymore, and we called the emergency line at the medical practice and waited for the doctor on call to call me back.

When they called back around 2:00 a.m., they quizzed me as to how serious it was, and I begged them to come and help. Dr. Maitland, our family doctor, attended about an hour later; he spent about five minutes in the room with her and prescribed her some painkillers. I was standing outside her bedroom waiting anxiously to find out what was wrong.

When he came out, he looked at me sternly. His words to me have remained with me to this day. His time was for "real patients with real problems."

I was fourteen years old and had no idea what to do. In the nineties, you respected the doctors and believed they were wiser and more knowledgeable than you. We didn't have google or an online medical diagnosis to rely on. We had to just trust what *the professionals* said and instead just watch her cry in pain until we could get to the pharmacy in the morning.

The following day, after an exhausting night, we took her back to the doctor's. Dr. Maitland was not available, but there was another doctor on duty, a lovely lady with a caring aura. She took one look at Mum and insisted she was taken straight into hospital. However, she didn't stop there. This doctor came with us to the hospital and told the doctors there that Mum was going nowhere until they found out what was wrong with her. She was forceful, demanding, and was not taking no for an answer. For the first time, someone was taking her seriously, and the relief for us kids was like the world off our shoulders.

So, instead of sending her home, the hospital kept her in and tried that bit harder. A strong enema later, they had cleared the bowel and were able to do the scan. It didn't take them long; they found something. A few more tests confirmed it, and those words that everyone feared were spoken. "You have cancer."

Christmas was just around the corner, and Mum had gone from working three jobs and running a busy house to struggling to find energy to move. She couldn't continue working and was struggling for money. We helped where we could, but the well was running dry, and our small salaries were not filling it. So she cashed in the only thing of any value she possessed, a small life insurance policy with a cash value of around £500 ($900).

All she wanted was for us kids to have a happy Christmas, so she cashed in her policy and put the money toward paying some bills and buying a few small presents and food for Christmas Day. As usual, she wanted to look after everyone and battle through her pain. She invited my grandparents round to enjoy the day with us.

Christmas Eve arrived and unfortunately, she was having one of her bad days. Bad days during chemotherapy are spent throwing up, lying on floors completely exhausted, unable to eat, and if not high on morphine she would be in agonizing pain. I got her as comfortable as I could, waited until Adam had fallen asleep, and then went straight into Santa duties.

Christmas was always a special time for our family. And no matter how many ups and downs my life has had, every year, I still always strive to make Christmas as magical as possible. That evening, I wrapped the presents Mum had managed to get, and I tried to follow the family soup recipe as best I could. With my grandma and grandad coming for Christmas lunch, I wanted to prove I could do this.

Christmas morning arrived. I excitedly jumped out of bed early to make sure everything was set for Adam. Before waking him, I went into check on Mum. I prayed she would be having a good day and she could enjoy Christmas. But as I entered the room, I knew my wishes were unanswered. Mum could not even get out of bed. She had to stay upstairs as we got Adam out of bed and watched his excited face as he realized Santa had been round. He ran upstairs, one present at a time, to excitedly show Mum, and she mustered all her strength to be excited for him.

As he played with his toys, I got working on Christmas lunch. I really did try hard, but I'll be the first to admit, the food, well, it wasn't the best. Mum came downstairs long enough to play with her food and throw up the little she did eat, before retreating back upstairs. My grandparents pulled out their best Oscar-winning performances as they pretended the burnt, bland disaster was delicious before heading home. Thomas went back to his Sega Mega Drive console. I cleaned up, bathed Adam, read him a bedtime story, and kissed him goodnight. I kissed Mum goodnight, got myself into bed, and said a little well done to myself for the small success of my first solo-run Christmas.

January came, and Adam's sixth birthday was approaching. Mum had now moved in with my grandparents in order for them to take care of her. No matter how hard I tried, it had become too much for me— now working two jobs, looking after Adam, preparing for exams, and running the household. I wasn't giving her the help she deserved.

On the day of Adam's sixth birthday, Mum was not well enough to come to the house for the little mini birthday party I had arranged, and we couldn't take him to her, not the way she was. But she did call to wish him a happy birthday. Adam spoke to her briefly on the phone before returning to play with his toys.

Grandma stayed on the phone, and I asked her how Mum was.

"Not good" she told me. "The cancer has spread to the liver, and the doctor has told us she may not be with us in six months," she added with an eerie calmness.

As I watched Adam play with his toys, my heart began to break a little. But a huge part of me would not accept what my grandma had said. I'd watched enough movies to know doctors got it wrong all the time. She was only thirty-six; people didn't die at thirty-six, especially single mums with three kids. She would be OK.

CHAPTER SIX

❧❧❧❦❧❧❦❧

LOSSES

I took on a third job to help support my older brother. He was ready to attend university, and I wanted him to do it without having to worry about the household income. We still looked after Adam, and I still went to school every day—well, almost every day. My exams were quickly approaching, and Mum was getting sicker by the day.

My days would start around 6:00 a.m. I would get up; get dressed; get Adam's breakfast ready; wake him; get him dressed, cleaned, and fed; and walk him to the childcare provider. Then I'd hop on the bus to school.

I went to a private school, which was very unusual for a girl from my neighborhood. Mum never wanted us to attend the local school, and this school gave a certain number of scholarships each year. I'd taken the scholarship exam when I was eleven and had passed, qualifying not only for a full scholarship but also for a sum of money that was given each year to pay for my school uniform and supplies. But with this privilege came the burden of expectation. I knew she'd worked hard to get me this opportunity, and I didn't want to blow that.

The school was accommodating and gave me a locker so I could leave my school uniform there, change for work, and head straight there when school finished. It was three hours at my first job and then straight to my evening job. My older brother would collect Adam on these days, and I would usually get home around midnight before starting it all again.

I was permanently tired—until one day one of the older guys who worked in telemarketing with me offered me something to "perk you up." I had tried marijuana, and I'd said no to anything else at the previous crossroads I'd faced. But this was different. Times were different, and I needed help. He gave me amphetamine, and I quickly realized it kept me awake, kept me functioning, and saved money on food. It made me feel great; it was just what I thought I needed.

The guys in the office were nice to me. They knew my vulnerabilities and played on them. I was so used to looking after everyone else, I craved that bit of attention and to feel someone cared for me. One night after work, one of the salesmen offered me a lift home. He suggested we stop at his place. He was in his twenties, and I was fourteen. And just as had happened to my friend Wendy years before, my innocence disappeared that evening.

Things got tough for my grandparents too. Mum was struggling to get out of bed and was reduced to bed baths. She still had her pride and hated her parents doing this. Mum decided she wanted to go into hospice. The hospice was slightly out of town, and my fifteen-year-old self, still in denial that she was dying, was not making as much effort to visit as I should have been.

One Saturday night in April 1998, Thomas was staying home with his girlfriend, Adam was at my grandparents, and I headed out for a night out with friends. I had a good friend at this time, Louise; we'd met while working as telemarketers together. She was a year older than me, and she just accepted me for me. She wasn't like the other posh kids at school, who looked down on me for having three jobs. She wasn't from my neighborhood, calling me a snob for going to a good school. She also had a tough time at home. And as a release, we partied together.

We partied with the older guys from our work. They would happily take us out and supply us with drugs to make us forget the real world. We went to the local nightclub. I didn't need a fake ID. I looked and acted older than most in the club did. I was soon on the dance floor. It was my release from all the immense pressures in life, just me and the music.

I came home that night at 1:00 a.m., but I wasn't finished and decided to head back out again. I headed out the door at 1:15 and didn't come home until 5:30.

My big brother shouted for me to come to his room. I was thinking I was in for a lecture about the late time. I went into his room, trying to hide how pinned my eyes were. But he didn't yell; instead, he had a look of lost sadness across his face. "Mum's dead," he told me quietly.

The world stood still for a moment, and it took a few seconds to process what he had just said. She was thirty-seven years old. She had passed away at 1:20 a.m., moments after I'd gone back out.

I felt an incredible emptiness, I still had drugs pumping through my system. I ran out of the house with tears streaming down my face. I started to walk. I walked around for what felt like hours. I had grown up in a place many would say wasn't the safest of neighborhoods, but I didn't care. I had never been afraid of where I grew up. I walked and I walked and eventually walked home.

I couldn't sit still. I immediately went to the cupboard and took out all her files and started clearing out all the paperwork. I then worked on the reading for the funeral—all this before my dad arrived at 10:00 a.m.

We had to then go to the hospice, take care of all the formalities, and say goodbye. I remember being in the room with her. She lay there still, her tiny little body finally at peace. They had not closed her eyes, and that image never left me.

I knew I wanted to bury her in her wedding dress. That was a day she was so happy and looked so beautiful. Days before, on a morphine high, she had told me she didn't want "to go into the fire." I had no idea how to decide upon cremation or burial, but the wedding dress and her words made up my mind.

I never realized then how big an impact not having a mum would have on my life. I remember the day of the funeral like it was yesterday. "Rainy Days and Mondays" by the Carpenters played as we said our final goodbyes. I never cried that day; I kept my focus and knew I had to be strong for Adam. I told him tales about Mum and how she had gone somewhere she could look after him properly and how she would always be with him.

Adam's dad and his family came to the funeral. They told me that day they planned on applying for full custody of Adam and moving him to England. I was now fifteen years old and damaged, but I wasn't broken. I was strong. And I told them it would never happen. I refused to accept that they could come back into his life and take him away. His world was here, with me, his brother, school, family. Why would they even consider putting him through more losses?

At thirty-seven years old, my mum died not knowing what would happen with us. But I had promised her I would always look after him. I'd made her that promise, and I fully intended to keep it.

Two days after the funeral, I sat my first of eight exams. I had not been to school for months in the run up to this, and study had not been at the top of my priorities. I sat all the exams and achieved the equivalent of As and Bs on them all. I should have been over the moon. But there was nothing; I was struggling, and I was empty inside.

Months passed and I worked hard to pay the rent and feed us all. I was still regularly taking amphetamine to help keep me awake. I rarely ate, and my weight was plummeting.

The summer arrived, and I received a letter saying Adam's dad and his family had taken their case to the Scottish courts. To the courts, it was a loving and willing father and his middle-class family versus a fifteen-year-old who had no one supporting her case. Even my own dad wouldn't back me, as he didn't want me giving up my life to take care of this kid; he felt that was what was best for me. I never really stood a chance. But I fought. I fought until the end.

Adam's dad won custody of him. My heart was broken. I couldn't bear the thought of losing him. But a date was set for collecting him, and I had to prepare. I received the notification—August 19 would be the collection date. I had to have him ready. His father, mostly absent in his life till this point, would be taking him away to live in England.

I had become very sick. I was eating next to nothing. My blood pressure had dropped. I had bad anemia. I didn't sleep. So, the week before he was due to be collected, I went to the doctor's. The doctor did all the routine checks and broke the news to me that I was pregnant. I was so skinny I couldn't believe it. My periods had stopped, but I had put it down to not eating and laxative abuse that had begun all those years back and had progressively gotten worse ever since.

Upon examination, it was confirmed I was more than four months pregnant, and the dates tallied back to the time of Mum's passing. The "father," a man in his late twenties, was one of the guys from the office. I never knew what had happened to me was abuse or illegal, and the doctor never questioned how I'd gotten pregnant or offered support or help. I was fifteen years old, and now I was seventeen weeks pregnant. I felt completely numb.

The doctor, the same doctor who had shouted at me months previous for dragging him out when mum was in pain, took an unbelievably blasé and dismissive approach to me. He asked me if I wanted to "keep it or terminate it." Just like that. He offered no words of support or reassurance, just laid the decision on me to deal with. How could I keep this baby? I hadn't been able to keep hold of my brother, no matter how much I'd fought; I had failed him. So, I felt I had no choice but to terminate. I had no one by my side, and the doctor impatiently looked at me for an answer. He booked me an appointment at the clinic and handed me the appointment slip—August 18, 1998, the day before Adam was to be taken away from me.

"Anything else?" he said before opening his door to show me the way out.

I checked into the hospital alone and told no one. My best and only friend had just told me she was moving away to take a job two hundred miles away. She left the day before I went into the hospital. I checked in the afternoon of August 18. The nurses started the procedure, and contractions soon began. I remember being told very little about what to expect. I was told I would be in pain, but no one explained what would happen next. I was given a number of different medications to induce labor. A few hours later, it started. Eleven hours of pain followed—contractions and feelings utterly alien to me, and then, suddenly, I felt a huge urge to push. There was no one around, and I was scared and in pain. It was now the early hours of the morning of the nineteenth, and I had been told to only go to the toilet in a bedpan, so I went to the bathroom.

Just then, the urge to push was impossible to resist. Pain surged through my body. And suddenly, this tiny thing fell into the bedpan. My natural instinct kicked in, and I picked it up. I didn't want to leave it in there. I could see it was a baby. I could see tiny little fingers, and I held this tiny, tiny body in my fifteen-year-old hands. My heart filled with pain and sadness.

What had I done? I was crushed. But I still couldn't cry. I didn't know what to do.

The nurse burst into the room and was furious at what she saw. I was holding this tiny body in my hands. She was shouting at me, telling me I shouldn't have done that on my own. I should have buzzed the buzzer. She told me to drop "it" in the bedpan. She took it away, but not before telling me "he" wasn't anything to worry about.

My little boy.

I checked myself out that morning, saying someone was waiting in the foyer. No one was waiting for me. There was no one. I had to get home to see Adam. In incredible pain, extremely weak, and dizzy, I headed to the bus stop. I got home just in time for his dad to arrive to collect him. Thomas was annoyed that I had been out all night, and Adam was excitedly telling me his dad was taking him on an adventure. I was already so tired and emotionally exhausted.

We sat for a while as his dad told me how amazing Adam's life was going to be and not to worry about him. *Maybe he's right*, I thought to myself. *What kind of mother would I be? What kind of person am I? Maybe all this is for the best.*

He packed up the car. I hugged Adam; I never wanted that moment to end. I said goodbye and watched as they drove away.

I turned to Thomas. I guess part of me wanted my big brother to hug me, to tell me everything would be OK. But he was dealing with his own pain, and he had a tribe of friends who were waiting for him, ready to support him. He told me he was going out to meet his friends.

"OK," I said, and off he went.

As the door closed, I sat on the couch, still in the same clothes I'd worn at the hospital, still in pain, still numb. I felt the need to cry, but I couldn't. I sat back on the sofa and closed my eyes and said goodbye to my babies.

CHAPTER SEVEN

※⁓⁓⁓⁓⁓⁓⁓

MAKING CHANGES

The days and weeks passed. The numbness I had felt had progressed to constant feelings of desensitization to the world. Nothing felt real anymore. Nothing gave me joy, pain, excitement; there were no feelings. My social circle consisted of all the people I worked with, older people, especially men. They were the same men who had come into my life when Mum was very sick, and I was very vulnerable.

My vulnerability was not something these "friends" wanted to protect or help; to them, it made me easy prey, and they would use alcohol and drugs to ensure they could get exactly what they wanted. I was fifteen and they were all in their twenties, thirties, even forties. They knew how to make you feel accepted, make you feel one of the group.

Knowing the difference between right and wrong then was not easy. I found it difficult to understand anything in life. When I was fourteen, I would usually go to work straight from school. My school uniform was a school blazer and kilt; it was a well-known school uniform in Aberdeen and unmistakable. My boss at the time allowed me to come to work in my school uniform, as, before I was given a locker, I often didn't have time between school and work to get changed. I was good at my job. I was given a supervisor role at fifteen, and I thought I had some respect.

Our shifts would sometimes go on until 9:00 p.m. And one night, my boss, a guy in his thirties, asked me to go to a party with him, a team celebration. He was charming and would show me pictures of his family. He made me laugh and made me forget about everything that was going on.

I went to the party. When we arrived, he took me into a room; there was no party in this room. I was very nervous. This guy was different; he was my boss, and I looked up to him. He tried to take off my top, but I was still very self-conscious about my burns and scarring, so I pulled it back down. He was OK with this, which, my fifteen-year-old self felt grateful for. *That was kind of him*, I thought. Here was another man using my pain to fulfill his needs, and all my young desensitized mind felt was gratitude that he let me keep my top on.

The following Monday at work, I arrived as usual, and he asked me to go into his office. He told me he would have to let me go, as the head office said I was too young to work there. I was young, vulnerable, and open to abuse. *But* I wasn't stupid. I knew he was worried about what had happened and the potential consequences for him. But I needed this job. I could not afford to lose it. I told him I would not say anything about what had happened if I kept my job. He agreed, and I added a lesson to my life.

I thought about Adam and my mum all the time. I would do anything to distract my mind. One Friday afternoon, I asked my friend to skip school with me and go on a shopping spree. She knew what that meant. We were going for a five-finger discount. At the time, I didn't know why I did this. What I would steal, I never wore. I took dresses in the wrong size and makeup I wouldn't be seen dead in. I later learned that shoplifting is a clinical issue, often associated with grief, loss, and anger. It is a coping mechanism often seen as "filling the void."

A few shops into our spree as I was leaving a store, I suddenly felt a huge hand on my skinny little shoulder. The security guard had caught me. He took me to the store's office and called the police. This would be bad enough, but my problem didn't end there.

Inside the pocket of my handbag, I had a handful of individually wrapped grams of amphetamine. This was purely for my personal use, but it was enough to constitute not only possession but also intent to supply. I was fifteen, but in Scotland at the time, you could still be tried as an adult if you were to turn sixteen before the trial. I was terrified.

Once at the station, the police quickly discovered the drugs. And as my older brother was officially registered as my legal guardian, he was called to attend my interview. He was not interested and did not want that responsibility. He told the police I wasn't his problem and that our dad would have to deal with me. This did not make my brother a bad guy. He just had his own self-preservation to deal with. We had to look after ourselves, and that was what he was doing.

The police called my dad's work. Dad was a bus driver, and a call was put out to the radio on his bus to say his daughter had been arrested.

I sat in the jail cell. I was tiny. I remember the wooden slats of the bed I was sitting on and how my whole body fit onto just one of the slats. I never ate, and I had so much self-loathing. I thought I was overweight, disgusting, useless, and ugly. I had zero self-worth or self-confidence and no one around me to tell me any different.

During my interview with the police, they quickly worked out that I was just a very lost, very sad, and very damaged little girl. I didn't need punishment. I needed help. They let me go with a caution and a small fine. They told me to be careful and stay away from the people I had been surrounding myself with, and they told my dad to get me the help and support I needed.

When I came out the custody doors, my brother and dad were sitting in the waiting room. I will never forget looking into their eyes—there was a mixture of disappointment, guilt, and sadness. I never wanted to be the reason for making someone feel like that, and I knew I had to make changes.

Adam had been gone three months, and my life was spiraling out of control. The pain of losing him was not fading. It wasn't getting any easier. I knew deep in my soul I could not live without him. That evening, I sat at my dad's house, the first time I had ever stayed the night at his house. We sat up all night talking, and he could see how much pain I was in. I told him about the men and the baby, and he knew I was lost. I told him I needed to be with Adam. I was almost sixteen and could legally leave school. He wanted me to forget about Adam and get on with my own life, but he also knew this was my decision, and I would do what I needed to.

I made the plans, packed my bag, wrote a letter to school, said goodbye to my home, and boarded a train south.

Adam's dad's family lived in the most idyllic location. A beautiful tourist area in England, it seemed like the dream place to live. Tourists flocked there in drones every year to take in everything this place had to offer. It was the perfect place to start my new life, with the bonus of having Adam back in my world. This was my fresh start, and I thought it was the happiness I had been looking for. I could see Adam every day. I had escaped the bad memories, and I was ready for the new adventures. Adam's dad allowed me to stay with him until I got a job and a place of my own. I was eating healthier and not relying on substances to see me through the days, and with my baby brother around, life was good.

Although I'd only just turned sixteen, I already had five years on my résumé, so it didn't take me long to pick up work, I got a job chambermaiding at a local hotel. I began socializing with new people and enjoying life. I was a young city girl now living village life, and for a while, I had the best of times.

Working in a tourist town meant working long, tough shifts. This was usually followed by long parties. It was very much a work hard, play hard environment. I was able to see Adam whenever I wanted. I was making money, making new friends, and feeling healthy. Everyone was friendly, life was so much fun, and no one knew my past. No one knew or needed to know all the sadness from before. I was just Alana having fun.

Workers came into the village for short working holidays, so the staff turnover was high, and friends would come and go. There was no social media then. So, if you didn't keep in touch as a pen pal, chances were, you wouldn't hear from those fleeting acquaintances again once they left. There was a constant turnover, which, as someone who wasn't great at forming bonds, worked perfectly for me. I thought I'd found somewhere I could fit in and finally be happy.

For the next year, I worked in various bars, restaurants, and hotels. I washed dishes, pulled pints, and learned a great deal about the leisure and hospitality industry. Living in a town like this was like living in a large version of Kellerman's in *Dirty Dancing*. To the guests, it was the picture-perfect scene. But backstage, all sorts was going on.

I was still very young and living in a very grown-up environment. After I turned seventeen, I got on an NVQ program for bar management. I loved being behind a bar; that thick countertop gave you power and protection. You had what they wanted, and you had the power to say yes or no. I could go into the whole psychology of the public house, but that is definitely a whole other book!

I started working in a local pub glass collecting and waitressing. It was a typical English pub—open fire, real ale, pie and chips on the menu, a pool table, and a good selection on the jukebox. The staff was all lovely, and the head chef and I quickly got close. He made me laugh, and I would get excited to come to work to see him.

After a while, we started dating; the eleven-year age gap wasn't an issue. He seemed to really like me, and that was always enough for me.

The first time he hurt me physically, we broke up. But in no time, we were back together. I still had little to no self-confidence or belief in myself, and this makes you very attractive to predatory types. If I could have learned from my mum's mistakes or had the strength in myself to walk away, maybe I could have avoided the next crossroad in my life. But I didn't, and this mistake was about to change everything.

CHAPTER EIGHT

STANDING UP

Mondays were generally staff's day off in the town. So, as the tourists began to go home, the teams who had been working hard all weekend were ready to party. Happy hours and two-for-one offers were always good on a Monday, and you would usually find the workers were all out daytime drinking.

I was still only seventeen, and all my friends were a lot older than me. We had a few drinks in the town, and then one of the guys suggested a house party. This was pretty standard for a Monday afternoon. There was always a party somewhere. As we arrived back there, the guy I had been seeing went to the kitchen to make drinks with one of the other guys. I stayed in the room with everyone else, chatting, laughing, and having a good time.

The guys soon came back in with drinks for everyone. They were specific about which one was mine. I had had a few drinks in town at this point but, within no time of sipping the drink he had served, I felt sick and dizzy. I stumbled my way up to the bathroom. The next thing I remembered was waking up on the bathroom floor with the door banging off my head. I had passed out in the bathroom, and he and his friend were trying to push the door open, but my head was blocking the way.

They managed to get through the door, and they carried me

through to his friend's bedroom, telling me I needed to sleep it off. I woke up some unknown amount of time later in his friend's bed, and I knew something wasn't right. It was dark, and I was completely disorientated. I called for the guy and asked if we had been in the room and if we had "done" anything. He said no. He said no one had been in the room, and no one had come upstairs. But I knew I could feel something had happened.

I started to panic, thinking of who was in the house. I pleaded with him to tell me if he had been in, and he began to get angry. He took me downstairs and asked everyone in the party if they had been upstairs. They all told me no, and nothing was wrong; I had been asleep, and no one had been near me. I tried to be calm and put it to the back of my mind.

Just then, a friend of one of the guys called him. He asked if she would speak to me, as he thought a female could calm me down more. He passed the phone to me, and I started to speak to her. I didn't really know her; I had seen her around town a few times, but that was it.

Immediately, she could sense the distress in my voice. She dropped what she was doing and quickly came to meet us. She spoke to everyone, and they all said nothing had happened. After a while of speaking to me, she said, "Alana, I think we have to go to the police."

I arrived at the police station that night and gave my statement to the policeman. There wasn't much I could say, as I didn't even know if anything had actually happened. I was then transferred to an examination center, where I had to wait for the on-call doctor to arrive to examine me. The doctor, a man in his midforties, had been woken up to do this, and he didn't hide the fact that he was angry. He was very grumpy and was not gentle at all. This was 2001, and things were still very draconian.

He placed a white sheet on the floor and told me to stand on it and strip. He sat there asking me questions as I began to take my clothes off. He then told me to get on the bed and put my legs up as he placed all my clothes in a bag for evidence. He conducted the full exam—I now know it to be known as the "rape kit." I cried the whole time he was doing it; it was humiliating. The questioning was intense and upsetting, as I didn't have any answers. The police confirmed there was evidence of sexual activity—something I had no recollection of.

All the guys there that evening were taken in for questioning. One by one, they were interviewed, and most didn't know anything. However, when it came to the two men who had who had found me lying the bathroom floor after the drink they gave me made me sick, they both immediately said they had had sex with me that evening, but it was fully consensual. When they were asked if I was awake, they both replied, "No." When asked why they believed this to be consensual, one replied, "Because she's my girlfriend," and the other, a man almost forty years old, replied, "He said it was OK." As I was his friend's girlfriend, and he was given consent by his friend, he took that as all he needed.

I'm sure the policemen conducting the interview experienced a mixture of emotions at this point—shock, bewilderment, maybe even anger, and some disappointment in their fellow so-called men.

The following day, however, after seeking legal representation, both men instructed their lawyers to retract their statements. Claiming the statements were given while they were under the influence and with no representation, they changed their statements and claimed I was fully awake and had given full consent.

The police were very frustrated. They knew the truth, having listened to the full truthful confession the night before. The case was sent to the Crown Prosecution Service (CPS).

One of the hardest moments for me was when I had to make the call to my dad to tell him what had happened. Dad was over three hundred miles away from me. He borrowed a friend's car and drove all the way down. My dad was devastated. He demanded I come home. I stubbornly said no. My reason for being there had not changed, and I wasn't leaving Adam.

At the initial hearing, both of my assailants pleaded not guilty, so the case went to trial. I spent the next ten months in that town during the buildup to the court case. This town thrived on the tourist industry, and the community as a whole didn't like anyone bringing unwanted negative attention to their good, wholesome image. They would do anything to avoid that type of story getting out. Verbal abuse was hurled at me walking down the street. I was called a liar, a slut, a prostitute. You name it; it was said. I couldn't go into stores, cafés, even the local post office. I lost my job, my home, and my friends. All the happiness I thought I had found was gone, all because I gave a statement to the police saying I had no idea what happened that night.

Over the years, there have been so many examples of the prioritization of protecting the crime, protecting the abuser, and protecting the scandal over protecting the actual victims and stopping it happening in the future. Saville, Weinstein, Epstein could all have been stopped a long time ago if the focus was on truth and justice, instead of pride, ego, and profit.

Over the coming months, a number of other girls came forward, and their stories were similar and frightening. Yet one by one, because of the threats and intimidation by the townspeople, they all pulled out and dropped their cases. In the end, I was the only one left speaking out.

The police were extremely frustrated, my dad wanted me just to come home, and my friends (the few I had left) were worried for me. The girl who had taken me to the police station that night had to leave town due to the abuse she was receiving. Her boyfriend, too—one of the other guys there that night who spoke up and didn't remain silent—was also physically attacked.

I have always been a strong advocate for justice and have never backed down from bullying. My whole life, men had been getting away with taking advantage of me. But this time, something had changed. This wasn't just about me; other people were getting hurt. And that was enough to make me fight on.

I remember being about eleven years old when I wrote a history essay on the Ku Klux Klan. We didn't have Google or the rest of the internet back then, so I spent hours in the library reading articles and books on the history of slavery and racism. I wrote a powerful report (which I still have now). And once I had finished, my innocent eleven-year-old mind was determined that, one day, I would end racism. It was so simple in my mind; hating someone due to skin tone was so crazy for my head to understand that, surely, I could make others see the illogic of such a stance too. I still have that simplistic, ideological mindset; I believe in right and wrong, and it's that mindset that would get me through this trial. No matter how much convenient logic people used and how they can try to spin things, truth and justice had to prevail. I needed to believe that.

In the run-up to the trial, my two assailants both continued with their story that what had happened that night was consensual. Although their story changed many times, my version of events never changed. It was pretty simple. I had no idea what happened that night. They took their defiant attitude all the way to the court date forcing everyone to go to trial.

Then on the first day of the trial, one of them finally pled guilty. He was moved to a sentencing date. He later told everyone in town he'd only pled guilty so he would get a lesser sentence. And, yes, you guessed it; they believed him. What a hero.

The other was willing to plead guilty if the CPS dropped it to a lesser charge. The CPS did not want to do this, and they spoke to me, giving me the choice. I decided that day that I had to take my stand, tell my truth. I was eighteen by this point, so I stood up in court and was face-to-face with this guy—this forty-year-old man—and he was directly across from the stand staring straight at me. His mum and fiancée were in the public gallery shouting out the occasional derogatory comment toward me.

I had to relive every moment I could remember over and over again. The hardest thing was not remembering. I wanted to give answers, but I had no idea. Every part of my life was dragged through court, and I was showered in shame. His barrister was a woman, and in all honesty, I did not think she was particularly horrible to me. In a way she seemed actually empathetic.

What I didn't find difficult was telling the truth; you don't need a good memory if you speak your truth. She did attempt to bait me a few times, but I rarely allow people to get me worked up. I am very well known for my ability to keep calm and for being unshakable. I guess that comes hand in hand with desensitization.

After a four-day trial, the verdict came back. He was unanimously found guilty of indecent assault. But as for the rape charge, it was a hung jury—nine jurors said guilty, and three were unsure. This meant we had to go to a further trial.

The problem, however, was the judge in the first trial had asked for the verdict on the indecent assault charge first. As the guilty verdict had come back unanimous *before* the jury had announced it was hung on the rape charge, in the retrial, he could no longer be classed as a person of good character (he'd been convicted of indecent assault). This amounted to him being unable to receive a fair trial for the rape charge. The judge, therefore, had no choice but to throw out the rape charge.

A sentence of twelve months was given to my first perpetrator, and eighteen months to his friend. Both were placed on the sex offender's register. I vividly remember another trial going on at the same time. A novelist named Jeffery Archer was given four years in jail for perjury. He had lied in court during a financial case and was sentenced to four times the jail term one of my offenders was given. This was where I learned that telling lies about cash is classed as a worse crime than abusing a woman's body. The laws written by men valued cash over women.

I knew changes needed to be made. But how? I was approaching nineteen years old, and the entire world confused me. I was driven, passionate, and determined but also had a great deal of self-loathing, pain, and disassociation from the world. I would often turn to drink, and that often made me feel in control. I could never commit to a relationship but casually dated a lot. Anyone who got too close, I quickly pushed away; and I was never, ever intimate when I was sober.

I thought a lot about the trial and all the other women out there who had gone through the same things I had, who were still going through it. I never had feelings of anger or revenge, but I wanted change. I often hear that, when someone is wronged, the immediate reaction is to want revenge, a desire for retaliation, or a need to teach the perpetrator a lesson. But let's say someone shows up late for your party, and your response is that the next time they have a party, you will show up late. What you think you're saying is, "I'll show them." But what you're really saying is, "I want to be like them." By replicating the actions of someone who's wronged, you are replicating the bad that was inflicted upon you. If someone wrongs you or does you harm, consider the reasons, think of the positives and negatives, remove any possible negatives, and make your next decisions based on your own well-being and growth.

If someone yells abuse at me because I accidentally pull out at a junction, my options are to argue back or smile and give a wave to say sorry and have a nice day. The first option brings rage into your life, while the second doesn't allow the anger in and adds an extra smile to your day. If someone hurts you, you can hurt them back. Or you can stop, walk away, and maybe try to understand the reasons for their actions and help them. Or, if necessary—if someone is causing you damage—you can cut the person out of your life. If someone is late for your party, for their next party, show up five minutes early and let them know you appreciate the time they spent planning this party and that you don't want to miss a moment. You'll have replaced the anger and hatred with a lesson in respect and positivity.

Revenge and hatred can eat you up; it is a cancer you allow to infect your body. Forgiveness allows you inner peace and freedom from the pain and anger. Allowing yourself to forgive releases you from a great deal of stagnant negativity and allows your energy to attract more positivity in your world. Once you have this energy in your world, use it to make the changes you know the world needs. My journey in helping others started during that court case and will continue for a very long time.

CHAPTER NINE

PLACES TO GO

Events in 2001 changed the world; with the court case, the year also changed the course of my life. And 2002 was a whole new world—the internet was just coming into its own, people were doing more and more online, and I was spending time looking at images of the world. I wanted to see everything. I remember listening to the travelers who would come into town and hearing their stories. I wanted to have stories of my own to tell.

Now it really was time to get out of this town. I had nothing left to prove. Adam was getting older, and I didn't feel I was giving him anything. His dad had his own way of bringing him up, and we never agreed on it, but he was his dad. I had to let go at some point, and this was the time. It was time for me to go.

I went to a local internet café and found the site www.anyjobanywhere.com. This was the site for travelers who were looking for work abroad. I applied for various jobs at far-flung locations from the Isle of Skye to the Bahamas. The first one that got back to me was a small family-run pub in Skibbereen, a small town in Southern Ireland. Perfect, that would do nicely. A few days later, I packed my bags, and I moved to Ireland. It was my next shot at life. No one knew me. I was starting afresh, and I was going to enjoy every moment.

I worked for a lovely and typical Irish family. Three generations of the family all still worked in the business, which consisted of a pub, a restaurant, and a B&B. The matriarch of the family, Angela, ran the show. She was a small but tough Irish lady; she worked you hard, and you had to put your shoulder to the wheel, but she also looked after you well. She made sure you sat down and ate your stew at lunchtime and took your breaks, no matter how busy it was. She took no non-sense from the punters and demanded respect.

The father, Paddy, was a lovely old man who would sit in the evening playing his accordion while all the locals would sing along. Hospitality service is very important in Irish traditions. It was not enough to pull a pint; it had to be served perfectly, you had to have a conversation with the customers, you only charged when they were happy, and you could be serving six to seven people at a time—so memory was important. You could not be precious just because you were a woman. If a barrel needed lifted, you rolled up your sleeves. If the drunk guy needed carrying out, that was your job too. It was hard work, but some of the most enjoyable years of my life were spent here. I ran the bar like it was my own, and the family would pretty much leave me to it. When it got busy, they would muck in. When it was quiet, they stepped back.

They say you haven't known a real booze-up until you have been to a proper Irish funeral, and they speak the truth there. I remember my first one. In rural Ireland, one pub is selected for the wake, usually the deceased's favorite one. The day our bar was confirmed for the wake after the passing of one of our favorite customers was the day I was to learn how it really worked. The bar opens in the morning, and food is served after the funeral service; the bar does not close again until the last man standing. After hours, it becomes a lock-in and reopens again during regular hours.

I was excited to see how it played out and how long into the night they would last. Twelve hours passed, and it didn't look like anyone was ready to give up. By the eighteenth hour, a few were failing, but the majority were still going strong. By hour twenty-four, I was beat; I needed sleep. I swapped shifts with one of the family. I went home and had a few hours' sleep but was keen to see how it was all going, so I freshened up and rushed back as soon as I could. To my shock, about half the bar was still standing, still drinking, people of all ages. I got straight back behind the bar and carried on working.

After three days of drinking, the last man standing passed out at the bar and was carried home by the team. I sat back exhausted after being taught a lesson in stamina; these guys were hard-core!

The Irish are definitely an all-or-nothing group of people. They party hard, laugh hard, and love hard; but, man, can they fight. I learned this one evening. My shift had begun like any other one; all the customers were having a good time. We had a group of guys who worked overhead power lines staying in the B&B, all Scottish guys, so it was nice to hear familiar voices. The locals were all enjoying some good banter with them when a group of travelers came into the bar. They were all English travelers and were already a few drinks in on their night out.

So, what do you get when you mix a group of Scottish men, English men, and Irish men with a lot of alcohol? A good old-fashioned brawl! I popped through to change a barrel, and when I came back, one of the travelers had gone behind the bar to help himself to a pint. One of the locals scolded him for this; the one person these guys had great respect for was the person who served them the beers, and you never disrespected her. They were incredibly protective of us. I walked back in just as things were starting to kick off. I did my best to cool the situation. However, the whole bar was now involved. With thirty to forty guys in the fray, I was staying well out of it.

The young daughter of Angela, a girl no taller than five foot two and weighing about the same as a small child, decided she was going to jump in. She went straight into the middle and was hit by the group in seconds. *Great*, I thought to myself, *I can't leave her there.*

I pushed passed as many of them as I could to get to her. She was lying in the thick of it all, out cold on the ground. I used my body to protect her and used my best Scottish Gerard Butler Spartan-style voice to tell them to get out of the way. But I was now right in the thick of it too. I managed to get the crowd away from her and dragged her to fresh air. I got the doors opened enough to get all the travelers out.

I and a couple of the more sensible guys had managed to separate the groups and close the doors to them outside. The trouble was, one of the Scottish lads had been pulled out; the guys were howling at me to open the doors so they could help him. I had no choice, but in opening the door, I got pulled out myself. The street was now wild with fists flying and bodies falling everywhere. I saw one guy on the ground and a group of guys kicking him. He was receiving some pretty serious blows to the head, so I ran over to get his assailants to stop. I got down to protect his head, and one guy came over and started punching my arm over and over again. It hurt for sure, but he was just punching the same spot, No harm was coming to me, really, other than it bloody hurt. I turned my head and made eye contact with him. When he looked at me, it was as if he had been in a trance; my eye contact woke him up, and he just went away.

As the sound of sirens approached, the groups dispersed. Unbelievably, there was only one hospitalization. One guy's head was cracked open, but he fully recovered after a few days. It was a new lesson for me about men; they had a lot of pent-up aggression that they really enjoyed disposing of.

Funnily enough, that incident never changed my opinion of the place. I still loved Ireland; the scenery, the hospitality, and the people were all amazing.

The family also had a couple of grandchildren, and they hired au pairs to help with them. I got to know a number of them over the few years I was there. I met a girl named Jenny from Florida. I promised I would visit her there one day. Another, Katya, was from Bulgaria. That went on the list too. I wanted to see the world. I loved being in Skibbereen, but I was keen not to settle down in one place.

I found a new job in Killarney, County Kerry, managing a hotel, bar, and nightclub. The interview was intense. The hotel was old and creepy. The owner here was a terrifying woman. She was very old-school Irish; she wore all black like a ghost from some old horror movie, she never smiled, and she seemed to really dislike me. So, it was to my great shock and surprise when she offered me the job. I suspected later, from what I could tell, she didn't really like anyone. I always wondered what her story was. I knew there was one there but never found out.

This place took busy to a new level. It was like nothing I had ever experienced. The hotel was always full, the bar was always packed, and the nightclub was jumping every night. Four different live bands were playing at any one time, all from different Irish music genres. The place was always packed to the rafters, and from the moment the shift started, you did not stop—exactly how I loved to work, a hundred miles an hour.

I found a room via an ad in the local shop. The house was lovely and easy access for work. The guy lived by himself, a slightly strange dude who had intense OCD. I once left a teaspoon in the sink, and he wrote me a letter explaining the rules of the house. I was never there though, as I worked so many hours at the bar, so his issues never really affected me.

One night, just before I was due to start my shift, I received a phone call telling me my grandma was ill; she was very sick. Grandma had been deeply sad since mum had died four years previously, and she'd had her fair share of illnesses and health problems. I received this call on Wednesday. The next flight I could get home was on Monday. But by Sunday afternoon I got the call to say she had died; I never got the chance to say goodbye.

My grandma taught me that nobody was better than anyone else. She told me my scars would never heal, but they would be an excellent tool for weaning out the bad guys in the world. She wasn't wrong. I once walked into a pub. A guy I was dating had his back to me and the door. He was discussing with his friends how disgusting my scars were, how much they "creep me out!" I remembered my grandma's words; it was a quick way for me to say goodbye to this tool.

Grandma's funeral was to take place in Aberdeen. I decided that was a good time for me to leave Ireland for good and find my next place. I was sad but excited to see everyone again. Adam's dad took him to Aberdeen for the funeral, and he sat in the procession car with me. But this was not the same cute little six-year-old boy who had left Aberdeen four years earlier. My baby boy was angry and filled with hatred and frustration. I didn't know if he was angry with me for leaving him, if he was having problems at home, or if it was something else; he just wouldn't talk to me. He was ten years old, and it broke my heart to see what life had done to him. I obviously blamed myself.

I asked his dad what was wrong. He said Adam was just a moody kid, and he had a good life. I could see that wasn't the truth. But if he wouldn't talk to me, what could I do?

I was back in Aberdeen now and had still not decided where I would go from here. A few weeks after the funeral, I received an unexpected letter in the post. It was from the criminal prosecution compensation scheme. Apparently, I was entitled to be "compensated" for my sexual assault. I never understood this. Why did you get money for something awful happening to you? I was never offered counselling or support, but I received £3,200 as a "sorry-you-were-a-victim" payout.

It was more money than I had ever known, but I wanted to get rid of it quicker than I'd received it; it was dirty money. Katya, the au pair from Bulgaria, had since returned to her home city of Sofia. She wrote to me asking me to visit, so I packed my bags and made Bulgaria my next home. I stayed there a few months, but the wages and money were so poor there was no point in working or trying to stay much longer. I traveled around the country and saw most of Bulgaria before setting off on my next adventure.

I traveled Europe for a while, visiting various places and spending the money before heading back to Aberdeen. My big brother decided he wanted to go on holiday to see a friend in Australia. He was still leasing our family home, so he asked me to stay there while he went away.

When he returned from the holiday, he told me how much he loved it. I could see that look in his eyes, and it was a look I knew all too well. He had seen life outside of the pain and memories. I told him, before he lost that urge, to go book a ticket and get the hell out of here. Our grandad, an amazing man who had lost his wife and daughter in the last few years, helped my brother fund his trip. He adored my brother; he was the first boy in my grandad's life after having four daughters himself. And despite the fact he knew he would miss him like crazy, he knew it was the best thing for him. My brother was incredibly nervous. But together we went to the travel agent. He booked his flight, and within a few months, he was gone and never looked back.

I decided to stay in Aberdeen and keep the house. Adam would come visit in the holidays, and I tried to settle.

I spent a few years working various jobs, including one as a traveling door-to-door salesperson. It was a commission-only job, selling restaurant discount cards. Twelve hours a day, rain, wind, and snow, I was knocking doors. Sometimes, I sold just enough to pay for food and accommodation for the night. Other days, I was clearing £150 to 200 in a few hours.

All the other salespeople were men, a nervous position for me. However, my time in Ireland had given me a much thicker skin, and I didn't take shit the way I used to. I worked hard, made money, and earned my colleagues' respect.

One day, after a particularly tough few winter months, an opportunity came up for a position as a finance account manager at a loans bank. I had no experience but thought, *Give it a go, Alana. Have a little faith.* I went to the interview and got the job. The pay was low, and I was paid over £5,000 lower than everyone else in the same position (they were all men). But I knew it was the experience I needed.

One requirement, however, was I needed a driver's license, and I may just have ticked the box saying I had one. Oops. OK, *not to worry,* I told myself. *How hard can it be?*

Learning to drive in the United Kingdom is not an easy process. Everyone must learn manual and automatic and sit a theory test. That side, the intelligence side, I had no problem with. It was the driving test that was about to teach me a lot about failure.

CHAPTER TEN

LEARNING TO FAIL

My first true lesson in failure was also a lesson in humility. It was my first attempt at my driving test, and if it isn't obvious, I failed. The feeling was alien to me. I had never failed before. I was highest achiever in primary school and had gained a scholarship to one of the top schools in Scotland. I was junior accounting student of the year and chess champion. I sat my exams days after my mum's funeral and passed them all and nailed my theory driving test no problem. But now, I had failed.

I called my dad straightaway, and he laughed. "Oh you're not used to this, are you?! Toughen up. This is what us normal folk have to deal with."

I didn't want to deal with it. This sucked. So I booked straight in for my next test. I studied my score sheet to see where I'd failed and how I could plan for the next test. I was ready for it.

The day came and—*I failed again!* What was happening here? I was failing, and I couldn't control it. I didn't want to be a failure. How did I stop this?!

I studied the score card again. Pages and pages of notes were taken. Then for a third time, I failed again. I was getting frustrated and worked up. I tried again, and lo and behold, I failed my driving test for the fourth time.

Should I just throw in the towel? Were there some people who could just never pass? What the hell was wrong with me?! I knew how to drive. I knew the theory. So what was stopping me?

I had approached the last four tests the same way; I had used academia to assess what was going wrong, and nothing was changing. It was then it hit me. It wasn't my ability to drive. More knowledge about driving wasn't going to help me. The problem was I had no confidence in front of this person sitting beside me. The driving instructors, all men, filled me with dread; they would sit deadly silent watching my every move. This was not a position a girl like me ever enjoyed being in. I was being judged, and I didn't like being judged. But I couldn't give up because of this reason. I couldn't quit because a man was making me uncomfortable. This was a mental barrier, and I had to break through it.

My next date arrived, April 26, 2004, the six-year anniversary of my mum's death. Was this a good sign or a bad sign? As always, I would choose it to be a good sign. I arrived at the exam center and sat on the bench outside watching all the stuffy examiners coming in and out and wondered which grumpy soul would be greeting me. I had prepped my mind ready for it and was employing a lot of breath control as I awaited my judge and juror.

Just then, a woman caught my eye. She had a lovely aura about her, blonde hair like my mum's, and a welcoming smile. She walked toward me, and I moved up as if to give her a seat. "Alana Killin," she said in a soft, kind voice.

Yes, that is me!

"Are you ready for this?" she asked.

Yes! Yes, I am.

I felt at ease. I felt comfortable. I didn't feel judged or awkward, and this lady actually spoke to me. We chatted about general day-to-day things, and she ended up telling me how she was in the middle of treatment for breast cancer. The journey passed quickly, and we pulled back into the center. She looked at me with her beautiful smile and said those words I had been waiting for. "You've passed!"

I hugged her and wished her all the best with her future and treatment. She walked away, and I thought of her as an angel. This feeling was the best, and my four failures previously had only made this achievement and feeling all the more amazing. I had to go through the first four failures to learn lessons. I improved my game; I learned how not to let others' presence influence my actions and that my mindset is just as important as my mind's knowledge. Mostly, though, I learned how to fail and learned that not only was it not a bad thing, but it was also a necessary stage of the greatest of achievements.

CHAPTER ELEVEN

FINDING MYSELF

I had accepted the finance manager position, and now I didn't have to keep pretending my car had broken down. Within my first week, I was given a brand-new company car anyway. So my first ever car was an Audi A3. It set a precedence.

I met some amazing people working in this role, but no one more so than the lady who would go onto become my best friend. Sarah was a single mum from around my neck of the woods; she was smart, sassy, and definitely my type of person. She quickly became a solid part of my very small friendship circle, a place she still holds firm. We have lived many adventures together. No matter where we are in the world, we are never that far apart.

We loved working there together, but the bank started closing branches, and we were offered redundancy. Sarah got a new job, but before long, she was off to Australia to start a new life with her little girl. I was sad to see her go but would never allow her to miss the opportunity. She grabbed life, and I was proud of her.

I took this as a sign that I had also become stale. It was time for something new. I was offered a job in another finance company—this one with slightly better money and prospects. So, I accepted. Within months, however, I realized I had missed the signs. I had itchy feet again. I was in a comfort zone, and I didn't sit well there. So I decided it was traveling time again.

Before I left, though, I wanted to give myself some security, both financial and personally. I was still living in the same house my mum had lived in, so I applied to the local council for permission to buy it—a privilege that had been brought in by the late Margaret Thatcher. The old social housing stock was being sold for cheap, so I got a good deal. This was my first step into property investment. Once the deal had gone through, I gave my notice at work, and I rented the house out. This also gave me some income for setting off on my travels again. With Sarah and my brother both now in Australia, it was easy to decide where I was going.

I traveled Australia for six months, visiting my brother and Sarah. I got to see they were both happy and settled in their new lives, and that was all I needed to know.

Life, to me, was about adventure and making the most of every day. When I arrived in Sydney, the very first thing I wanted to do was go shark diving. I found a place that allowed you to do the dive without cages. The only thing that scared me was getting into a wetsuit in front of the hot instructor; other than that, it was only excitement.

When I got into the tank, the sharks were immediately intrigued; they came straight up to me and were soon swimming around me. I later found out that it was their feeding day. Sharks can go two or three days without eating. So as this was day three, they were happy to see us. I remember the very distinct feeling of being in that tank with the sharks—so peaceful, so serene, and so safe. I had never feared animals. I am not stupid with them either; it's about respect. You always know where you are with the animals; even if that is in a place of danger, you know. You can trust them in that respect. I never wanted to leave that tank, and that experience will live with me forever.

The shark experience, along with climbing on top of the Sydney Harbour Bridge were cherished experiences. But when I would look around, it was always just me. I saw others there—couples and best friends all celebrating these moments together; then there was me, giving myself a wee high five.

Don't get me wrong. I met some amazing people. But at the end of the day, when the doors closed, it was just me. I was very used to being alone. People traveled in pairs and groups and had bonds and friendships that I had never had. Life can get pretty lonely when you have lived the kind of life I had. Trust and openness were not up there with my top traits, so it was easier to just go it alone.

On one evening, I was sitting in a local bar, Manly, just outside of Sydney, and I heard this voice next to me. It was a very familiar accent, the unmistakable sounds of a girl from Aberdeen, Scotland. I turned to see this beautiful, redheaded girl sitting next to me, a big beaming smile, and she introduced herself.

Marion had grown up about fifteen minutes from where I grew up, and we were similar in age. We immediately clicked, and we were both traveling on our own. Over the next few months, we had many adventures together before eventually going our separate ways. I went back to Scotland, and she continued around Asia. Social media was just taking off at this point and we were able to keep in touch. I'm now not only still friends with this girl, but over the past seventeen years, she has grown to be one of my closest friends. I don't think she ever actually knew how important her friendship was to me at that point. She made me believe in myself and never judged me. She was an incredibly special part of my life, and of course, she still is.

Upon my return home, I was immediately offered my job straight back at the finance company, heading up their serious debt-collecting division. Of course, this was a dangerous job. But as usual, I enjoyed the challenge.

I used to look at other collectors' tactics, and it would often leave me in dismay. I remembered being a young girl, Friday afternoons, hiding under the windowsill when the "provie man" came around. These loan companies preyed on the desperation of single mums, desperate for money just to keep their heads above water, money they could never afford to pay back, and they were set up for a lifetime of hiding under the windowsill.

This was now my job, and I saw it differently than did the other collectors. I would spend hours with the debtors, or clients as I would respectfully call them; a lot of the time was after hours, off the clock. I would sit with my clients, trying to work out a way out of the desperate situation they were in. Sometimes, all they needed was those outside eyes to look in and work out what could be done. They didn't need threats and intimidation; they needed support and empathy.

There was a woman who had lost everything because her husband died of cancer. They had no insurance, and when he fell ill and lost his job, their income plummeted; they couldn't keep up repayments on their home. She had lost everything, and now she was being chased for the debt.

There was a young lad who had just made a few silly choices in life. He had borrowed from Peter to pay Paul, and he was now only nineteen with a ruined credit rating and no idea how to pay off his debt. He was scared, and he would lash out when the intimidating male collectors would approach him.

They all had a common thread; they could see no way out, and no one ever took the time to help guide them out of the black hole they were in. I treated everyone equally and gave them all whatever support I could offer. I would sit them down, and we would come up with a plan together. I made them feel like they were no longer alone; sometimes, it was all they needed.

Empathy pumps through my veins, and I was finding I could never switch off from their pain. I loved my job, but after a while, the job was getting to me. Soon, I realized I had to find something new. I tried simple things to invigorate me, like signing up for freefall rappel off the Forth Road Bridge in Edinburgh. It was for charity, and I think I may have been drunk when I agreed.

The morning of the jump, my colleague turned up to collect me at 7:00 a.m. The unfortunate thing for me was I had been partying until the small hours, and the two-hour drive took its toll. By the time I arrived at the jump location, it took all I could muster to not chuck up over all the spectators down below. I decided then maybe a new job would be a better idea.

A role came up as a manager at a local bank. I spoke to a few people and was told things like, "No, don't do it," "You don't know enough," "You're not qualified enough," and, "This is way above your pay grade." It was like being told to stay in my lane, be comfortable, know my limits, and avoid testing them.

This was never me, and I didn't believe in limits. Their negativity was all I needed to reinforce my positivity, so I picked up an application and applied for the job. People will set limitations on you based on what they believe they can achieve. If you listen to them, you are setting your bar by other people's beliefs and standards. Set your own bar, and then aim a bit higher. After three interviews, I was offered the job.

Working in the bank was not easy. I was a twenty-five-year-old blonde girl, with no qualifications and no experience, and this made me a target from numerous angles. Other managers treated me differently, and the staff was often told by senior staff to ignore me. On the first day, my regional manager introduced me to a large older woman with a very powerful presence. He told me she was going to shadow me for a few weeks; she had been seconded to the branch for the past few months while they tried to find a manager, and she was the perfect person to buddy with me. *Great*, I thought. *Some help is always good. I will absorb all her knowledge.*

She, however, had other ideas. She was not familiar with or a lover of the "women supporting women" movement. She took an immediate dislike to me. She told me I was too young and would fail at this job. That would have been fine if she had left it there. But she went on to prove she was right by deliberately trying to sabotage anything and everything I did.

On one occasion, she asked me if I needed help with anything in preparation for my first staff meeting. I thought this was a breakthrough, an olive branch; she was offering to help me. I told her stocks, shares, and bonds were not known to me, and I was getting very confused trying to learn it all so quickly for the meeting. If she could assist with this, I would be very grateful. We entered the boardroom for my first staff meeting. I began presenting to them. I asked if anyone had any concerns or questions. She raised her hand and said, "Alana, can you explain a bit more to me about bonds?"

I couldn't believe it. She completely threw me under the bus—what a complete bitch!

Unbeknown to her however, I had been reading a bit about stocks and bonds, being they were my weak spot. Also, I was the queen of improv! I was able to chat enough to sound like I knew what I was talking about.

I had to grow an incredibly thick skin. She would pull many more tricks like this. But I never demanded respect, I firmly believe respect is to be earned. So, I led from the front, got my hands dirty, solved problems, and respected my staff, and I earned the respect I needed. It was true that, as a young woman, I had to work a lot harder than others to earn it.

At the same time, as I had been offered the job at my branch, the other branch of the bank in the city, which was smaller than mine, also got a new manager. A guy in his forties with the same level of experience as me immediately came in on a salary £10,000 more than I was offered. Within months, he was struggling to run his branch. The job was incredibly demanding, with a lot of targets. But when the financial crash of 2008 hit, being a banker became an incredibly difficult position to hold. It wasn't long till the pressure got too much for him, and he was signed off with work-related stress. I was asked to step up and run both branches until we found a replacement. I was delighted to accept, being given a £5,000 per annum supplement to take on the extra responsibility. Before long, I was running all three of the branches in the city, and we were winning awards.

I was often told to get my head out of the clouds, you can't do it, be realistic. Realistic is another thing I never really understood or took to. Life is short; why be realistic? Why not take chances? Why not risk everything you have for the expectation of getting everything you ever wanted? Realistic, similar to impossible, just means it hasn't been done yet. If you don't try, if you don't push, if you don't fail, you'll never really know. Create your own reality. It was difficult to keep this mindset when everyone around me opted more toward living in a negative energetic space. It wasn't until later in life I realized, to reach your own potential, sometimes you have to remove these people. They could be family or very close friends, and it will be hard. But ultimately, it will be for the best.

I had bought my first house when I was twenty-two and another few since then. I worked my way up the rank in the bank. I worked all day and partied all night. I was comfortable living this way. I was flying high in the corporate world and building my empire. However, I had stopped planning my bigger dreams. I forgot about that niggling inner feeling I always had that I was meant for so much more in this world.

One Thursday evening in 2008, I got a call through to my office from my auntie. She had arrived at my grandad's house to find him on the sofa. She realized very quickly he wasn't just sleeping and had passed away. I rushed round there and walked in to see him peacefully "asleep" on the sofa with his dog, Tanya, loyally by his side, I would never have expected her to be anywhere else.

My heart broke once again. This man was one of the good ones. He was a true gentle giant, a gentleman, and a man who always made you feel safe. He was the kind of man who was always turning his hand at DIY, and I would often find him round my house making things and doing repairs. When my bath panel broke, he went out and picked up some scrap wood and repaired it.

When he met my grandma, she already had a child. It was the fifties, and he was told to steer clear of her. Instead, he adopted the child, married my grandma, and went on to have three more girls. When a friend of his insulted my grandma back in the day, he punched him, knocking him to the ground. He immediately reached down and picked his friend up; took him indoors; and cleaned him up, reminding him never to disrespect her again.

This guy had respect and showed it too. Even in my twenties, he still called me "toots" and still saw me as an innocent little girl. He never knew what had happened to me over the years, and this was just how I liked it. Losing him from my life hurt so much. But in a way, I knew how sad the last eight years had made him; losing his daughter and then his wife, he was a lost soul. He missed them both every day they were gone. But now he was at peace and with his wife and child.

A few months later at work, I sat contemplating how I had settled into this position so easily and that I was fully in my comfort zone. The zone is not a place I enjoyed being in. It's an easy place and a place that is meant to be full of contentment. But for me, something was always missing. I always struggled to find that contentment. When I worked door to door, and it was freezing cold, rain pouring down on me late at night, I would look in the windows of the happy families all warm and cozy, the smell of teatime wafted out the door whenever they would open it, and I always thought, *These guys have it sorted.*

Now, it wasn't the food, warmth, and watching soaps on the television I envied; it was their ability to be happy with that. My yearning for more always exceeded my desire for a simple life. I needed to travel again, but I did enjoy the job. I had to take a chance.

I approached my boss. And despite the fact I was now running three branches single-handedly, I told him I needed to take a month off work.

He said, "What if I say no?"

I looked at him, and he knew the answer.

He granted the leave. So, I went online; I booked a flight to Miami and a return flight a month later from Los Angeles. What would happen in between was anyone's guess. It was May 2009 when I set off. I jumped on a plane to Miami, picked up my one-way rental convertible Chrysler, and set off on a road trip of discovery and adventure some would call "finding myself."

I immediately fell head over heels in love with America. I loved the warmth and kindness of the people, and everyone was intrigued as to why I was out there on my own. I met some lovely people every place I stopped, but I never stayed longer than a day or two.

Savannah, Georgia, was a memorable place. While dining at one of the oldest restaurants in America, the waiter kept staring at me. Eventually, he came over to me and asked me why I was dining alone.

I explained to him about my trip.

He turned and said to me, "'Ma'am, if you were my girl, you'd never dine alone."

I came from a place that had very few gentlemen left, and compliments were few and far between. I never realized at the time, but this encounter set a precedent. It was a small step for me—toward realizing my worth and beauty inside and out—and that was no bad thing. I continued my trip, which took me to some amazing places across America. The South left fond memories in my heart—the spirit of New Orleans, the kindness of Alabama. The West revealed the openness of California and the craziness of Nevada. I never planned where I would go or how long I would stay. Sometimes, I would check into a motel, pick out the next point in the map about 200 miles away, pick a hotel nearby, and then drive there.

One evening, my planning pinpointed me in the direction of El Paso. So, the next morning, I jumped in my white convertible and drove the 250 miles to the hotel I'd booked in El Paso—or so I thought. As I drove through the city, I entered a bridge. I was concentrating far too much on the satnav and not enough on where I was actually going.

I drove across a big bridge and noticed some guards, gave them a little wave, looked up, and, oh, "Welcome to Mexico."

OK, well, I'd always wanted to see Mexico, and it was another country to check off the list. Ciudad Juárez sounded like a nice place.

I drove through the next checkpoint and pulled over to see where the hotel I had booked was. I looked at my phone, which, in 2009, was still a pay-as-you-go phone. I had crossed borders and crossed the country.

Then it happened. "Searching for signals." This phone would not work in Mexico. So, now I had no signal, no idea where I was going and no idea how to speak the language. I was also blissfully unaware of the unfortunate drug war that was raging in Mexico or that Juarez was delightfully known as the murder capital of the world. So, we now have a Scottish blonde in a white convertible sports car, on her own, in a city plagued by drugs and murder, no phone, and no idea where she was going. What could go wrong?!

I decided to just drive and try to find the hotel I'd originally booked. I knew it couldn't be far, as it had been very close when I'd still had signal, and I had a vague recollection of the route. I drove into the city center.

I'd never seen anything like it. It was so busy, so fast, and so confusing I thought I would never find my way. I channeled, the force, my higher powers, and a few prayers and kept driving. By some wild miracle, there ahead of me was a sign for the hotel. I drove up to the gates very pleased with myself. As I approached, I noticed soldiers approaching me. They started shouting at me, and then one pointed a gun through my window. They were both shouting in Spanish, and I eventually got them to understand I was staying at the hotel that night.

They allowed me in, and I parked up the car. I figured it was maybe just the way in Mexico, armed soldiers at the gates.

I checked into the hotel, and the woman at the desk was convinced I was a journalist. When I explained I was a tourist, she told me to have my sleep and then get back in my car in the morning and get out of town ASAP. She explained the president of Mexico was staying in the hotel that evening, and this was why the hotel was so heavily guarded. She told me about the troubles in Mexico and, in particular, Juarez and explained it was not a safe place to be. It was too dark to leave tonight, but I should get out when morning came.

I have to admit, I found it a bit exciting, and I was pretty pleased with myself; despite not speaking the language or knowing anything about the place, I'd pretty much breezed my way into the hotel. And at dinner that evening, I was sat in direct sight of the president. I am not a Sicario; however, if I had been, he would have been in trouble.

The next morning, after a lovely Mexican breakfast, I hot tailed it out of there. As I approached the US border, I saw in the cold light of day what Juarez was really like, and I was very much looking forward to getting back into the United States of America. Mexico is an absolutely beautiful, friendly country. But like everywhere, it has its trouble spots, and this was one of them.

My car slowly pulled up into the checkpoint and a very handsome US border patrol guy pulled me aside and started questioning me about my trip to Mexico. The conversation basically went like this:

> "So, ma'am, you drove into Juarez, the most danger-
> ous city in the world, by accident, stayed one night,
> and traveled back?"

> "Yes, officer." By this point, I wasn't altogether con-
> vinced myself.

Needless to say, he was highly suspicious of the possibility of me being a drug mule, and I reckon if he had the option, he would have bet his house on finding a huge stash of Colombia's finest stuffed under the seats of my ride.

He quickly called in the dogs, and for the next two hours they pulled apart my car and went through all my cases. My underwear was sifted through and sniffed by lovely canine troupers and a vast number of guards, all eager to find my major reason for my day-trip to Mexico. I actually felt sorry for them when they found nothing.

My lovely handsome guard began chatting with me towards the end, and once it was confirmed I was not the next Pablo Escobar, the officer gave me a telling off. He followed this by a request for me to stay in El Paso for the evening so he could take me for dinner. Even though this would definitely be a great "how-I-met-your-mother" story, the sheer embarrassment of the past few hours made me want to get out of there as quickly as I possibly could and never return. So, this would be one love story that was just not meant to be.

I spent the few days before memorial weekend in Las Vegas, leaving for LA on Friday. What's funny is my future husband was actually in Vegas the day after I left, and we had a sliding door moment, missing our first chance for an encounter. I partied with the Playboy Bunnies in Vegas and was invited to the white party at the Playboy Mansion. I never did go to the party, but I'm sure it would have been a great night.

I spent a few nights in LA and the final night in Pasadena. I dined in a fabulous restaurant, took my last sip of wine, looked at the stars, and said to myself, *Dream achieved. I'm ready to go home.*

I remember the flight home from LA clearly. I was filled with happiness. I would always look back after this trip and feel I understood what "finding yourself" meant. I had found this inner spirit in me that was going to be hard to take down. I got off the plane, after thirty days of traveling, in a white dress that was a bit worse for wear by this point, no makeup, and looking very disheveled.

A young man approached me and said to me, "I'm sorry to bother you. But I just had to tell you I think you are the most beautiful girl I have ever seen."

Was he drunk? What did he see? What was different about me? What had changed?

That was the moment I realized beauty truly comes from the

inside out; if you ooze happiness, kindness, and love, it shines through to your aura and makes others see you in special ways.

I was back into work that Monday morning and was quickly brought back down to earth with a bang. I was behind the counter in my bank covering for one of the tellers, and a woman approached the desk. I wished her a good morning and asked her how she was doing today.

She snapped back at me, calling me patronizing and idiotic.

I asked her why she would say that, and she said, "No one is that happy on a Monday morning." Therefore, in her head, I was clearly mocking and being rude to her.

It struck me; some people really do love misery. I put it out to the universe there and then to, *Please don't ever let life make me like this. Please let me always see the joy and happiness in the world.*

CHAPTER TWELVE

❧❧❧❧❧❧❧❧❧

FINDING HIM

I carried on working in the bank and, over the coming months, bought another property to add to my portfolio. I was climbing the ladder in my career. I bought myself a sporty little car and felt like I was really enjoying life. One thing was clear, however. I often felt lonely.

I was twenty-six years old and had never really had a proper relationship. When it came to dating, if the connection did go anywhere, I would quickly put up barriers and become cold, making the interested party lose that interest very fast. I had the nickname of "the ice queen." I typically worked with young people. I was only a year or two apart in age from my staff. However, I often felt much older.

Public holiday weekends were a rare treat and meant we didn't have to work Mondays. This inevitably meant Sunday sessions! One particular August public holiday in 2009, I was ready to party. It was one of the girl's twenty-first birthdays, so a group of us planned a big one. A couple of friends and my cousin Steven, who was my partner in crime at this time, threw on our best outfits and headed out. We headed to the nearest pub, and we were straight on the shots; there was a lot of drinking, a lot of dancing, and equal amounts of fun. Heading for the city center, we honed our radar on the Soul Bar, the place to be on a Sunday session.

I vividly remember entering the bar from the front entrance. We had a quick cocktail and shot, but not much was happening. So, we headed for the rear exit. This was the exit that took you to the good clubs in town. We'd all started to head out this door, when suddenly, I had a feeling that stopped me in my tracks; something told me to go back.

"Guys, let's check out the other side of the bar before we go."

I can never explain what that feeling was but can only say it has happened more than once in my life. Call it gut feeling, call it intuition, even psychic ability—whatever the reason, I stepped around the corner, and there he was.

A group of guys was not an unusual sight in Aberdeen, the oil capital of Europe. We were more than used to the three-week-on, three-week-off crew that would rock up and throw their money around thinking they were Billy big bollocks, acting like they owned the place, then leaving town. But this was different. One particular guy definitely stood out for me. Was it his inner beauty aura calling to me? No, I won't lie; it was all about the tattoos and muscle. I was definitely into him, but I played my usual aloof, cool self and pretty much ignored him and ordered another drink.

It didn't take long for the group to clock us. One by one, they approached us and got blown out until this mound of tattooed muscle eventually asked to buy me a drink. My response was to tell him I was perfectly capable of buying my own drink. The girls with me that evening were both very attractive lap dancers, and as they swooned over this Jason Statham look-alike, I played it cool and pretended I had no interest.

With his rippling biceps all inked up, I found it hard to keep up the façade. He was persistent and asked again to buy me a drink. I told him he should stick with the other girls; he told me it wasn't the other girls he was interested in. My first coy smile broke, and I accepted his offer. We had a couple of drinks and chatted the night away.

The guys asked where it was good to go in town. The girls and I looked at each other with cheeky grins. We knew exactly where we were going—the same place we always ended up, the strip club. Funnily enough, this was the one place we could go for an after-hours drink where we didn't get hassled. We knew all the door staff there, the girls were our friends, and no one bothered you.

The group all jumped at the chance. We grabbed our coats and headed off to the club. Whilst there, I couldn't help noticing that this guy, even when surrounded by beautiful girls, could not avert his eyes from me.

We danced the night away, and I walked him back to his hotel. We talked and talked and didn't want the night to end. He invited me in, and of course, I accepted his invitation. His room was probably the only single-bedded hotel room in Aberdeen. We sat and chatted until I got tired. I jumped into his bed and told him he could sleep on the floor. I apparently immediately began to snore, and I'm guessing that was the point when he fell in love with me.

He had to leave early the next morning for his course, so he sneaked into my bag, found my phone, and self-dialed, furtively obtaining my phone number. I woke to a text from him telling me I was sleeping beautifully (I have my doubts), and he didn't want to wake me but wanted to see me again. I was still dressed in my little black dress from the night before, and it was a Monday morning in this city center hotel. I did not fancy the walk of shame in this dress, so I found his jeans and T-shirt and called a friend to collect me.

He called that evening, desperate to see me again. I now know it was likely because this was the only change of clothes he had, and he needed his favorite jeans back! We spent the next four days together; we wined and dined, played pool, and partied. He told me he was in town on a demolition course. He also told me he was a Special Forces soldier. Naturally, I didn't believe him but played along anyway.

His final evening in town, we headed for dinner and then onto my favorite thing to do with a guy like him—pool hustling, letting him teach me how to hold the stick, how to stand, what the colors meant, because I'm just a girl who has no idea how to play pool, because, well I'm just a girl. Then once the mansplaining is done, I go to work and enjoy the fallout.

This guy, though, he didn't want to play for money. He placed a bet with me and told me, if he won, I'd have to promise to visit him at his place in England. If I won, I'd get his watch. I didn't know at the time, but the watch was an SBS watch, one of only 250 in existence; the stakes were high. I agreed, never thinking he would beat me or believing we would see each other again.

This guy was Dean Stott, and he was the first to beat me. And a bet is a bet. He got to keep his watch, and I promised I would see him again.

Dean left Aberdeen on Thursday afternoon. I remember this day very clearly, as it was that day I received a full blow to the face—literally. Not long after Dean had set off, a customer came into the bank and began verbally abusing my girl who was serving him. Now he wasn't particularly irate, but he believed this was how one should talk to women. He was a fairly new customer, who'd arrived from Pakistan a year earlier to work in the oil and gas. I very politely explained to him that he could not talk to my team in that way and that he must honor them with the respect they deserved.

He replied with an explanation that still floors me to this day. "Respect?" he yelled at me. "They are women. What respect?!"

I actually couldn't believe what I was hearing. What year and what country was I in? Once again, I explained very politely that all my staff, regardless of age, gender, race, or religion, deserved to be and would be treated with respect. If he was unable to comply with this, he would no longer be welcome in the bank.

He demanded to speak to the manager.

"I am the manager, sir," I said in a similar tone to the countless other times a man had said this to me.

He looked me up and down and sneered. "You can't be the manager. Where is the man?"

Well, mate, in that context, it looks like I am the man, and I have had just about enough of you. It was time for him to leave. "Sir, I am going to politely ask you to leave. We are no longer willing to serve you today. You may return to the branch when you are willing to treat my staff with the respect they deserve."

He told me that would never happen, and I had no authority to tell him what to do. After one more ignored warning, I instructed the young girl he had abused to close his account and issue him a check for his balance.

He persisted with his explanation (which I believe he firmly believed) that, as a woman, I had no authority—that was until I presented him with his closing paperwork and the check with his final balance. I asked him to leave the bank and advised him he was no longer welcome to bank with us. He refused and was advised that I did not want to involve the police, but I would if I had to.

The staff, both male and female, were delighted with these actions, as up to this point, they had previously been told that the customer always came first and to always look after them, even when they are rude. This customer had been abusing the staff for a long time. His behavior, along with that of a number of other customers, had gone unchecked. One girl had even had a stapler thrown at her head, and the customer was not reported, as he had a very high balance. This was never going to be acceptable to me. A person should be able to come to work and be safe and respected at all times, regardless of gender or how rich the customer was!

I handed the customer all his documents and advised him it was time to leave. He looked at me with a very sinister look in his eyes. I asked what he would like me to do with his card. He quickly snatched the card from my hand, and before I knew what was happening, he rapidly punched his fist into my face. His bank card was still in his hand, and it cut me straight across my lip; blood immediately started to flow.

I turned away, and the whole branch stood still staring at me. The bank hierarchy had drummed into us during many training sessions that we must never get physical with a client; even if they hit first, any retaliation would result in a job loss. But when pain and anger combine, it's very difficult to keep your cool, and it crossed my mind that I was on my own, with no idea what this guy's next action would be.

But just as quick as that thought crossed my mind, Virendra, a personal banker from India jumped up and got straight between us, stopping him from coming at me again. Another colleague called the police. While we waited for the police to arrive, the guy did not leave the bank. Instead, he stood firm, saying he was well within his rights to do what he'd done. Even when the police arrived, he was adamant he was in the right.

The police arrived, and after speaking with him, they told me that the "gentleman" was sorry and that any charges would result in him losing his job, as he was just here on a working visa with an oil company. The police advised me to let him off, as he didn't mean it and was sorry.

I stood there, with a burst lip and blood on my clothes. I knew he had no remorse whatsoever but felt incredible pressure by the police to leave it. They clearly didn't want the paperwork and didn't see the incident as a serious one. I agreed not to press charges as it was only me who had been hurt. I later regretted this, as I thought of the other women who he would encounter who didn't have witnesses or others defending them.

Dean, the guy I had just spent four days with, had only just left, and he called me to tell me he was already missing me. I answered by telling him what had just happened. He was determined he was turning around and coming back to sort this out. I told him that was very kind, but I was more than capable of looking after myself. He agreed but told me he didn't want me doing it on my own anymore, and maybe I could meet him halfway.

"Maybe," I said.

"Just remember," he said, "you lost the bet."

A bet's a bet, and I lived up to my promise. Within the next few months, he had visited me again in Aberdeen, and I visited him down south. What I remember most about my first night out with him and his friends at camp, his Special Forces friends, was the politeness and manners they afforded to the women. Despite being a group of squaddies, when they were in my company, no one cursed or used offensive conversation. It always makes me laugh when I watch reality TV shows or movies with Special Forces guys in them; they are constantly shouting and cursing. I personally know a lot of these guys, and I never actually heard any of them say a rude word, not in front of me. How they're portrayed on screen just wasn't how they behaved in reality. They wouldn't let me buy a drink, and they were very protective. This was very alien to me. I was used to men with very little respect for women or girls and had come to expect that kind of behavior. It was incredibly hard for me to succumb to this new dynamic; I was very used to having the power and control; however, it felt nice. What was wrong with a bit of chivalry? Sure, I could buy the drinks and hold my own in a sailor's conversation, but—even though my inner feminist rebelled—this was actually a very welcomed change.

Later that evening and out of nowhere, I found myself stopping him dead on the street, I turned to him, looked him in the eyes, and those three words I never thought I would say just fell out of my mouth.

He looked straight into my eyes and said, "Obviously, and I love you too, have ever since the first time I saw you." He kissed me and then carried on walking, like it was the most casual thing in the world.

I still struggled. Could this be true? Did true love really happen? The next few months were blissful happiness, not in the normal way— not in the "I've-found-the-one-I'll-marry-and-we'll-have-a-house-wi th-a-white-picket-fence-full-of-kids-and-cute pets" kind of way. It was more that I'd met someone who thought I was none of those things. I was crazy and wild and had ideas way beyond my station and still believed anything is possible. I had met a man who thought just like me and loved me for that.

***

Christmas approached, and over in Australia, my older brother had met a woman, fallen in love, and was preparing to say his vows. I was so excited to go over and tell them all about my new guy. The excitement was only intensified when, a week before I left for Australia, Dean closed down the opening night of a nightclub, got down on one knee, and proposed to me. He had no ring and no speech prepared. "Meet Me Halfway" by the Black Eyed Peas played in the background and had no real relevance to us. But it was a no-brainer. I loved him, he loved me, and we had felt this way since day one.

I spent the weekend telling friends and family the ice queen, the eternally single girl, was off the market. A week later, I headed to Australia for the wedding. My friends, dad, family, and baby brother were all there, and my excitement quickly turned to dismay. To many, I was still the messed-up Alana. I was not meant to settle down. I was meant to end up alone. I was most definitely not meant to meet the man of my dreams, fall in love, and have all my dreams come true. It didn't fit. It was wrong. It was not meant to happen that way.

I heard it and felt it enough it even convinced me. I called Dean from Australia and told him it was over, it was never going to happen, and it was a pipe dream. I was never meant to be that happy girl whose dreams all come true. Forget it, Alana. It's not you.

I flew back from Australia, and it was a matter of weeks before my little brother would turn eighteen. Eighteen—where had that time gone? I knew I had loads to do, but after a thirty-hour flight I couldn't wait to get home and catch up on the *EastEnders* Christmas special, under a blanket, drowning my sorrows over my lost love.

Landing at Aberdeen Airport, I felt the cold air fill my lungs. I took a deep breath and was prepared for my road ahead. What happened to that guy—the handsome, funny, charismatic Special Forces gentleman? He had run for the hills, right? Negative, ghost rider, this guy loved the chase, and there he stood at Aberdeen arrivals, a pile of belated Christmas presents in hand, a big smile on his face; he was not giving up on me.

My inner child filled with joy. I was bursting. Could this be it? Had I really found him?

Obviously, in usual Alana style, I contained the excited child, walked up to him, shrugged my shoulders, and said, "Hi, how are you?"

He smiled, threw his arm around me, took my bag, and said "Come on, crazy. Let's go home and watch *EastEnders*."

I smiled as my heart filled with pure love. Yep, let's go home.

CHAPTER THIRTEEN

NEXT LEVEL

Now that I'd finally let go and realized it was OK to be happy, things just became easier. One thing about Dean was he was the mirror of me. He believed nothing was impossible, and he believed in the pursuit of excellence. As we'd missed Christmas, we decided to have a late Christmas with the family—my aunt Molly, my dad, my brother, and some friends. I was to borrow a nice big dining table from a friend, and I would cook up a feast and finally get that happy Christmas.

That morning was perfect. The snow had settled. All the food was prepared and ready to be cooked. And guests were arriving in a matter of hours. Dean went to start the van to go and collect the table we were borrowing from a friend, but the van wouldn't start. The weather had frozen something within the engine. I won't pretend to know what the mechanical issue was, but my issue was no van, no table, no dinner.

"Where is the table?" Dean asked.

Why does that matter? It's not here, and that's the problem. But if you want to know it's about two miles north, the snow is waist deep, and the table is solid oak.

"Give me the address and keep cooking," he said calmly.

I had no idea what the plan was, but I kept cooking as he'd said.

A couple of hours later, guests were arriving, and food was ready. I was clock-watching in a big way and starting to get nervous.

Then my brother shouted through to the kitchen, "Alana, come and look at this!"

I ran through to the lounge, looked out the window, and saw in the distance this figure, waist deep, ploughing through the snow with a huge, solid oak table on his head. His tattoo-covered, bulging biceps had never been more obvious. Local kids pelting him with snowballs to add to the mix. He was like a superhero rising through the ashes, carrying the world on his shoulders. *Who is this guy?*

I remember watching him walking through the snow that day, and it was the first moment I really believed that the law of attraction was real. I had dreamt of this character. I'd never settled for anything less. And here he was—someone who shared my very mindset, who didn't understand "can't" or "impossible," who made no excuses and went for it. I felt like I might have met my match. He had walked to the house and then walked the two miles through the snow with this table on his head—a table that I could barely lift the side off the ground. The skin was peeling off his bald head, and his arms were numb. But he told me later he could see how important it was for me to have the table there, so he had to make it happen. I just loved that attitude—the positivity and can-do approach to life.

When you surround yourself with positivity, your own positivity will struggle to stay contained. Having very negative people around you all the time will make even the happiest, most positive person struggle to remain upbeat. I experienced this for many years—surrounding myself with the bad, the negatives, the cant's, the don'ts, the ones who love the word *realistic*—ultimately, the drains. They will drain you of all your energy and your zest and, most importantly, your self-belief. This is not a deliberate act of giving or receiving but more a natural effect of the law of attraction.

The best alternative is to surround yourself with the radiators of life, the go-getters, the achievers, the ones who act, the ones who radiate positivity. You can't help but let your own "I can, I am, I will" flow. Bringing this man into my life had done that.

One evening as we shared some cheese and wine, we were chatting about my career. Dean gushed at how incredibly proud I must be to have become a bank manager so young. I felt the guilt creep in immediately. I looked into his eyes and knew I could never lie to him. I immediately confessed that I was not proud. I had taken the easy option. All this—numbers, banking—it was my comfort zone; it was what I was good at. It wasn't what I wanted to do.

"So, what do you want to do?" he said.

Note the *do* you want and not *did* you want. What I always wanted to do was work fighting crime—serious victims unit, FBI, SOCA, MI6. I wanted to be a crime fighter, to help vulnerable people, and to take down bad guys. I loved anything that helped fight injustice and right wrongs. Truth be told, I still never knew exactly what I wanted. When I was a little girl, I loved to write, and I was obsessed with movies; the art of storytelling fascinated me. I had always had so many imaginary career changes in my head that the only thing I knew for sure was that I wanted to help others.

"That's what I wanted," I started to say, before he stopped me midsentence.

"Want," he said. "That's what you want."

That evening, I came home from work to an email from him with a link attached. I opened the link, and there it was—an application form for MI6.

I called him straightaway. He told me he had spoken to a friend at Whitehall, and if I got the application over to him, he would check it out. It was that easy, and I knew this—I had known it since I was a young child. I always had an inner voice telling me I was capable of so much, yet the inner voice was too often drowned out by a sea of other voices telling me, "Keep your feet on the ground," "Your head's in the clouds,' "Those things are for others, not us," "You can't do that" and *"That's not realistic."*

These days, if you want to get my back up, use that last word; that is the quickest way to evoke one of my speeches on what realism really means. But back then, after so many years of being surrounded by negativity, I had forgotten my inner voice. Still, I completed the application, had a chat with Dean's friend, and sent it off.

The application process was obviously long, with numerous

stages. I got through to stage four before receiving the letter saying, at this time, I had been unsuccessful. I was disappointed for sure. And just like with my driving test, I was ready to try again. However, the letter I received said I could only reapply after two years had passed.

I wasn't going to wait around. I was a girl whose mum had died at thirty-seven, so to me, every second in life counted. I called Dean, and on his next trip, we sat down and discussed it.

"How about going private?" he suggested. "Help people and take down bad guys, our way."

We began to look at options.

Days later, while at my office, I received a call from Dean. "Alana, I have to go away. I can't tell you where or why. But I just wanted you to know I love you."

Due to the Official Secrets Act that Dean had signed to join the Special Forces, he was not allowed to discuss his mission. However, one thing I am renowned for is investigating. I quickly jumped on the internet and looked up what was going on in the world. The main story I kept coming across was the kidnapping of a British couple, Paul and Rachel Chandlers. They were sailing on their yacht from the Seychelles to Tanzania when their vessel was boarded by Somali pirates. This was the exact type of work Dean's team would be sent in to deal with.

There had been a number of kidnappings in the region, and people had been warned not to travel. Their yacht was later found off the coast of Somalia, and it took over a year for the couple to be released. I remember watching it on the news and then a report coming in saying the yacht was found empty. Dean returned shortly after that, and I asked him if this was the task he had been on. He just gave me a look.

What I found very interesting was the delay in getting anyone out to the yacht. Four days went by between the distress signal and the yacht being found. I often wondered if it had anything to do with our prime minister and the president of Somalia being in deep talks in London during these four days. Maybe it was just a coincidence?

Whenever Dean came back from missions, he would always take me on little trips. One weekend, he invited me to Twickenham in England, where there was an annual rugby match played between the Army and the Navy. The whole town prepared for the arrival of 150,000 squaddies and their partners. I couldn't believe it when I arrived—thousands and thousands of incredibly drunk and incredibly happy people were there. I had a suspicion many attended not for the rugby but, rather, for the giant reunion this was.

We were watching the match inside the stadium, and Dean was texting away on his phone.

"Who are you texting?" I asked.

"My mate," he replied.

"He will be outside soon and wants to meet you."

Cool. I was up for that. I loved meeting his friends.

We grabbed a beer and headed out to the parking lot. As I approached his friend, I clearly recognized him. I knew Dean was friends with Prince Harry but had no idea he was at this event. And here he was. He reached out and shook my hand, and his energy was very warm and open. "Nice to meet you," he said.

We chatted for a while, and I remember countless people coming up to him trying to chat. He was very courteous and polite with every one of them. I wondered how he managed that. I had only been there thirty minutes, and it was driving me crazy. Even when people would come over with recording devices that were clearly visible, he remained polite.

My mum had been a big lover of Princess Diana, and as Diana's style would change, so would my mum's, from clothing to haircuts. I remember my mum crying the day Diana died. It was almost a year later when mum also found her wings. When you lose a parent young, you immediately have a connection with others who have been through the same and can understand your pain. That day, the first day I met Harry, I knew he had a good heart. And he was a good friend of Dean's and had a true mate in Dean.

CHAPTER FOURTEEN

❧⸙❧

TIME TO STEP UP

Dean was preparing for his next tour of Afghanistan and had to deploy to Oman for pre-tour training. He took off for Oman, and I used this time as my own mini pretraining. I'd never had an issue being alone or a desire to have a partner with me 24-7, but I had also never been in love. I knew the separation would be hard, and I had to prepare for him to leave for six months, with possibly no contact.

Late one evening, I got a call informing me Dean had been in a parachuting accident and was in a bad way. My heart completely sank, even though this was just a training tour; I remembered that Dean had lost one of his team the weekend we'd met. He was killed during a training exercise, so I knew the possibilities.

Dean was jumping HAHO (high altitude high opening), and his leg had got caught in the rigging line during the jump. When the line pulled, his leg went with it, tearing muscles and ligaments. He was thousands of feet up in the air in agonizing pain, slipping in and out of consciousness. He had to land on one leg, and when he landed, it was clear this wasn't good. He told me he immediately yelled, "Medic!"

He was taken straight to hospital. They tried to air evac him. But just at the same point, the eruption of Eyjafjallajökull happened in Iceland. The volcanic ash caused air travel to shut down over Europe, and we couldn't get him home. Dean was stuck in a hospital bed in Oman, with only tramadol for company.

After a week he called me. I remember the call very well. This was a different voice, a different Dean. "I'm out," he said, "They won't want me like this. I might never walk again. What am I going to do?"

My superhero, my force of positivity, my driver sounded faded and broken. I took a deep breath, and I knew I had to step up. It was my turn. I had to be the strong one now. "Dean, we will deal with this. We will get through it together."

The waiting game was a nightmare; all we wanted was to get him home, where we could work out what to do next. It took two weeks to get him home. He was picked up by an evac plane from Afghanistan and taken to Selly Oak Hospital in Birmingham. I remember the first time I saw him. It was scary. He looked so skinny and pale. He looked sad. His radiation of positivity wasn't glowing anymore. I knew then that we had a long road ahead of us.

We had only been dating for about seven months, and everything had just changed in a flash. There wasn't a lot of specialist medical support in Aberdeen, while Selly Oak and Frimley had specialist centers who could give better treatment options to Dean. There was no question. He needed me, and he needed to be where he would get the best treatment. I spoke to my boss and put in for a transfer.

I was quickly offered a branch manager's role in Guildford, Surrey. And within a few weeks I packed my bags, rented out my house, and said goodbye once again to Aberdeen. I found a nice apartment for us, and we moved in, preparing for the long journey ahead.

The injury had taken Dean's spirit. He had lost physical abilities, but it was the change in his mental state that was the toughest challenge. The anger started to show more and more. The smallest things would set him off, and it was reaching a boiling point. Dean's squadron had gone off to Afghanistan without him. During the tour, one of Dean's team was lost, and Dean blamed himself. Somehow, he believed, if he had been on the tour, his friend would not have died. The funeral was tough, and Dean struggled to hold it together.

At the bar afterward, the drinks were flowing, and the champagne was popped, celebrating his life. Dean's friend Ant popped a bottle and offered it to Dean. By pure accident, the bottle hit Dean's tooth and cracked it. Dean erupted. He grabbed Ant by the throat and lifted him off the ground, and I could see the red in his eyes. I had no idea what would happen next.

My calm talking kicked in and he let him go. There was no hard feelings from Ant but, rather, concern over Dean's quick temper. Dean didn't understand where the anger was coming from, and I didn't know what to do.

Every morning, I would wake up, and for the first few minutes, I would be on eggshells until I worked out what mood he was in that day. One morning, Dean got up and was excited to make breakfast. He was in a good mood, and it was great to see. He was smiling and headed into the kitchen. After a few minutes, I heard a loud bang, followed by the awful sound of Dean shouting and hitting things.

I went to the kitchen, nervous as to what I would find, what had happened. I walked through the door and looked around. I saw Dean. He was shaking with anger. His face was red and sweaty; the red mist had firmly descended.

I tried to speak to him, to calm him down and to find out what had happened. Has someone called him? Has someone else been hurt? No one was here. What had happened?

Just as a million thoughts raced through my head, I looked at the floor, and there was a broken egg lying there. I looked back at him, and his eyes had started to well up.

"I broke the egg," he said as his lip trembled. "I'm not a man. I can't even make eggs. What am I worth?"

I looked him in the eyes and wrapped my arms around him. I held him tight, as if I was never letting go, and I promised him I would sort this; everything was going to be OK.

His career was over. Everything he ever knew—the military life he was raised in, followed by the career path he had been so proud of—was gone. I couldn't let him dwell. We had to plan for the future. I thought about the conversation we'd had after MI6, and I got out my BlackBerry and set up our first security company. I then registered us both on a close protection course with Anubis, a protective security course provider.

Anubis was one of the most prestigious private security courses. The course was tough, and the trainers were experts in their field. Dean was already fully qualified in close protection. However, as with many military courses, his didn't transfer over to civilian qualifications. It was a four-week intensive residential course, and once complete, you were a fully qualified close protection officer (bodyguard).

There were many reasons we wanted to do this, one of my reasons being my passion for fighting sex trafficking of women and children. The Haiti disaster had not long hit, killing an estimated 316,000 people and orphaning children in the thousands. Orphanages were being set up, and child traffickers quickly followed. Whenever there is a major disaster such as an earthquake or tsunami, you will find criminal gangs quickly moving in. Children are incredibly vulnerable when law enforcement is overwhelmed, and they are alone—either separated from their parents or orphaned. Traffickers specifically target disaster zones.

I had a call from someone asking if I could help find people to provide protection to rescuers who were trying to stop what was going on. The people trying to help automatically had a price on their head, as the traffickers were offering $5 to locals to stop them. They needed security but could not afford the average $300 per man, per day price tag.

I made a number of calls and was incredibly shocked no one was willing to do this work pro bono. I wanted to become a bodyguard so I could be the one to go and help when needed. And luckily, Dean and I are cut from the same cloth when it comes to our passions and desires to help people.

Both Dean and I passed the course. We both scored the same marks. However, my report was labeled "Very Good," and Dean's was "Excellent." I queried this, and I was told he was Special Forces; he would automatically score higher. There were only two women on this course of thirty plus people, and I was basically being told I never had a chance of scoring higher, as I wasn't in the Special Forces; I was female, and only men were allowed in the Special Forces. You could say I was pissed off, but I wasn't really surprised.

During the course, the day after our conflict management

training, we found out that I was pregnant. The pelvic thrust and Japanese choke holds all of a sudden didn't feel like such a good idea! The pregnancy wasn't planned, and we discussed our options. This baby was made from love, and it was to be part of our family. But this wasn't going to be easy. I had given my notice to the bank before starting the course, so I was now out of work. Dean's recovery had started, but he was no longer useful to the military, so he was at the bottom of the list for treatment. We waited months for hospital appointments and almost a year for his first operation. We had just embarked on this new career, and I was guessing there wasn't a high demand for pregnant bodyguards!

To save money, we had moved back to camp. We weren't married, so we had to stay in the singles' quarter. I was pregnant and huge (I put on seventy pounds plus with each of my children). Dean's knee was braced up, and he needed room to lie down. Dean's room in camp was slightly larger than a single bed but not quite a double, a three-quarter, if you will. At night, he would take cushions from the communal block sofa and lay them on the floor, giving me the bed to sleep. In the morning, we would wake and reset the room before the other lads got up.

Dean had free reign around the camp, but I wasn't allowed anywhere except the block and the training field outside. Dean would spend his days in the NAAFI lounge or down at the gym with the other lads, while I would be in the room watching really terrible daytime TV. It was incredibly lonely.

I never really fit in with the other military wives out on the patch. I spent a lot of time with Emilie, Ant's wife. I distinctly remember speaking with her one day, and she told me, "Alana, when this baby is born, your life will change 100 percent. Dean's life will be no different."

I didn't understand what she meant at the time; I do now.

Dean was starting to get treatment and was working in the recruitment cell. We were building up our security courses, and next for me was maritime security. The issue of piracy in the Gulf of Aden was a hot topic at this time, and maritime security was becoming a big, lucrative business. Dean spoke with a friend who ran courses and got himself booked on one. He managed to get me on too, which was lucky, as they now require documented sea time to even sit the course.

I decided to go for company security officer as well as ship security. "Company" allowed me to run teams, and that was what I was looking at doing. I was seven months pregnant and on docks, climbing rope ladders and boarding ships. The academic side of it was in depth, and a lot of the Marines struggled with it. When I first arrived, they'd all looked at me like I had two heads; not only was I the only woman there, but I was seven months pregnant! However, when it came to academia, the guys really struggled. I happily helped them, and by the end, I felt I had gained their respect.

My instructor signed me off and shook my hand. "It was great to meet you and get to know you," he said. "You really surprised me, and I wish you all the best for the future." He then delivered the killer blow. "It's such a shame. You would have made a great CSO."

"Would have?" I asked. *What does that mean?*

"There are no female toilet facilities onboard most of these ships, so they don't allow women on board."

So even though I had passed and had all the certification, I would never be able to do the job I had trained and qualified for because I was female. Yep, that pissed me off too.

CHAPTER FIFTEEN

※ ⁓ ⁓ ⁓ ⁓

MOLLIE

Spring came, and Dean was preparing for his final days in the military. I was weeks away from giving birth. We didn't know where we were going to live, how we would support ourselves, or what was going to happen. We decided to move back to Aberdeen, I still had property there, and we could live in my old family home, the first house I had purchased years before. We could stay there until we decided our next move. We had very little money, so much so that we couldn't even afford an aerial for the TV.

Dean took a task in Libya a few weeks before my due date. Neither of us wanted him to miss the birth, but we needed the money. Civil war had started to kick off in Libya due to Arab Spring. Arab Spring began on December 17, 2010, when Mohamed Bouazizi, a street vendor from Ben Arous, Tunisia, set himself on fire following the confiscation of his goods and the ongoing abuse by a municipal official. Anger and violence erupted following his death, and protests spread throughout the country. People wanted an end to brutal regimes and dictatorships, and the actions of the Tunisian people soon inspired much of the rest of the Arab world, including Libya

While Dean was in Libya, the civil war intensified, and NATO and the Libyan Government declared a no-fly zone across the country. I was days from giving birth, and we thought he wouldn't make it home for the birth of our first child. But luckily, days to go, he made it on time.

I went into labor with Mollie at 7:00 p.m. on Friday June 10, 2011. I had made a playlist to play during her birth. I wanted her to come into this world surrounded by love and positivity. My midwives, Emma and Sharon, were lovely. Mollie was one of Emma's first births, and she and Dean were very chatty.

By about 9:30 p.m., my contractions were getting more painful, not that you would know. I'm not very vocal when I'm in pain, unless I stub my toe—then you'll hear a few expletives! Dean and Emma were busy discussing AC/DC and various other bands. I tried to interrupt their chat by explaining I needed to push.

Sharon heard me and said, "No. You have barely made a sound. You've not even started yet."

"OK," I said, "but maybe you can just check, as it really does feel like I need to push!"

Sharon did a quick check. "Ten centimeters!" she yelled, "This baby is coming!"

Dean looked at me in total shock.

Then within minutes and the worst but best pain I had ever felt, I had this beautiful tiny baby in my arms. She latched on immediately, and as I held her little hand, I waited for that gush of love that everyone talks about. But in all honesty, my feelings were of immense protection, an overwhelming need to protect. *While I walk this earth, I will never let anyone hurt you. I will protect you with my every breath. I will teach you to be strong so, one day, when I am no longer here, you have everything you need to protect yourself; to stay strong but kind; to help others whenever you can; and, most importantly, to be happy.*

We stayed in hospital for a couple of days, and then, discharged on Sunday evening, we headed home to begin our life together as a little family. I remember that drive home, sticking well below the speed limit and not taking my eyes off her for one second.

At home, we got settled into bed, with some DVDs for comfort, as we had no live TV. Then Dean came in with his suitcase. "I'm sorry, babe. A job has come in. I need to leave tomorrow morning. Flight's at 5:30 a.m."

I was terrified; could I do this by myself? I didn't have many friends with all the moving I had done in life. Mum wasn't here. How was I going to do this? But he had to go. We needed the money, and this was his job now. So, as had become standard, I showed no fear or concern. I simply nodded my head as I rubbed his arm. Looking at him with a reassuring smile, I handed Mollie to him and began helping him pack his case.

Dean left for Guinea the next morning at 4:00 a.m., and it was just me and Mollie. We walked down to the local Blockbuster video store and rented the entire seven series of *The Shield*. It probably wasn't the most child-appropriate collection. But, hey, she was three days old, and perhaps she could learn some future tools for life. I missed contact with the outside world. I had no TV antenna in the house, so it was always DVDs.

I remember deciding to get the aerial put in; it was £98 and seemed such a huge amount of money. But for the sake of my sanity, we decided to go for it. Once it was installed, I was able to watch normal TV. We lay in bed for days; it was a special time. She was the most content baby, rarely crying—so much so that, when she was around a month old, I took her to the doctor's concerned about her lack of crying.

"Be grateful," was his only reply to this new mum.

I remember catching an episode of a TV show called *Real Housewives of Orange County*. With so much time with just me and Mollie, I would get engrossed in the episode and loved watching the ladies and their lives. It looked like a beautiful part of the world, and my desire to live in America had never left me. I said to myself, *One day, I am going to live there.*

Dean returned from Guinea. His trip had been successful despite an arrest and interrogation. He received a presidential apology for that and was given a gift to say sorry. Dean handed me the gift on his return. It was a giant fertility statue. I looked at Dean, breast milk still leaking through my T-shirt and my Kegel strength still requiring vast improvement. "Really?" I said.

He just laughed; we both laughed. I still have that statue, along with a host of other gifts we have been given over the years. The following few months the pattern would continue. A job would come in, usually last minute; Dean would accept; I would help with the planning, logistics, and business; and Dean would go and execute the task. It was sporadic, random, and fast-paced. But mostly, it was an incredibly lonely time.

When the first task to Libya had come in, I never realized how much that country would consume and shape our lives. I had only really heard about Libya during my time in Bulgaria. My friend's mum had worked as a doctor in Libya and had treated women for some horrific injuries during her time there. At the time, Libya, to Westerners, was another possible cash cow. When Arab Spring happened, it was the beginning of some of the biggest revolutions of Africa and the Middle East, but with the uprising came so much destruction.

At home, I would do most of the planning for Dean's trips. He conducted travel and evacuation planning and risk assessments. Every week, I would sit and write the *Libya Focus*; I would research real-time incidents, gather intel from various sources, and write the report to send to Dean's clients. The first few times I sent it, I would sign off in my own name, and not once did I receive a response.

I changed tactics, signing off as Dean Stott. Without exception, I would receive a reply. Feminism was never something I jumped on board with. I believed in equality but only if it was under the same standards. A female firefighter, for example, should be given the same exams and tests as her male counterparts, including what she has to carry, as, in real time, the weight advantage won't come into play. I didn't believe we were all equal, but I believed we should all have equal rights and chances. We all have our strengths and weaknesses, and we should nourish those qualities in each other. Improve your weakness if appropriate to do so, but if not, focus on your strengths and what you can do with them. However, I was becoming more and more frustrated by the level of respect I received as "Dean Stott" for the same work completed by "Alana Stott." That was another thing that just pissed me off.

It was a decision I subconsciously made very early on that I would build up Dean, his career, his life, and his passions. I would look after Mollie, run the businesses from the shadows, take care of Dean, and support him to succeed and flourish. I really did have an all-consuming love for him and could see every bit of potential in him. Every bit of self-doubt he used to get, I would dispel. The injury had changed him, and he needed me to keep reminding him of the man he was and still is.

The first task was to help with this transition from the military. It was true, in June 2011 he walked out of that camp for the last time. But cutting the cords of the military was a whole other matter and a series of mammoth tasks. First task, civvies—wow that was a mission. Trying to make him realize we are all not lazy, useless, undisciplined, boring losers was not easy. He struggled to believe he would find friendship outside of the military world; it was all he'd ever known.

Next, I had to make him realize just how remarkable he was. He truly believed all soldiers, especially Tier 1 SF soldiers, were the same and that he was nothing special. This was so far from the truth. Dean had many gifts. He was intelligent, personable, thought outside the box, and could take orders but was a leader too. The world of close protection and security was beginning to get saturated, but this never bothered me. I had met plenty of operators, both SF and others, and no one was a patch on him. There was always something very obviously different about him; only he couldn't see it.

The next and biggest task I had was to teach him about trust. I am a firm believer in trust and forgiveness, but you still must be very careful. The first thing to trust is your gut. The digestive system is directly linked to neurological functions, which links with the energy of the universe, and your true gut instinct will always tell you what you need to know. Dean was incredibly trusting. He believed when someone said they would do something, then they would just do it. Why wouldn't they? He believed, if someone was helping him, they weren't expecting something back or it wasn't for their own purposes. People should always help people and just pay it forward, shouldn't they? He had a beautiful way of looking at the world, and I fully agreed that this was the way it should be. However, I was more than aware this was not always the case.

Given Dean's skill sets, there were many leeches out there wishing to take advantage, throwing Dean into the danger zones while they reaped the rewards and benefits. I very quickly became known as the "bitch" of Team Stott; I would constantly block these people, even facing arguments with Dean himself on the matter. Trust me, I would say, they are only out for what they can get. Dean was a commodity to them. To this day, my gut on this matter has never failed me. And Dean, well, he still has that innocence that I love, the belief of the good in people. But that's what I'm here for, and it's why I'll probably always be known as the "bitch."

Dean worked the circuit for many years. Jobs would come in. I would deal with the business end, report writing, and Dean would take on the task. I guess that's where the "brain and the brawn" titles came from. We had often been told that having a child would change everything. We wouldn't be able to do what we did anymore—no traveling, no adventures, no fun. But Mollie fit very nicely into our world. We never experienced that end-of-freedom feeling. WE never did. Emilie's words from all those year back were clear now. My world had done a 360, but Dean's, well, he was still able to do anything he wanted; she was so right. As women, we make it so their lives can continue as normal, better even. I made sure we could carry on doing everything we had planned, and I was lucky enough that Mollie was the angel she was.

The Special Boat Service Association (SBSA) boxing ball was an event that took place every December, where serving members would attend and accompany guests who had paid up to £15,000 for a table. As a serving member, Dean had attended two of these events. Following one of these evenings, Dean had returned home to me and said, "Alana, one year, I want to be one of the guys buying one of those tables."

Mollie was six months old when we got our first table at the SBSA boxing event. He believed it, and we made it happen. We sold off the other seats to cover the costs, and Mollie came with us to the Grosvenor House Hotel in London, a very exclusive venue that was more glamorous than anything I had ever seen. Dean had invited his friend Harry to the table, so you can imagine there was a lot of attention on our table.

Mollie stayed upstairs in the hotel bedroom with a nanny. One problem—she had never left my side. She was not happy. Security was high in the hotel as the prime minister of the United Kingdom was also in attendance, so the elevators were out of action. I spent a large part of the night running up and down the hotel stairs in heels and a ball gown, feeding and comforting Mollie. I had a beautiful silk gold dress on, and on one particularly embarrassing check after I had run up to feed her, I returned to the table where I was sat next to Harry. I noticed the breast milk had leaked onto my dress. Milk on silk is not good, and I had these incredibly noticeable wet patches I had no way of hiding. There were 1,200 people, all staring at the special guest sitting next to me, and I wanted the ground to open up. Harry, as always, was the perfect gentleman and pretended like he could see nothing.

Our world had most definitely changed, but it never stopped; we just made it work. Mollie was ten months old when one of the most prestigious super yacht shows in the world took place in Singapore, bringing all the big players in the world of super yachts and maritime security together for one week. We had no babysitting options, so we booked our flights and all went together. This was a big opportunity for us to gain some contracts and network, so we would just make it work.

Mollie was still breastfeeding, so Dean would have to do a bit more of the one-on-one meetings without me. But we all attended the larger networking events. We were blessed to have a child like Mollie. She was so good—never cried, never complained. As long as she had Mummy nearby, she was happy. Team Stott hadn't changed for the worse; it had just gotten bigger and better.

My family and friends never quite got it. They knew me before and always saw me as the independent, ambitious girl who was capable of doing anything she set her mind to. Now all that ambition and drive was firmly directed toward Dean; very few people could understand why I did what I did. I grew up in Aberdeen in Scotland, the oil capital of the world. So, I was surrounded by "oil wives"—women who usually didn't work and whose husbands were on rotational work, home for two, three, or four weeks and then away offshore for the equivalent period of time. When I joined the military wife's world, it was very easy to see the similarities.

I call it the "military/oil family cycle," and it usually works like this: Husband leaves. Wife adapts to him being away. Initial feelings of loneliness and pining for her love give way to the setting out of a plan for the period ahead. Usually, this is a goal, which will depend on the length of time away—anything from losing a few pounds to learning a new language. (It should be noted that I didn't often see the goals achieved; and I could talk about that forever, but it's probably another book.) As the time goes by, the wife hits the settling-in period. She has adapted to life without him, and the "single mum" life becomes the new normal. Then comes the homestretch, the run up to when he is due home. There is a mix of emotions. She's excited for him to come home but nervous he'll mess with her routine.

Husband comes home, and there's a slight bit of awkwardness. (It was at this point I always saw the issues.) The wife is usually uneasy. Of course, she is excited to see him and has missed him, but she now wants him to fit straight into her world without messing it up, while the husband is nervous too. He has spent weeks, sometimes months away. Changes have happened, and home doesn't always feel like his home; he is having to fit into their world and is expected to immediately fit in. This stage of decompression is often overlooked by both sides, and this is always the stage where resentment and arguments can occur.

Settling in phase soon comes, and everyone starts to feel welcome and like a family again; things become normal and a routine sets in. Then comes the inevitable, the time when he has to leave again. Nerves kick in, and both sides have their own reservations. Once again, either side is not always understood by the other, and again snapping and arguing can occur.

He then leaves, and it all begins again.

This roller-coaster life is definitely not for everyone. I have seen many examples of this life, good and bad. On the worst end of the spectrum are the wives who fell in love and then, during the many cycles, eventually fall out of love. Some stick at it, especially in the oil world and often because of the lifestyle and money, while others find different outlets to cope—adultery, drinking, depression; I've seen it all.

But then there is the other side of the scale, the beautiful side, where a couple makes it work. My grandma and grandad were one of those couples. He was merchant navy and then offshore and was so madly in love with my grandma he just couldn't wait to get back on shore. When he got back on shore, he had one blowout; this was a time where he went to the bar and had a good time with his friends. Once that was over, then it was family time.

For me, it was different. Firstly, Dean's rotations had never been regular. He could be away for a week and then home for a day and away again. On one occasion, he had been away four weeks and arrived home at 10:00 a.m.; by midday, a call had come in, and he was on the 6:00 p.m. flight out again. Secondly, I was never an idle; I was always working on our businesses, properties, and charity work so never had time to mourn his departure. The hardest part was always trying to gain normality. Things like booking a holiday were next to impossible with our lifestyle. We could never book anything, as he could never turn away work. So anything we ever did had to be spontaneous. Or, as was often the case, I would go away with Mollie on my own, usually visiting friends or family.

In 2012, London had been awarded the Olympics, and this was a big deal for the security world. We had secured a gig with Visa, so Dean was on duty throughout the whole of the Olympics. This was great for us, as it ensured us a regular income; a monthlong contract was the equivalent of a regular income.

When it came to the finances, Dean had very little involvement. Stress about money was something he didn't need, and it wasn't necessary to burden him with it; I had always kept it away from him. To this day, I would bet he doesn't know who we bank with or what bills we have. Many would say this burden should be shared. However, I have never quite agreed with this. I always found this side of things easy, and I can handle the stress of money well. I never saw merit in the theories that "misery loves company" or that "a problem shared is a problem halved." If I need to vent, I know he is there. But for the most part, I've got it.

Money was tight, but when the opportunity came for me and Mollie to join Dean for a couple of events during the Olympics, I knew I couldn't turn this down. So, Mollie and I flew down to meet Dean. I remember the journey very distinctly. Dean asked me to bring down a couple of things for him, including his tuxedo, which he needed for a black-tie event, and a bag of his things he had left behind. I therefore had to fly down with my suitcase, his bag, his suit carrier, the push-chair, the baby, and the baby bag.

Dean had spoken with me earlier that day and said that taxis were quite expensive and that it would be better for me to get a train from the airport to the city. I didn't disagree. Looking back now, I often laugh at myself; I never have taken the easy route!

So, there I was, baby and bags in tow. And to top it all, I had agreed with Dean's ex-wife that I would pick up his kids and have the three kids while I was in London. A friend of a friend had given us keys to their late mother's flat in Hackney, and I would stay there for the week. I got myself (by some minor miracle) into the center of London. At the tube station, I got off with Mollie in the push-chair, the suit carrier over one arm and the suitcase in the other, the baby bag over my shoulder, pushing the pram with my other hand. And then, oh lord, stairs!

I stood at the bottom of the stairs and had no idea how I would get up there. I couldn't believe how many people walked past, especially young men, and offered zero help. I began to panic. Just at that point, a woman, probably in her sixties, came along and offered to help me. I was deeply grateful, and although we never said much to each other, I could feel the female solidarity.

Arriving at the flat in Hackney, I was once again met with a flight of stairs. I managed to shuttle everything upstairs and arrived in the hallway, avoiding eye contact with the drug dealers and trying not to let Mollie breathe in the clouds of marijuana smoke circling the air; it was not good. I had to call and tell Dean's ex-wife that there was no way the kids could come here; this was no place for kids. I called Dean, who at that precise moment was sitting in his five-star hotel in the heart of London. He was a bit annoyed that I couldn't take the other kids, and I quickly put him back in his box.

This wasn't Dean being an asshole. He just didn't understand, Dean has a way of believing I am some sort of superwoman, and nothing should phase me. It confuses him if I find something difficult. I cried that night, and I did not sleep!

Dean managed to join us for a long weekend during his task, and we headed down to his old haunts in Devon. Dean's old friends were lovely, but I always felt uncomfortable. He had been married before, and I felt I had to prove I was more than just another of Dean's conquests. They never treated me badly, quite the opposite; it was just my own insecurities. Mix this with a major loss of identity following motherhood, a career transition, immense feelings of loneliness, and stress about money and security, and my mental health was taking a bit of a beating.

As we drove along the Cornwall coastline, I will always remember looking out the window and feeling empty. I could never show this to Dean. I had to be strong for him. I knew he was fragile with his transition and his injury. I had to keep up the front. But inside, I was crumbling. I didn't know what it was, but something was missing, and I was sad.

CHAPTER SIXTEEN

❧❧❧❧❧❧❧❧❧❧

BECOMING MRS. STOTT

Soon after the Olympics, Dean returned to Libya, this time into Benghazi. Benghazi was always more of a worry than Tripoli; there was so much more unknown. I was now very used to disassociating myself from situations and adjusting to Dean being away; however, I did spend most of my evening heavily researching the areas Dean was entering into. Nothing was sounding good about Benghazi around this time.

Soon after Dean arrived in the country, the American embassy was attacked, and the American ambassador to Libya was assassinated. Dean had to evacuate his clients while navigating the chaos that ensued. I was home with Mollie who had just turned one year old. I was busy preparing the weekly Libya report as news reports started to pop up about what was unfolding on the ground. I contacted the other SF lads to see if they had any updates or reports, and so far, they had nothing. A few hours would pass until I finally got the call with a status update from Dean. That was all I ever needed, that one check-in.

I found myself living in that circle, either waiting for Dean to come home, preparing for him to go away, or waiting for the safety check-in—just waiting and preparing. I tried to add other things into my daily life. I began studying criminology, started working on rental properties and taking on little extra jobs—anything to fill the void.

There is no better void filler than planning a wedding. So, along with everything we had going on, we set the date, December 14, 2013. Dean would continue to be away more often than not, so conversation around the wedding would generally be me asking what he thought and him replying, "Whatever you want. I'm easy." This used to be infuriating. I just wanted him to feel the passion I had for it.

It is clear to me now I had such a passion for planning the wedding because it was my void filler; his life was full of purpose surrounding the work he was doing. The civil war was getting more and more intense. Libya was a full war zone. It became more his life than home did.

My family didn't always approve of how things were with him so, instead of talking with them, I would be completely on the defensive and, in turn, would put walls up with them. My maid of honor didn't like the lifestyle or approve of things so just stopped talking to me. I didn't know what I had done and actually to this day still don't know; she has never talked to me again. I never heard from her in the run-up to the wedding, and she didn't come to the bachelorette party. The strangest thing was she did come to the wedding. She didn't speak to me or Dean, and I have never seen her since.

Luckily, my younger brother's girlfriend, Lorna, stepped up; and, as far as stand-in maids of honor go, she was the best!

The guest list for the wedding was definitely exciting. We had people from all walks of life there, from my old neighborhood to Prince Harry.

We booked a beautiful Scottish Castle in Auchenblae, near Montrose in Scotland. We would later learn this had more meaning than we knew. The castle was on hundreds of acres of hilly land, hugely populated by beautiful deer and majestic stags. We rented the castle for the whole weekend. I was to arrange all the catering, flowers, decor, and a horse and cart to take us down to the little chapel at the end of the road. The chapel was to be filled with candles and romantic lighting. The room was filled with blue and white flowers. The groom and groomsmen, who were all UK Special Forces, three SAS and three SBS, were to wear Help for Heroes tartan. I was to walk down the aisle to the soundtrack of *Braveheart*. We would dance the night away to Scottish music, and then a Bon Jovi tribute band would be booked the following day. And we were to dine on the venison caught by the groom party earlier in the day. It was to be the perfect fairy-tale wedding.

As the wedding approached, the guest list began to dwindle, Dean's dad found out two months before the wedding that he had cancer, and his sister didn't feel she could travel while her dad was sick. Prince Harry was in the middle of the Antarctic on a charity mission, Dean's friends were being called on duty, and we even had one who was in prison! Dean was concerned about it. But for me, so many people I wanted with me wouldn't be there—my mum and my grandparents all would be missing, so I couldn't get stressed about the others, as they were at least still around.

I had to arrange all the accommodation and move people around to make sure they were happy and comfortable; it became a day about pleasing everyone and making sure everyone was OK. We arranged shuttles back and forth to the airport, and as more and more of the Army lads arrived, Friday evening soon became a party. We had hired karaoke. The castle had games and pool tables. It really was the stuff military reunion dreams are made of! The girls retired to bed early, but the boys held a full all-nighter. I had no issues with this, as, for me, it was, again, making sure Dean was happy; as always, it was making sure everything was perfect for him.

The day of the wedding arrived, and my post on Facebook read, "It's not about how hard you hit, it's about how hard you can get hit and keep moving forward; how much you can take and keep moving forward. That's how winning is done. Today I won!" This was completely true. I was marrying the man of my dreams, the man who understood me; who was tough; who knew what it was to strive, to dream, to believe, and to make it happen. It was a quote from my hero Rocky played by Sylvester Stallone (who, just like his character, is equally my hero), and today I was marrying my very own hero.

The morning of the wedding, all the girls woke up excited. So we drew the curtains, we could see the weather was not going to be our friend. The rain had come down, and it was drizzly and wet. The horse handler called and said the mud would make it too difficult for the horses to come and pull the cart. At this point, we had no way for the girls to get down to the chapel.

A knock on the door came. It was Scott, Dean's best man. "Problem solved," he said. "We are going to do it."

"Do what?" I asked.

"We are going to pull the cart!" The groomsmen had all come together and decided they were going to pull the cart all the way down the hill to the chapel.

The castle manager immediately began freaking out. "No way," he said. "Health and safety would never have it!"

Scott put his arm around him. "Don't worry, mate. It will be fine!"

As I sat there getting ready, again my focus was on the bridal party. My girls, Lorna, Sarah, and Una, were the most beautiful bridesmaids ever. Mollie was the flower girl; it was so amazing to be able to share this day with my baby girl.

Mollie, however, decided to choose this day to become the spawn of the devil. She was doing absolutely nothing I told her to do and was being completely uncooperative. However, Ewan, the castle manager, had magic powers and just took over. He waved his wand, and within seconds, Mollie was in her dress and ready to go. We all headed down to the chapel and my dad was there, at the entrance, waiting for me.

As everyone sat down waiting, I thought of my mum again. What I would have given to have her there. But let's be real; she most probably was. My dad walked me down the aisle, and Dean and I said our vows. It was beautiful and magical, but I definitely didn't soak it in enough. I guess no bride ever does. I always regret not getting the wedding videographer, but £2,000 was a lot of money and not affordable at the time.

Following the vows, everyone returned to the castle. Santa arrived, and the kids all had a great time receiving gifts. The wedding breakfast was amazing, and we ate the deer the men had hunted earlier. The speeches were funny, and my dad got all of two words out before bursting into tears and bowing out! The rock-ceilidh band played traditional Scottish music mixed with modern music, and everyone danced the night away.

I barely remember speaking to Dean, and even when we did head to bed, I'm pretty sure he would have much preferred to hang out with the guys downstairs. There was a serious case of FOMO going on there!

The next morning, I got up to find the groomsmen still drinking, some of the lads passed out on the stairs, and Dean's stepfather asleep in the position he landed in after falling down the stairs (not a pretty sight of a man wearing a kilt!). The military wives had already started on the tequila, and I knew we were ready for another big session. The Bon Jovi tribute band arrived, and I was ready to party.

I had the best night dancing away to Bon Jovi, one problem being Dean was off with the lads. I wasn't angry; it was rare for them all to get together, and you never knew when or if it would happen again.

The following day, we all checked out of the castle, and we were ready to start our new life as Mr. and Mrs. Stott.

CHAPTER SEVENTEEN

THE ARAB SPRING EFFECT

A few weeks after the wedding, Dean's dad took a turn for the worse, and a few hours after his sixty-seventh birthday on January 1, 2014, he passed away. I knew Dean was devastated. But what he exhibited to the outside world was the tough Dean, the stoic Dean. It was even more stoic than I had witnessed before. He put on an incredibly untouched front, and as his sisters and dad's partner got busy planning the funeral, Dean faked his nonchalant attitude. He wasn't involved in the planning of the funeral; I knew how much he wanted to be part of it, but I said nothing and allowed it all to unfold.

He wore his military lovats to the funeral and stood there without a tear and never flinched. I remember when his dad's partner asked him for money for the flowers while at the wake. It was horrible; he was brokenhearted, and the concern was on the fifty pounds for the florist. I still said nothing and allowed him to maintain this stance.

A few hours afterward, we were home, and a day later, he was off to South Africa on task. That year, he was home for twenty-one days in the whole year. In many ways, 2014 was the worst year of our lives. But in many ways, it was also the making of us. We had to hit rock bottom, face breaking point in order for us to build up again.

Dean was taking on more and more of the dangerous jobs no one else would do; every trip, he was returning with blood-soaked shirts and asking for me to remove the stains. He had no awareness of the blood and the fact no amount of Vanish stain removal would get it out. He didn't talk about what had happened and just got angrier and angrier. He would shout for no reason at random points and was never truly with us when he was home.

During one of his trips to Libya, he called home, and all I could hear was gunfire. He managed to tell me that things had gotten really bad, and then he told me he was taking heavy fire. I could hear the bullets like they were flying through the phone. My dad was over and playing with Mollie. It was a Saturday evening, and I tried to stay calm. The shots got louder and louder until Dean shouted down the phone that he had to go, and the line went dead.

I didn't know if he was alive or dead. I waited and waited. I called his business partners, who were all out drinking up the profits, making money while Dean took all the risks. They had a blatant disregard for Dean's well-being.

I received calls from the SBS and SAS asking me if I had heard from Dean, telling me the shit had completely hit the fan in Libya, yet no one had heard from Dean. They needed crucial intel. Hell, I just needed to know if my husband was alive or dead. I imagined everything. I thought of the conversation I would have with Mollie in her later years; of telling his family that he died doing what he loved; of meeting other people and having to listen to their dull, boring existence of a life while futilely trying to live up to the man who was once my husband. It was torture.

My dad went home, and I was left overnight, just me and my thoughts.

At 9:33 a.m. the following morning, the phone rang. I grabbed for it quickly and felt immense relief when I saw it was Dean calling. "Hi, babe. It's me," he said, with not a care in the world, as casual as you like. "You OK? How was your weekend?"

I remained calm. "Dean, are you OK?" I asked.

The reply was what shook me to my core. "I'm fine, babe. Sorry. I fell asleep when I got back to my room late last night. It was a bit late to call you, as I thought you would be asleep. But all is good. How are you?"

How am I?! My desired reply was that I—and the entire British Army, among others—had spent the entire night worrying about him, so, no, I most certainly was not sleeping while he was casually having a nap! No, no, I was not in the slightest bit OK. However, what I actually replied was, "I'm fine. I'm glad you're safe."

This was the issue now; Dean had become so desensitized to normal life and normal feelings that he genuinely didn't see wrong in his actions. Since his father had passed away, it had become even worse. He refused to show any kind of emotion, and I didn't really question it; the truth was, I had also become desensitized. This was also now my normal; everything I ever wanted to say I didn't for fear of upsetting him. Since the accident, his moods were so up and down, and the constant feeling of walking on eggshells had just become normal. I lived a very single and lonely life, and the person I loved the most was not opening up to me as much as I wasn't opening up to him.

I kept myself busy with work, but my passions for helping people still burned bright. I began working with a rape crisis center and also qualified to become a member of the Children's Panel Scotland. This was the equivalent of social services family court. The people would sit on a panel and make decisions on children's lives. This was a rewarding and difficult job. It was voluntary and you can imagine the type of people who sign up for this work, especially in an oil-rich city. It was usually retirees or bored housewives. Most had never entered the areas where the children grew up and had no idea about life below the breadline. The decisions were always made on a majority basis, and often my decisions were overridden by the other two members.

I remember the day I knew I couldn't do it anymore. I had seen so many amazing kids pass through the system, but one kid stuck with me. He was fifteen years old and was in front of the panel for lying on a job application and bunking off school. The boy had been in the system since before he was born. His mother was using drugs and alcohol while pregnant, and he was born addicted to opioids and had alcohol fetal syndrome. He was placed in foster care when he was seven days old and spent years back and forth between his mum and the system.

At thirteen, he had finally settled with a foster family, when his mum returned, saying she was clean and wanted him back. He got to know her and was returned to her care.

One month later, she died from illnesses caused by years of abuse. She knew she was sick and had wanted to spend her last days with her son. She never put his needs first, and following her death, he was back in the system. The foster family he'd found happiness with was no longer available, so he began the usual bed-hopping again. He never attended school and was hustling his way through life. He decided to find himself a job, earn his own cash, and get out of the system. So, he wrote a CV, lied about his age, and was given an interview. His hustle worked, and he was offered the job—until they found out he lied.

The amazing thing was his potential employers were so impressed by him they still wanted him but needed the approval from the panel to allow him to leave school at fifteen. He sat across from us; the panel consisted of a middle-aged man, a retired schoolteacher, and me, all with the best of intentions but all with different ideas of what was best for this kid. Both the man and the teacher said he was to return to school and finish his education. I explained to them that this kid had not attended a day of school in six months, his attendance record was poor at best, and this was the first time he has shown some real initiative and drive. These skills should be praised, not squashed. They went on to say that he had lied, and this type of behavior should never be rewarded. They both refused to sign off, and I was overruled. He was crushed. I never quite got the look in his eyes out of my mind.

I continued to work for the rape crisis center, but that, in itself, was also taking a toll on Dean and me. Aside from the juggling act I was performing with my work, Libya, Mollie, our businesses, and general life, the work in the center itself was harrowing. Dealing with five-year-old kids who've been raped was one thing; another was dealing with long-term abuse victims.

One such case I will never forget. A young lady had been referred to me by the police. She was a key witness in a historic case against a pedophile, and her testimony was crucial. The issue, however, was she did not believe she was a victim; nor did she believe anyone else was. The perpetrator was her own father. Along with all the other victims, he had also been abusing her since she was a baby. She was now in her twenties, and she told me they were in love. Her mum was dead, and she told me he loved her, and she loved him.

The hardest part of the sessions with her was when she started to realize that what had been happening was not normal, not real and that she was a victim. Everything she believed came crashing down on her. The trauma in this circumstance ran incredibly deep here. I did all I could to support her, but everyone at the center worked on a voluntary basis, meaning turnaround and unreliability were high. The work was incredibly demanding. But helping was always my passion. And I could handle demanding in order to save at least one girl.

Libya soon descended into complete destruction. On July 13, 2014, the Libya Dawn coalition launched an attack on Tripoli Airport; the militia led a coup d'état operation against the Libyan House of Representatives in order to seize control of the airport and, therefore, Tripoli itself. The airport was completely destroyed in the fight, and embassies from around the world began evacuating Libya, some by land and some by sea. On Dean's first ever trip to Libya, his gut feeling had told him things may not end well. We discussed this many times. We set down plans so that, if this happened, Dean always had a way out. He bought a load of weapons on the black market and cached them in multiple locations, perfectly positioned so that, if he ever needed an escape plan, they were accessible.

The Canadian embassy found itself in a position it could not get out of; a number of diplomats and military personnel were trapped, and the embassy called upon Dean for support. Dean had an incredibly unique skill of befriending the locals. He treated them with respect and, in turn, was treated with equal respect. This was true for any country Dean entered. The first thing he would do would be to form bonds with street-level locals. Governments and suits do not know a country; street peddlers, doormen, bartenders, and shoe shiners—these people are the ones in the know.

Dean had a main fixer, who had inside knowledge and connections everywhere. He began the move of the embassy, incredibly low key, using safe houses of friends along the route to the Tunisian border.

I had been taken into hospital for further work on my burns. The minute I woke from the anesthetic, I picked up my phone and laptop to find out what was going on. I had no details or updates so ran a quick check of Facebook. Dean's partners, who at the time had taken a hefty payment for this mission, were on Facebook, and I saw pictures of them in a bar in London, throwing back wine and champagne. Dean was paid next to nothing for his role; this wasn't his incentive. But I would have at least hoped that, if only for their enrichment, they would have kept tracking him, kept him somewhat safe.

No one was tracking him.

Dean made it from Tripoli to Tunis with only himself and his fixer; no weapons were needed or used, and the only enemy contact was a handshake or two along the way.

I had expected Dean to come home to me at this point. My operation had rendered me unable to use my left arm, and Mollie was still only two years old. A couple of days passed, and I saw receipts from Paris and London show up on the credit card. Instead of coming home, he had joined some of the team at a bit of a party following their escape. It was natural they saw him as their hero and wanted to party. But for me, I just wanted him to prioritize me and come home as soon as he could. But, as usual, said nothing and told him to enjoy himself.

A few days later Dean returned, and I cooked him a steak and champagne dinner. He began to eat and enjoyed a drink, but still, he was distant. There was no acknowledgement of what it took for me to make the dinner, how much pain I was in, that I had done it all one-handed. Even getting ready, washing my hair, I'd had to recruit my friends to help. I never wanted him returning to a messy house or wife; no matter how much I was hurting, I kept it all locked away.

Dean was home, but things were different. I didn't feel like he was really home. I tried everything I could to make him happy, but the distance was ever present. One day, he told me he missed Libya and missed helping people. He told me of the troubles in Jerusalem and the Gaza Strip and how he wanted to go and help. I asked if it was work, and he said he didn't see there being money in it. He really had no idea how much debt we were in, how much I struggled and juggled; now he wanted to disappear again to help people in another country.

Funny thing was I got it. I felt that way about the world too. I saw so much pain and destruction, and every time I witnessed it, I just wanted to go and help. For me, however, there was no wife at home who would look after everything, pay the bills, raise the kids, run the businesses, and keep all the usual day-to-day things away from me. I didn't have that luxury; Dean did. I told him it was his choice, and he had to do what made him happy.

He began to make plans to leave. This time, I told him, if he left, I couldn't guarantee I would be here waiting upon his return. He looked at me completely shocked. He'd never thought I would say these words.

I called my brother to come and collect Mollie; pulled out a bottle of port and two glasses; slammed them on the kitchen table; and told him, "We need to talk."

This time, we did talk. We talked, and we talked, until we couldn't talk any more. As the sun set, we put everything out on the table and were still talking as the sun rose in the August sky. Two things had become abundantly clear. Dean hated it every time he left us, and I showed no emotion. And I hated it every time he left but acted like he wouldn't be missed. We could not believe the revelation. Neither of us had been happy, but neither of us was willing to say the words. For years, we had both been pretending that life was great, while inside, we were both miserable. We had not only not been communicating but had also not been comprehending each other's needs.

It was time for change. Dean came to work with me in the property developing business. As for any security jobs that came in, we discussed them together and only took on the ones that benefitted us as a family. I blocked any and all attempts from others to use Dean's name for self-enrichment. Dean was able to save face, as my crown of being the bitch was shining brighter than ever; and among those types of people, I was more than comfortable with that.

Dean went to Somalia on one occasion. Mogadishu is renowned for being incredibly dangerous, and most personnel, including US and UK forces stay behind the perimeter. Dean's task did not allow for this; he had to go inside the gates. A group of older SAS men who were stationed there got pretty annoyed with this. This worried Dean, as he never wanted to disappoint his peers. He spoke to me, and I explained that this was a jealousy thing; he had to realize, in this world, he was the best of the best.

Dean entered Mogadishu, and on his first night there, a car bomb exploded outside his hotel. This was perfect! One of Dean's tasks was to discern the fastest route to the nearest hospital; when the ambulance arrived, Dean immediately jumped in his car and followed it. He reported back to me, and we were both delighted to have this element ticked off. My dad told me I was crazy for not being more concerned, and I told him, "Dean is working with me now. The risk before was lack of intelligence and backup; that risk is negated.

You hear a lot of people talk about taking a positive from a negative or living your best life; dream, believe, achieve, have zero negativity—all the usual clichés. However, very few have examples of *how* this is achieved. They make it out to be a mindset you can just create. But participating in talks and seminars—while I agree can help, to an extent, as you'll learn a lot about how a particular person does it—won't enable you to learn what living your life in such a way means. You can't truly learn until you're in it. It's about hard work, actions, doing what others won't, facing your fears, having a moral compass, holding true to your integrity, perseverance, and always helping others. Until you have lived these actions, no number of daily affirmations will change you.

CHAPTER EIGHTEEN

WHO DARES WINS

Dean continued to jump between the occasional task and working with me in the property developing world, but he found this world incredibly difficult to work in. Aside from the mundane days of architectural meetings and council checkups, he found civvies were a different breed altogether. In the military, when someone says they will do something, they usually do, as, let's face it, someone's life will usually depend on it. This is not so true in the real world; requests need to be chased, promises are not always promises, and people will step all over each other to get what they want. I was also finding it difficult to see him so bored and hated to see that glazed look in his eyes. But to add to that, I was also increasingly frustrated as to how it was affecting my position. When Dean would come to meetings with me, the contractors would always address Dean; even when it was me asking the questions, they would reply to Dean.

This was Dean's first real experience of misogyny and sexism in the workplace. Following one architect meeting, we were heading out the door, and he turned to me and said, "Does that hurt?"

I looked at him. "Does what hurt?" I asked curiously.

"When they treat you like that?" he replied.

He went on to explain how he had watched me work day and night, build up my business, negotiate, research, draw up plans, build amazing properties, and yet, when he was in the room, they treated me like I didn't exist. "I was just curious if that hurts you?" he ended.

Hurt was probably one of the feelings. But frustration was probably more accurate. No matter how much I proved myself, the glory could be taken away in seconds at the sight of Dean. I don't have a big ego, but I did yearn for just a sliver of recognition and respect. Truth was, I had become accustomed to just ignoring it, getting on with the task, and fighting for my seat at the table. I couldn't battle every misogynistic guy out there; life is far too short. I just had to keep growing, working hard to achieve, and moving forward. But I knew I needed to get Dean into something else. This mundane life would kill him faster than any bullet ever would.

One day, we received a phone call from a television producer, Andrew. He wanted to run a concept by Dean. He had been given Dean's name as being the best of the best in security and in Special Forces. He explained he had this concept for a new TV show and wanted to discuss it with Dean. Andrew flew to Aberdeen from London to discuss it further. The concept centered on putting regular people through the Special Forces selection process. They had the idea, but the formula was all over the place. Dean sat down with Andrew for hours, discussed various ways to adapt the show, to make it more authentic, and to show the viewers what it takes to become Special Forces without actually giving away any secrets.

UK Special Forces training is known as the toughest in the world. It was used as the basis for US Navy SEALs training, and it's known around the world that only the best of the best can pass it. The selection process is six months long and includes aspects such as hill phase, jungle phase, and interrogation. You have one shot to pass (unless removed for medical reasons), and it's ruthless. The SAS and SBS take the same six-month course, and once complete, the SAS are badged. The SBS, however, have to go further to then complete their boat handler and Special Forces diving courses before they are signed off, making SBS selection tougher than any other course.

My experience of living in camp and witnessing the work of the SBS is that they are very unassuming and incredibly humble. Humility is one of the main traits of the SBS. So how would it be possible to make a TV series using real guys? They generally didn't like the limelight. Alarm bells were ringing with me because of this. I knew Dean would never do it unless he got the sign-off from the Ministry of Defense (MOD) and, more importantly, his peer group.

Dean continued to develop the concept, and the finished article was pretty impressive and lined up to be a great show. All he was awaiting was the sign-off. Soon after, we received a letter in the post from the MOD, saying the department would not sanction Dean taking part in the show. I asked Dean if we could appeal, but he was adamant that, if the MOD had said no, he would not be doing it. He would never compromise his integrity or reputation.

He had spent a lot of time on this and was proud of what the show could become. He didn't want to let the producers down, so he told them he would find them people who would do it. They had to be badged guys, either from SAS or SBS, but the selection pool was small, as there were not many who would be willing to compromise their reputation.

Dean set up a group chat, but there were only a few who were interested without the MOD sign-off. There were a couple of guys who, for various reasons, were able to do it and were not concerned about doing it without sign-off. Two of them stepped up immediately. Dean ran their names past Andrew and made the introductions, and they both jumped at the chance of being involved in the show.

SAS: Who Dares Wins was commissioned by a network in the United Kingdom and, subsequently, was franchised to a number of other countries, including the USA. Dean was delighted he was able to help. But even then, with my very limited experience in the industry, I knew Dean had just helped create something amazing and would receive no credit for it.

When season two was commissioned, Dean was once again asked to join. However, he had now seen the reaction of the lads within the units and had witnessed the fallout. Friendship and integrity are everything to Dean. So, this time, he politely declined. Dean was never remunerated or credited for his work helping to create the show, but he took comfort in how he was able to help the guys he did help get that leg up.

This wasn't the first time Dean's love and respect for the British Army had been detrimental to our purse strings. Following Dean's injury and subsequent medical discharge, he was awarded a minor compensation. Given the level of his injuries, I said he should appeal. However, he absolutely refused. His reasoning at the time was he didn't want to take money that may benefit other lads.

A few years had passed, and I broached the subject again. This time and following the refusal for him to take part in the show, he was a little more open to the idea. I pulled all the files and evidence and told him I believed he fell into a higher tier. We did a bit of research and spoke to a few friends who had been successful in their appeals. We were advised to contact the Royal British Legion, who were an amazing support throughout. And finally, Dean was awarded the compensation he deserved.

Dean, however, still felt uncomfortable about accepting this; he felt he had not earned this money and didn't want handouts. Along with this anxious look, I could still see evidence of the lost look in Dean's eyes; he seemed to be lacking purpose. The SAS show had given him a distraction. But as that continued without him, he was now back to trying to find his way. The compensation appeal process provided further distraction, but he was still lost.

I was also at a loss as to how to deal with this, but it was never far from my mind. I knew I had to come up with something—and fast.

CHAPTER NINETEEN

✤✥✦✥✤

GROWING TEAM STOTT

Following a successful property deal, I surprised Dean with a trip to the Maldives. We rented a beautiful water bungalow, and on April 18, 2015, we renewed our vows. It was an incredibly special day, just the two of us and two witnesses. We drank champagne and discussed our future. The day produced the special memories and photos, photos we've never shared with anyone.

We talked about our family and how we loved our setup. But wouldn't it be cool if it was bigger? When his dad had become really sick, he had revealed that his dad had a sister he hadn't seen for over forty years. She had emigrated to Australia in the seventies, and he believed she may have already passed away. The family had managed to track her down, and Dean's dad was able to talk to her just before he passed.

His sister, Helen, had gone on to have two children of her own, Ken and Robyn, who both had two children. The whole family decided to come and visit us in September 2015. We had the most amazing time, and Robyn and I quickly became great friends.

Helen and her husband, Ian, agreed to babysit Mollie one evening while we all went out. It was a pretty heavy and wild night, and I woke up to the mother of all hangovers the next morning. Dean laughed but I wasn't laughing.

"I'm so sick," I complained.

"You're just hungover," he said with a clear lack of the sympathy I required.

This definitely felt worse than a hangover, but maybe I was just getting old!

The family left, and we promised we would return the visit and head over to Australia to see them very soon.

A few weeks later, I discovered that visit would have a plus one. It wasn't a hangover I'd had; it was morning sickness. Baby number two was on their way.

As a girl who had yo-yo dieted her whole life, I was consistent with one thing—being slightly overweight whenever I would fall pregnant—and this baby was no different. I was 168 pounds when I discovered I was pregnant, and if Mollie's pregnancy was anything to go by, I was preparing for a massive weight gain (70 pounds with her!). Pregnancy was definitely my one time in life when I didn't sweat the weight; my mothering instincts are incredibly strong, and good, strong healthy babies were more important than anything.

While Mollie's pregnancy had come with its own challenges, nothing could prepare me for what I had to face with this child. My business partners at the time took great offence to me falling pregnant; they enjoyed that I worked my ass off for their majority shareholding profit, and it terrified them to think any of that might change. Well, it didn't. I was only more determined to prove I could do it all.

The home we were renting at the time was not great, and I told Dean we needed to find somewhere more suitable. I say *we*, but this, along with almost every other responsibility, lay firmly in my court.

Lorna, my sister-in-law, who'd also discovered she was pregnant, three weeks after I did, came with me until we found the perfect home in a little village outside the city. It was ideal for a new baby. I signed on the dotted line before Dean had a chance to view it. Ever since the whole Libya and *"escaping to the Gaza Strip"* incident, I had sworn I would never be in that position again. I was too reliant on Dean and had put too much into creating his world. I had neglected my own growth. I needed to have my independence and not have my whole world revolve around making him happy. With this baby on the way, this was even more essential. This may sound harsh, but it was incredibly important for me to be able to look after Mollie, Dean, and this baby; and for that, I had to look after myself.

We were only ever in the position to afford one car. But as I was in the office every day, and Dean was coming in at different times, we decided, for economical and fitness reasons, we would purchase Dean a bicycle. Previous to this, he had only ever cycled on his paper route as a kid. We lived seven miles from town, so it was a great bit of physical exercise for him, something Dean always needed in order to retain his mental health.

I still had the feeling that he felt lost and disconnected. I could see it more and more often and could easily recognize the signs now. I was six months pregnant. Dean's thirty-ninth birthday was approaching. As I sat one day racking my brains as to what could be done, I suddenly had a light bulb moment. I knew what needed to be done.

I went to the store and picked up a book, a book that was soon to change our lives—*The Guinness Book of World Records*. Since our communication levels had rocketed, our new favorite thing to do was, every Sunday morning, sit at the breakfast table and make plans. We'd plan for the day, the week ahead, and the year. We'd talk about our goals and dreams and work out where we were with them. This Sunday morning, I pulled out the book.

"What's this?" he asked.

Well, he knew what it was, but I think the question was, *What do you want me to do with it?* Dean had lost the adrenaline he once had in the Special Forces. He'd regained it during his time in Libya, but normal life just wasn't bringing him the rush he needed. He needed a challenge. And what better way than to break a world record?

"What do you think I should do?" he asked as he looked at me, so I understood the literal meaning of his question. Translated—"Alana, tell me what to do please!"

There was one record that required one to eat more than twelve Ferrero Rochers in two minutes. Maybe I should go for this, I thought. But seriously, whatever it was, it needed to get his heart rate up, and the achievement needed to be incredible, almost impossible, or a world first.

As fate would have it, as we were discussing the different ideas and how we could use it to do some good, Prince Harry got in touch and told us that William, Kate, and himself were setting up a mental health initiative and suggested Dean may wish to fundraise for this at the same time. It was a no-brainer really. Dean could combine his passion for physical exertion and achievement, along with our joint passion for helping people and changing lives. It was confirmed, but we just needed the perfect challenge.

We decided we would raise £1 million pounds ($1.3 million dollars). So, the challenge had to reflect this. Running the London marathon just wouldn't cut it. A few days later, he came to me with an idea. A Scottish cyclist had broken the world record cycling from Cape Town to Cairo.

"That's good," I said. "But isn't it … well … a bit easy for you?"

Dean looked at me with pure bewilderment as I flicked through the book of world records. "It's over ten thousand kilometers. How is that easy?" he proclaimed.

"Well, it's not easy for me," I said, still studying the book. "But for you it doesn't feel enough … Wait here! Look." I pointed to the cycling page of the book—and the longest motorable road in the world, the Pan-American Highway.

"Where is it?"

This was a question neither of us would ever have to ask again. Over the coming month, we studied every inch of that road. We learned everything there was to know about it.

I was now in the full throes of pregnancy and planning one of the most extraordinary cycling and fundraising adventures to have ever taken place. All this while running three businesses, looking after a four-year-old, and keeping Dean laser-focused. I had my work cut out for me; that was for sure. My business partners, who at this stage were already annoyed I was pregnant, grew even more irritated about this extra work I'd taken on. When it came to these guys, they almost had a sense they owned me, and I had to do as they said.

There were cultural issues. I was a white woman, and, in their culture and their eyes, I was definitely beneath them. They felt they had all the power and did not like it when they felt anything was out of their control. This was nothing I hadn't dealt with in one form or another over the years, so I dealt with it as I usually did. I just got on with it, ignored the noise, and kept moving forward.

My final days on the run up to the birth were spent busily trying to get all the loose ends tied up and all the meetings that needed completed in the bag. We were still actively working on sponsorship, and every meeting counted. We had a meeting booked in and had arranged a Skype call with an associate.

During the call, my water broke; however, the main meeting was still to come. I felt the first contraction come, but I could tell it was not so intense. The meeting was in thirty minutes, and my contractions were incredibly far apart. Dean suggested we go to the hospital, but I said no; the contractions were way too far apart to cancel this meeting.

Thirty minutes later, I was sitting in Starbucks conducting a meeting with an important donor to the cause with contractions now coming quite regularly. As each contraction arrived, I would literally grind my teeth together, inhale deeply, listen intently, and breathe through it.

As we drew the meeting to a close, the breathing was becoming more and more difficult; I had to wind things up. With one last big breath, I calmly told the donor I was delighted he was on board, shook his hand, and said goodbye. He began casually chitchatting, and I politely told him I really did have to rush now; the contractions had now been coming at six-minute intervals, and I should probably be getting to the hospital.

I don't think I will ever forget the look in his eyes. Of course, he was super helpful to get us to our car. Yet, he was completely taken aback by the circumstances that unfolded. We are still great friends to this day, and he tells me he uses the story when trying to motivate his team. It has become a "no excuses" motivational speech for him.

We arrived at the hospital, in full pain mode, and were immediately escorted to the labor suite. They were braced and ready for this wee guy to join the world. As with Mollie, it began as a pretty quiet time; Dean used it as his opportunity to try to beat me at scrabble on the iPad. Every time a contraction started, he would pass me the iPad, as you only had two minutes to come up with a word. That was how competitive we were; not even labor would stop Dean trying to win.

I could hear women screaming from another room. The young doctor in my room, a trainee from Malaysia who was in the labor ward for the first time, asked me, "Why don't you make noise? It doesn't hurt you?"

I calmly told him that everyone deals with pain in different ways; some are very vocal and want everyone to know how much it hurts, while others keep it to themselves. This is true for both physical and mental pain. I was just a person who kept my pain to myself.

Dean, however, had begun to have a phantom pregnancy and had developed incredible back and pelvic pain. He was very vocal about this. All the midwives were fussing around him, and even I was checking he was OK between contracting and pushing.

I vividly remember the pain of the final stages with this baby boy; he was ready to cause some pain. As he entered the world, I fell 100 percent in love. This was the baby boy who'd been waiting to come into my life since I was fifteen; and now, he was here.

Dean held him in his arms with incredible pride and love in his eyes. "What shall we call him?" he asked.

I was far too tired to care at this point. "You decide," I mumbled. I knew what name I wanted; I had my heart set on Rocky, due to my love and admiration for all things Sylvester Stallone and boxing. But when Dean said, "How about Tommy?" it was just perfect.

Tommy was born on July 1, 2016, a hundred years after the Battle of the Somme, where a million soldiers were killed; they were named Tommies. My grandad, one of the most amazing examples of men I knew, was called Tommy, so the name was just perfect. Tommy was also born on what would have been Princess Diana's birthday. So Dean's first message after family was to Harry. He was delighted to tell him of the new arrival, and the prince was just as excited to hear about it.

Tommy was born at 3:02 a.m., and my first email that day was at 9:00 a.m. My partners were concerned about when I would re-turn to work and sent me a list of jobs that needed completing, all of which they were more than, or at least should be more than, capable of completing themselves. But not even the simple fact I had just given birth six hours ago would stop them.

It's pretty obvious to most that their actions were very poor; however, my actions were no better. I had not respected my own boundaries and, therefore, didn't enforce them either. This was true for my work and my home life. I was allowing people to abuse my own strong work ethics to support their own advantage. We got Tommy home, and I sat with my laptop to my side while Tommy fed on my other side.

This baby was different, though. He was hungry! Very soon, the breast wasn't enough for him, and I had to include formula feeds. This was never something I felt guilty about. I always said I would breastfeed but only if it was good for the both of us. My guilt, however, came from wondering if it was my workload that was stopping my milk from being as much sustenance as he needed to satisfy his hunger. That guilt has since disappeared, and I now know he was and still is just a hungry boy!

CHAPTER TWENTY

✦✦✦✦✦✦✦✦

PLANNING THE CHALLENGE

There was no postbirth mummy and baby time for me; it was straight back to work, planning the challenge, and working on Dean's fitness and nutrition. We had to learn about all eleven charities involved in the campaign, beef up on mental health and nutrition, discover all new ways of physical training, learn the layout of the Pan-American Highway and all fourteen countries involved in the journey and, plan it all around work and family.

We read book after book about cycling challenges and preparation, but Dean was always very insistent on asking the experts. No matter how much research I put into things, if someone came along who seemed more qualified or looked that bit shinier, he would always go with them, and it usually didn't turn out well.

The first training company he approached was highly regarded in the United Kingdom. However, I wasn't loving them. My first issue was that they wanted to charge a very high fee to work with Dean and still receive full coverage. Dean was adamant he wanted them, so we proceeded. I refused for the payment to come from the charity, so I said we would only do it if it came from our own pockets.

When it came to nutrition, the company was very used to dealing with aerobic athletes and endurance athletes but not a mix. This challenge would last for over three to four months and needed a new approach to nutrition. There was no one out there who understood this or who was willing to take the time to learn.

I took matters into my own hands and began studying sports nutrition. I learned everything I possibly could about the subject and eventually qualified as a sports nutritionist. It wasn't enough, though. I needed to replace the nine thousand to twelve thousand calories a day that he would be burning, and I had to do it quickly, as he needed to spend his time needed on the bike. I went on to study for an advanced sports nutrition diploma and learned all the finer details. I worked overnight while I fed Tommy in order to get the study in, not affect Dean's training, and still do my day job. Eventually, it paid off, and I was delighted when I passed the course to become an advanced sports nutritionist.

It didn't stop there, though. I spent hours in the kitchen like some mad scientist trying to perfect what he could consume and still keep him moving. Dean was a very willing guinea pig and was very polite when the recipes would go wrong. I created every type of smoothie imaginable. I even managed to create one with 150 grams of protein that was still drinkable. It took a while and a few vomit sessions but got there in the end, and it was so worth it.

As a girl constantly on a diet I had to be incredibly careful not to mix my meals with his, as that would have had disastrous consequences for both of us! I created meals that were easy to consume and full of good macros and calories, and Dean would sit at the table and enjoy every bite. I still don't think he realizes how much work it took to get there. But then again, that is true for pretty much everything. People tend to focus on the results rather than the hard work that came before this.

There had always been an old-school approach in our house. Despite us both being alphas, certain tasks were very stereotypical, and cooking was one of them. This was definitely the woman's job, as decided by both Dean and me. I enjoy the creating, and he enjoys the consuming!

The company we had chosen to do his challenge training prep

was falling more and more behind our pace. Dean and I would argue regularly, as he was being his usual self and not wishing to disappoint or offend, whereas I didn't have that same level of need to please. If you were not on board and moving at our pace, then you had to get off; the train was moving with or without you, and we had no room for stowaways.

Dean created a promotional video with Prince Harry, and I was furious to discover that he wore the company's brand in the video. They had charged Dean a hefty fee for their work and deserved no free promotion.

Dean is an incredibly driven individual, but he also has amazing amounts of respect for people with knowledge; if they are the experts in the field, he will take their word. This is something we don't share, as I am always questioning things. I guess this comes from having believed the doctors knew what they were doing with my mum.

I watched as they worked and got more and more concerned, so I started researching and training myself. One day, Dean's coach questioned his ability and told him he was "doomed for failure." This was enough for me. I told Dean they were not good for our positive mental attitude, and he needed to get rid of them. I had the backup plan already prepared, but I needed him to be the bad guy for once.

He contacted the company and explained it wasn't working and that we would find an alternative method. Swiftly following this, I introduced Dean to a company I'd heard a lot about. They were not national like the other company. However, they were highly recommended and ready for the challenge.

Dean was incredibly skeptical and refused to believe a local company could do this. So I arranged a meeting with Ken, the owner of Total Endurance, a local Aberdeen company who looked after athletes and Ironman contenders. Dean was immediately impressed by Ken, and when we discussed the fee, Ken wouldn't even entertain it. He believed in the challenge and the cause, and most importantly, he believed in Dean. He was happy with me being involved with the nutritional work and was never precious about sharing hints, tips, and advice. We had found the dream coach.

As the end of 2016 approached, Dean was approached again by

the production company involved in the SAS show. They said they had a new show coming up and wanted to see if Dean would be interested. It was about MI5 and the world of secret espionage. Dean explained that he would be too busy with the fundraising and the challenge to commit to anything long term; however, he would happily be an advisor for an episode or two. We agreed to this, as it was not a breach of any of his military ethics, and the release date was set for the same time as the promotional video with Prince Harry was to be released—therefore, it would mean some great exposure for the campaign.

We decided as a family to take a trip together before everything got too crazy with the campaign and headed off to visit Dean's family in Australia, returning the favor from their visit. As with everything, we had told them we would visit, so we did. We had an amazing time and, on our way back, had a stopover in Thailand. The issue was we both find it incredibly hard to unwind and switch off; we always know there is work to be done so feel vacations get in the way of that.

We jumped on the internet and changed our flight to come home three days early so we could really get into the campaign. There was so many costs involved in the setup of it all. During the process of establishing everything and creating promotions, we spent almost £50,000 of our own money, the money Dean had received as compensation for his injury. This was a tough decision, but we discussed it together. We knew how many people the campaign would help, so we decided it was worth it.

A few days after returning from Thailand, *Spies* was released featuring Dean as an advisor, swiftly followed by the release of the promotional video with Prince Harry. This was when things really blew up. We were inundated with offers of support from every angle and elements of support from every field, sponsors, donors, you name it. However, the offers often came with a clause, usually involving Prince Harry.

"We will give you free bikes if we can get a picture of Harry sitting on our bike."

"I'm trying to get my award from The Queen, so I'll fund this if you can get me that."

"If Harry can give a shout-out to my business, I'll give you a free tattoo!"

You name it, we had the offer! I had to filter through all the offers and try to select people I thought were genuine. Unfortunately, I had no experience in this and no understanding of the lengths people will go to and the deceit they will use to get close to fame and/or become famous themselves.

Our first offer of help came from a wonderful woman who'd dedicated her life to supporting charities. I think she gave us a false sense of security, as we believed everyone would be as amazing as she was. Needless to say, we were wrong.

Our next yes was to a medic who came with a great CV and a great offering of help. He wanted to come on the trip, supply all the medical supplies and extra support, and support the fundraising—all at his own costs. He told us that mental health was very important to him, and as he was so successful in life, this was his way of giving back. We were delighted by this offer, and even though we had many more medics offering help, his pitch definitely won us over.

Next, we had a bike mechanic who told us he'd taken part in similar expeditions and was an expert in his field. He was ex-military and was passionate about supporting mental health. He again wanted to come on board completely at his own costs and time and was incredibly excited to help.

We were then approached by an old Army guy who had taken Dean through training at one point. He told us about his successful career post-military, how he had built a multimillion-dollar empire. And now, being semiretired, he was struggling with his mental health and some past drug issues and was in desperate need of a project. Dean's love of the military and need to support guys kicked in at this point. We knew this guy didn't have any of the skills we were looking for; however, he could come in to oversee things. He'd also offered to fund some of the projects and come on at his own expense, so we agreed to help him and bring him on board. He had a friend whose partner was a sports therapist, and as muscle recovery was key, this was an area we needed help with. She was mostly excited about the adventure and being part of something incredible.

Everything in my life now seemed to revolve around the planning. My time was consumed with the challenge, planning, working, fundraising, the kids, and Dean. I had little to no time for the rest of my family, friends, or myself really. On the morning of the January 21, 2021, I came down for breakfast, and Dean was already downstairs. He was sitting at the breakfast table looking at me with concern.

"What's up?" I asked.

"I think you should sit down," he said.

When someone says that, you can pretty much be sure that what you're about to hear will not be good.

"I think you need to call your dad," he said.

I was getting annoyed and worried at the same time. I told him he needed to just tell me what was going on.

"Your dad has cancer."

With those words—the same words I'd heard about my mum exactly nineteen years previously to the day—I was right back to the fifteen-year-old girl I'd once been. I broke down; there was absolutely no way I could lose my dad right now. I called him and demanded he come over immediately.

He jumped in a cab, and as soon as he got out, I gave him the biggest hug. Sitting him down, I asked him a million questions, none of which he had the answers to. I insisted on attending the following hospital visit. I sat down with the doctor and a list of questions. I wrote down every word the doctor told me and then returned home and opened up Google.

I sat all night googling, researching, and learning about prostate cancer. I was pretty much an oncologist by the time I was done. I was now armed with the knowledge I needed and felt more equipped to help Dad. This wasn't a task my dad could take on alone. I knew he needed me to get him through this.

CHAPTER TWENTY-ONE

HOW TO ASK
FOR MONEY

Given the level of my workload and with everything I had going on, I knew I also needed help and decided to recruit an assistant. It needed to be someone highly adaptable, self-motivated, and driven. A friend of mine told me her sister, Frances, was looking for work. I had known this girl for most of her life and loved her. I had watched her work in hotels, bars, and restaurants, and she always stuck out to me as a great worker. I interviewed her, and we took her on. She had no idea what she was getting into at the time, but I can honestly say, it was the best decision I made. Frances became an integral part of not only the challenge but also my life. I always wonder if I could have done it without her. I am just glad I didn't have to live that reality.

There was a lot to do. Dean and Ken set into the training, learning new levels of fitness and terminology we had never heard of. Dean thought bike fit meant how fit you are on the bike; he had no idea there was a correct positioning. He learned about watts and cadence and how simple shifts in positioning can make all the difference.

We had no shortage of offers of kit, but what we really needed was a main sponsor to take on the challenge. It's funny how these things happen. At the time, I was working with a local contractor. He was very much into charitable endeavors and introduced us to business associates of his who worked for a large wealth management company. We met with him, and he introduced us to his CEO and company founders. We attempted to arrange meetings with these guys, but something would always come up.

During one of our trips to London, we had a free day. So, with me dressed in my white jeans, flip-flops, and pink Victoria's Secret jumper, we headed out to do the tourist thing. An hour into our excursion, we received a call asking if we could be at the would-be sponsor's office in Mayfair in one hour to pitch our idea. There was no time to change. So off we went; I was dressed in pink, ready to pitch for half a million dollars!

I often hear it said that appearance is everything, that one must be smartly dressed, and that a person will judge you in the first five seconds of meeting you. While this is true to an extent, I disagree that the clothes you wear are what is being judged in that first five seconds. A person's energy is the very first thing we become aware of; our gut reacts to that energy in the very first second; the gut then examines the rest. When good energy is combined with a smile, eye contact, and a good handshake, a person has made a good first impression. Then you might notice their clothes.

We entered the very impressive building a few minutes' walk from St. James Palace. The interior was like something out of *Pride and Prejudice,* and the doorman fit the stereotype. We were led up to the fourth floor and through the old Victorian hallways. Entering the room, it felt like I was walking into the scene from *Mary Poppins,* when the kids were taken to the bank to invest their tuppence.

We sat at the table, and two gentlemen entered the room. They wore suits that exuded wealth and were poker straight. I took a deep breath, stood up proud, extended my hand, looked them in the eye, gave a big smile, and introduced myself. Once seated, it was clear that time was money; they were not here to hang around. It was straight into the pitch.

Dean and I bounced off each other as we explained every aspect of what we were doing and why. We answered every question with enthusiasm, and they quickly loosened up and joined in our excitement.

Then came the awkward question. "What will happen if you don't achieve your goals?"

We had been asked this before, and each time we responded the same. "There is no plan B. We have an objective, and we will hit this target."

We knew the only way we wouldn't raise this money and break this record was death; even then, we would probably find a loophole.

We walked out of that room that day with full sponsorship; all the costs would be covered. What this meant for us was that every penny we raised through other donations would go to the charities. This was significant for us, as we'd been told that most fundraising efforts worked on the sixty-forty method, where 40 percent of funds raised went to costs and 60 percent to the causes. We were going to be one of a few who could give 100 percent.

This was incredible, and we went straight into the next stage—raise £1 million. Fundraising is not a game and is not something that should be taken lightly. Asking for money through donation and charity is no different than asking for money in business. There is a formula to it, and it is all about the planning, the homework, and the strategy. If you want to learn more about this, I have written a help book called *How to ask for Money*; it will give you all the tools you need.

For this challenge, we planned several events, from skydiving to fundraising functions to mini challenges. Mollie even cut off all her hair, raising almost £1,000, impressive for a six-year-old. It was very much a team effort; we worked together. Dean was out there as the face of the challenge, and I held my place behind the scenes, continuing to work night and day to make things happen.

We still tried to fit in family time, and for Dean's fortieth birthday, I got all his friends and family together in London and then took him and the kids to the Greek Islands. We hired a sailing boat and lived in it for a week, sailing around all the islands. We followed a fleet around; this was required for safety purposes. But mostly, we did our own thing. At the end of the trip, the crew awarded us with an award for the easiest breezy family due to our chilled-out nature throughout the trip. We never complained, did our own thing, and just got on with it. This was the very essence of our family dynamics. Put us in the toughest of situations, and this is where you will see us at our calmest. Sit us down by a beach with a cocktail, and we start getting all stressed and fidgety. We are all about the doing.

My own business partners were getting more and more demanding, as they were getting more and more annoyed by my other priorities—such as raising money and looking after my family. The thing was I gave 100 percent to everything I was involved in. It was only my own health and well-being that took a back seat. I was working around the clock, going literally days without sleep. I knew eventually something would have to give.

The challenge and campaign had become the priority above all else. Dean was in full-time training and was gone most days. His training would include hundred-mile cycles and meetings with his coach. When he was home, he would be sleeping or soaking his sore muscles in the bath. I had to ensure the food was ready when he needed it and he had everything he needed to keep going. I kept everything else away from him. Perfecting a nine thousand-calorie-a-day menu was not easy, but what was even tougher was hiding from him how tough everything was. We had made a pact following Libya to always communicate, but I felt that he needed to be laser-focused on this challenge. When it was all over, I could release to him. But for now, I had to keep it to myself.

Everything in the home was on my shoulders. All bills, all business affairs, anything to do with the kids, my family issues, my dad, his family, the planning of the challenge, the fundraising, social media—everything—lay firmly at my door. My friends were at their wits' end. They were constantly worried about my health, and they would sit me down on a regular basis trying to make me take care of myself more. I completely understood what they were saying, but they didn't fully get who I was. I was on autopilot robot mode. I had to keep focused and see the road ahead. I loved them so much for who they were and that they cared, and I still love them for that to this day. They will probably never stop telling me to slow down, and I will never stop telling them I am fine!

Our first fundraiser was approaching, an event at a very prestigious hotel in Aberdeen. Planning these things, one would normally enlist the help of an events planner. But no, I decided I didn't have quite enough on and planned the whole event myself, from guest list to talent searching to auction item sources; this was a full-time job in itself.

As I was concentrating on this, the newly formed support team was left with tasks to complete. This was where cracks were starting to form. The guy we'd put in charge of the operation was falling further and further behind. He was keen to take trips to Mexico and rub shoulders with the who's who of Central America using Dean and Harry's name but not so keen when it came to the pressure of the job. I knew he was working pro bono, so I didn't push him too hard. But at the same time, we had an objective to achieve, and we couldn't risk it failing for the sake of sensitivity. I sat him down and discussed with him the challenges he was facing, and we agreed I would take a number of responsibilities off his shoulders. My workload was piling up, and the balance was getting hard; and of course, I kept it well away from Dean.

The first fundraising event was a great success. We raised amazing amounts of money, got some real promotion of the event, and we were really starting to see some movement with the mental health campaign. The eight charities we'd been working with as part of the campaign had now become eleven. Contact, the potential military mental health charity, was another incredible brainchild of Prince Harry; it was to be a collaboration of military mental health charities. But for many reasons, including lack of support, he couldn't make this happen at the time. Harry's dream of Contact was never formed. Instead, we decided to split Contact's share between four military mental health charities—the Royal British Legion, Walking with the Wounded, Combat Stress, and Help for Heroes. All the eleven charities would sit under the umbrella name of Heads Together.

One evening, I received a message from one of Dean's friends. He'd heard from Combat Stress, and the suicide helpline for veterans had been given the go-ahead, largely off the back of the work so far. I was over the moon. There was no better feeling than seeing the direct impact of the work we were doing. In the short time we'd been running the campaign, we knew personally of two soldiers who had taken their own lives. I believe during the challenge we were hearing about a suicide of friends of friends an average of at least once a week. Every forty seconds, someone takes their own life, and this is entirely preventable.

The charity and their causes were now hitting home, and fundraising was becoming more a priority than ever. This was when things really got interesting. The Royal Foundation, who were in charge of Heads Together had now decided they didn't want the responsibility of accepting the money and distributing it between the charities. Heads Together was not an official charity in its own right, so we couldn't donate directly to them. So, they now asked us to set up our own charity, accept the money through this entity, and donate it directly to the eleven charities.

At this point, I had zero clue about running a charity, and I was planning on raising more than a million pounds. I knew this was going to be tough but honestly had no idea what I had in store. I had a genuine belief that working with the Royal Foundation would make the fundraising easier. How wrong I was.

CHAPTER TWENTY-TWO

SUPPORT, OR LACK OF IT

Working with the Royal Foundation was incredibly difficult. They were a small team of thirty-five people, and they were responsible for all the initiatives and ideas Prince Harry and the Duke and Duchess of Cambridge had and then, later, the Duchess of Sussex, Meghan Markle. It was difficult to stop any initiative brought forward by the team from growing arms and legs, and for Heads Together, it was no different. Every move we made had to follow a huge amount of protocol, even when it came to accepting donations; there was so much red tape it was exhausting. I understood that everything had to be done just right when it came to an organization like this. But often, actions were taken that defied logic. We were also met with a certain amount of animosity; I have my suspicions as to why that is, mostly related to the reason we'd come on board. Harry had brought us into this fundraising, and I may be wrong, but I don't think members of the team showed him as much respect as they did the other principals.

So, now we were working with eleven charities. It was a whole new ball game, as originally we only had to deal with one, Heads Together. We now had to deal with each charity individually. This was a challenge in itself. But it was a challenge we embraced. We visited every single charity and got to see firsthand the work they did. Every charity had a different function in the mental health sector. There were charities you were interested to learn more about and others that touched you to your very soul. When you see firsthand where the money you are raising will be going and who it will benefit, it gives you real fire in your belly to make sure you achieve all the targets you set. We knew, for example, every pound we raised gave one child access to a vital help line. Knowing fourteen thousand miles would help fourteen thousand children really helped us in our motivation.

Our visits with the charities were very emotional. It always left us feeling full of energy to help these people. We were never able to just visit and do nothing. We always had to help them feel we were really here to help. When we visited the family school, a unique, alternative, provision-free school in Central London for kids aged five to fourteen who'd been excluded from mainstream school due to serious emotional and behavioral issues, we were firstly struck by their environment. It was a beautiful, ninety-eight-degree summer day outside when we arrived at the inner-city building—a large gray stone building with no outside area or grassland. We entered the building and were first struck by how hot it was. We spoke to the fantastic staff there who told us there was no air-conditioning. They had no government funding and had to rely on fundraising and donors. As we entered the classroom, once again, the stuffiness and heat got to us first. These kids had serious psychological issues and had been removed from every mainstream school, and now they had to try to learn in this environment.

The first boy we spoke to was thirteen years old and had been in twenty-seven foster homes in his life. He told us he loved going to school but wanted fresh air.

Another lovely young man came straight up to Dean and said, "What are you going to do?"

Dean started talking to him about the bike ride and the challenge, and the boy stopped him and said, "No. What are you going to do for us?"

It floored Dean. Dean had grown up in a homeless shelter, and this really got to him. He knew all about empty promises and "do-gooders." We looked at each other and realized all this talk about bike rides and physical activity was wasted here. These kids didn't own bikes; and going out for fresh air in the areas they grew up in meant fear.

Almost instinctively and without us saying anything to each other, we knew what we would do. We spoke to the school, and they told us they were raising funds for a better facility, where the kids would have outdoor space; our funding would go toward this. That was great for then, but we needed to do something now.

Gibraltar Barracks was an Army facility thirty miles from London. Dean had spent time there during his service, and we'd stayed there for a while during my first pregnancy. It was a wonderful place full of acres and acres of countryside, wildlife, and streams. Dean made the call, and within hours, we had secured a day out there.

The kids would be taken by bus from the school and would spend a day at the facilities. They would learn about the work Dean had done and about the area and just spend time outside in fresh air. They got to play in the lake and do some adventure challenges. The day was special, but the eye-opener was the moment one little boy came up and pulled on Dean's coat. He lifted up his hand and said, "What is this?"

In his hand was a conker (horse chestnut). It was at that point Dean realized this child had never been in the woods. He had never seen nature. His life was spent inside the gray walls of London, from foster home to foster home and school to school. This moment in nature was everything to them. And for Dean, I believe it gave him that extra push for every pedal of the wheel.

Dean was starting to get into the zone. His focus was firm, and he knew what he had to do. We had pretty much everything arranged and ready to go.

One of the other major jobs was pulling together a documentary team. Naively, I'd assumed once we'd agreed to bring them on board, they would then be able to organize their own admin. I was wrong. The responsibility landed firmly on my shoulders—arranging all visas, flights, accommodations, and transport for the production team was for me to deal with. I'd also assumed the team would find the financing and handle the distribution. Again, I was wrong. I had to arrange this and, luckily, found a full financer. I was doing the role of a producer even then without realizing it. The workload was extreme and intense, but I held it and held it strong.

Frances, my PA was my backbone. She kept me standing whenever I felt like I would fall. If you were to ask Dean, I always stood strong. I was indestructible, I was superwoman. And that worked for me. He never needed to see me struggling; he had to stay focused.

Christmas came around, and I knew the time was coming to say goodbye to Dean. Tommy had not long turned one, and Mollie, six years old. It was going to be easy to explain things to Mollie. She was more than used to Dean being away; she'd been experiencing that since she was a day old. Tommy, on the other hand, was used to seeing Daddy all the time. Sure, Daddy was usually in Lycra, but for the most part, our little boy got to see Dean every morning.

December was incredibly busy, but we managed to get in some precious time with the kids before Dean was ready to go in January. Our main sponsor had arranged their annual conference for the beginning of 2018, and Dean had agreed to speak at the event. The meeting was presented at the O2 in London in front of ten thousand people, followed by a fundraising dinner to raise donations for the challenge. They had set the date for January 26, 2018, so we decided this would be the perfect time to depart, immediately after the event. We spoke to the whole team, and everyone agreed to leave on the twenty-seventh. Now we had a date, and it all became real.

There was pressure to make sure everything we said was in place was actually in place. Frances and I were working hard on the support vehicles. The major issue we had was the Darien Gap—a thirty-six-mile stretch of jungle between Panama and Colombia that is impassable. The Guinness rules allow flights or ferries across the gap only. The issue at the time was trouble between Colombia and Panama, meaning ferries were not crossing; this meant we could not get support vehicles across. Our only option was to get two sets of vehicles, one to be at the start line in Ushuaia, Argentina, and the others to be in Panama City, Panama. This was incredibly hard work to organize logistically, but we made it work. We ensured the team had vans in Argentina. Then we were to ship the three vehicles from Florida to Panama City. It was all set. Or so we thought.

The member of the support team who was assigned to operations had very little responsibility by this point, following our previous discussion. But one of the tasks he did have was to organize the kit to be ready in Ushuaia. He had decided to use a shipping company to move the kit—spare wheels, parts, sleeping bags and tents, and such. In hindsight, this could have been managed more effectively. But this was our first challenge, and everything was about learning. I trusted he knew best.

The kit was due to arrive in plenty of time for Dean's planned start date of February 1, 2018. However, the container was now floating in the middle of the ocean, and the paperwork was not correct to ensure release at port.

I spoke to the ops manager, and he was nervous; he knew there may be an issue, and the stress was now getting to him. On Christmas Eve, he emailed Dean to say he could no longer continue with the challenge. The moving forward of the date, even though only by a few weeks, had pushed him over the edge. I knew I should have been more prepared for this given his previous actions, but I had naively believed that soldiers, especially higher-ranking ones such as himself, could handle ever-evolving situations. As they say, a good plan only ever survives first contact. But it had become too much for him. I returned his email saying I was grateful for all he had done but agreed it would be the right decision for him to step down. I told Dean I would take over all his remaining duties. At this point, it was only really the shipping, but it had been left in a total mess—just another problem I had to resolve.

Christmas Day arrived, and we cherished the day, knowing the time was coming that Dean would be leaving us for four months. For Christmas, my gift to Dean was a box containing a letter for each day he would be riding. In each letter, I wrote heartfelt words, poems, inspirational quotes, and stories from the kids. Dean would discover the meaning behind the letters later.

I try to make every Christmas special for everyone; ever since that Christmas my mum was too sick to celebrate, year in, year out I strive to make Christmas special. This Christmas felt extra special. Dad joined us, as he did every year. He was now coming though his radiation treatment and doing well. As I served up the turkey, I lit the candle. This special candle comes out on special occasions. We light it as a way of bringing everyone we've lost to the table; it's a very precious tradition we hold dear. I wanted to hold on to that day and make it last forever. This was my family around the table, and I knew very soon it would be separated. But I smiled, played a few board games, made sure everyone had full bellies and sore faces from laughing, and I raised a glass to the future.

My day job as a property developer was still in much need of my time. I was back to work the day after New Year's Day. I'd just completed two developments of my own and needed them up, running, and leased out before Dean set off. I'd resigned from the work with my other business partners; they wanted too much for far too little. Every hour in the twenty-four hours in a day was incredibly precious to me, so I had to trim the fat. Breaking up, whether that be in personal or business life, is never easy. But if you're in a toxic situation or an environment you feel uncomfortable, you have to ask yourself, *Is this situation championing me? And am I championing it?* If the answer is no to either of those questions, then it's time to exit.

We cherished every moment of the first few weeks of 2018. Then the day finally came to pack the bags. Packing Dean's bags was a routine I was very much used to. But even this was like a military mission; Dean packed with absolute precision. He'd been on many tours before, but this time, I could see his nerves. He had told the world he was going to break two world records and raise £1 million. He had spoken about the UK Special Forces ethos of the "unrelenting pursuit of excellence"; he believed it so much we even bought the trademark. He had put his name to this, and he was going to make it happen.

CHAPTER TWENTY-THREE

THE JOURNEY BEGINS

The day came to leave Aberdeen. Dean and I were to head down to London together, where we would attend a number of events before he would fly to Argentina. Dean dropped Tommy at nursery and kissed him goodbye. He walked Mollie to school and gave her the biggest hug. I could see how tough it was for him. The kids kept it together. But for him, well, I could most definitely see his stoic nature cracking.

In the background, I was still working on all the other logistics. Frances had taken over the shipping issues and had managed to get answers on the arrival of the kit in Ushuaia. She flew down with us to London, and as we arrived in Heathrow, she pulled me aside; she was also well aware to keep everything away from Dean. She told me the shipment would not arrive now until the February 7. This meant either Dean would have to hold off on his start day, or we had to come up with another plan.

Dean was now fully psychologically prepared for starting on the first, and any delays could have an impact. When you are taking on a massive feat, something that's never been done before, psychological preparation is one of the main keys to success. He was fully prepared, so Frances and I had to come up with a new plan. We looked at the route map and other ports, and we found out the ship was due to stop in Chile on February 7 before arriving in Ushuaia a week later; the date for Chile would coincide with Dean and the team arriving in Chile if they set off on February 1 from Ushuaia. We spoke with the team and agreed they had enough kit to see them through the first week; they would then meet another team member in Chile, who would get the shipment sorted for them. It was not the cleanest way of doing it, and if I was to do it all again, I'm sure there were a lots of lessons learned. But for this challenge, we made it work.

The team member who flew into Chile to sort the shipment was a great friend of Dean, and I'd him as a great friend since my first ever trip down to Poole to visit Dean. He was in it for all the right reasons—to help us where he could, to keep the team going, to help production, and to support the massive fundraising effort. He was very much void of ego and simply wanted to be there to help. He didn't care about the Prince Harry connection and was a loyal supporter of Dean and what he stood for.

Our first job in London was to visit Harry and say goodbye. We met at Kensington Palace where he was living at the time, and we were met by some PR people who would be taking our photographs. This was my first time in the company of Harry where it was a formal setting, with people recording and taking pictures. Normally, we were in a much more casual setting and vibe. The conversation was super uncomfortable with all the camera flashes and note-taking.

At the end of the discussion, he asked the press and PR team to leave the room and immediately the atmosphere relaxed. I remember thinking at that time, *I wouldn't wish this lifestyle on anyone.* Having to behave a certain way, never being able to relax, having to be careful of every word you say, who you make friends with, being under constant pressure to perform—why anyone sees that as a glamorous life to be desired, I will never know.

Our next big task was the launch party. We had been kindly gifted a loft party house above St. Pancras railway station. The penthouse apartment was incredible and could only be accessed by a private butler-controlled elevator. Everyone involved in the campaign so far was invited. Frances and I planned out the evening and the speeches. *Hello!*, a UK weekly magazine, came along to photograph and share the story. I was pretty excited, as, growing up, I used to see the magazine on the stands and think it was incredibly high-end. The only time I ever got the chance to read it was when someone left a copy lying in the dentist's waiting room. I definitely couldn't ever afford to buy it, let alone live any of the lifestyles it portrayed. Now, I was going to be in it.

I remember the very day it was published; I was so excited, and my inner child wanted to share it with all the kids at school who used to tease me. But of course, the adult in me controlled that. It was still exciting though. The evening was a great success and the perfect way to launch the task. The owner of the penthouse, Lord Fink, attended, and we were incredibly grateful to him for his generosity in hosting the event.

The following day, we attended the O2 arena. We were ushered through to the VIP area, and Dean was given his own suite to get ready, I thought this was pretty cool, given the stars who had performed here. In fact, the last time we'd attended, it was to watch Bon Jovi perform; we most certainly had not gotten backstage then.

Dean walked out onto the stage in front of ten thousand people in his Lycra and told his story; he talked about the challenge and our fundraising target. I was incredibly proud of him as the whole audience gave him a standing ovation.

Afterward, Dean was to do a meet and greet in the private VIP area of the arena. As I watched him working the room, I knew he was a natural at this. Being in front of a crowd was where he belonged. I was in the background, and that was always good for me. As he mingled with all the top dogs in wealth management, the main sponsor's CEO approached him. He told Dean he was incredible and said he was proud to be part of the team and that the entire team was impressed by him. He told him once Dean had finished the ride, he would have him back next year to tell the story of his adventure.

We had to rush back to the hotel to get ready for the evening at the Grosvenor House Hotel in London, where 1,200 of the top executives would attend a huge fundraiser. I dressed in a beautiful ball gown, and Dean wore his tuxedo. We arrived ahead of others, and as the room started to fill, it was clear it was filling with tuxedos and very few ball gowns. It was incredibly obvious, this Mayfair-based company still had the feel of the bank from Mary Poppins—all suits.

I saw a woman arriving, and I was excited; thank god, I'm not the only one. I would have some support here. She approached me with a very stern look on her face. Dean was off chatting with someone, and I was standing alone. "Can I help you?" she asked.

I wasn't sure exactly what she thought I needed help with. But I told her I was fine and attempted to introduce myself.

She asked if I should be here and if I was looking for someone.

Still very confused, I told her I was sitting at this table with my husband Dean Stott.

"Oh, you're the wife," she said, as if being "the wife" made it OK for me to be at the top table.

I couldn't understand this coming from another woman. Where was the support? Where was the solidarity? Was she judging my inability to be at the table by the way I looked or just that I was a woman? I couldn't work out where her judgment was placed.

The answer was made clear later when she finally got into conversation with me—asking questions about my role as a housewife, military spouse, and mother. She could never imagine for a moment I was a successful businesswoman and was running everything on my own in order for Dean to succeed in all he did without distraction. No, she took one look at me and decided my capabilities were limited to being a housewife. It was then I vowed I would never judge another woman; I would always give her the chance to tell me her story and celebrate her successes.

The evening began with the CEO presenting to the team. He advised that pledge sheets would go around the room, and the company would match every pound donated—pound for pound. At the close of the evening, we had raised £265,000. With the pound-for-pound match, that gave us a total of £530,000 before Dean had even set off.

The company was to donate its match directly to the charities, including Beat, a mental health charity focusing on eating disorders. I was quietly delighted about this but unable to discuss my reasons. I knew I'd had a secret struggle with issues around food and weight all my life, and I knew how important this was. I had only learned during my time with the campaign that these types of issues were classed as mental health problems.

Dean was also over the moon. It was an incredible boost to the challenge to begin his ride over 50 percent of the way to our fundraising target.

The next morning, we awoke. And immediately "deployment" Dean and Alana set in—meaning we'd turned cold, distant, and detached. We were avoiding small talk and standing stoically beside one another, and neither of us shared emotions, for fear of upsetting or cracking the other. He was ready to go. I had to be ready for him to leave.

We arrived at the airport and unloaded all the supplies and cases. The production team was meant to also be there to film the departure but, ultimately, missed the timing. This was their first major piece of filming, and they missed it. Annoying as it was, I brushed it off so as not to worry Dean and made some excuses for them. The team was ready. I hugged them all, wished them the greatest of success, and told them I was available day or night for anything they needed.

Now it was time to say goodbye to Dean. Everyone moved away as I stood eye to eye with him. I embraced him, looked him in the eye, and told him to go and smash it. I told him to remember the letters, to take each day at a time, and to stay focused. I told him all he had to do was cycle that bike. I would be taking care of everything else, and he was not to worry about a thing. One final kiss, and he was gone.

As Dean headed toward "the end of the world" (the nickname for Ushuaia), I headed back to Aberdeen. Frances and I drove the six hundred miles back to Aberdeen, returning the team van along the way. I dropped her home and asked her if she was ready.

"Yep" she told me. "You just tell me what to do, and I'll do it!" This was said with eager anticipation, and I just hoped I could live up to everyone's expectations and lead this challenge through to the end.

The Argentinean time zone was four hours behind us, so I had to work across the two time zones. I'd planned how to handle everything going on at both sides, and I knew sleep would have to be rationed.

Problems began almost immediately. The team arrived in Chile and had to drive down to Ushuaia. This was another area I could have improved on; because I was concentrating on raising as much money for the charities as I could, I'd looked for the cheapest options for everything we did. I was basing things on how Dean and I would handle them, without considering that others didn't have the same mindset and resilience that we had. Things like flying economy class was not something some of the team was used to, so they were irritated by the journey. Taking a car ride after a long journey also bothered them. The hotel I had booked in Chile was not quite up to their standards and they were all tired, so the following day the car journey was miserable for them. I had to take all their points and respect them; this was definitely a learning curve for me. It's incredibly important to focus on the abilities of your whole team. The old saying "a team is only as good as its worst player" is very true.

Once they arrived in Ushuaia the team sat down with Dean and told him they didn't think he should set off until the kit arrived in Ushuaia. They felt they should not start until they were 100 percent prepared, and everything was absolutely perfect. Dean listened to them and was already starting to feel the effects of being around their mindsets.

He called me and said it would be a safer option. I had to get him out of that headspace, I told him to go for a walk, think about the planning and work that had gone into this, take his head away from the negative, and focus forward. It was like trying to decide the perfect time to have a baby; perfect doesn't exist! I knew Dean could do this on the bare bones. He had the three most important pieces of kit already there with him—his mindset, his strength, and his bike. Everything else was a luxury and would be picked up in a few days. The best plan only ever survives first contact. This was first contact, and he now needed to adapt. Sitting around Ushuaia would just drive him crazy. I told him to call me back once he had walked off the negativity.

Thirty minutes later, the phone rang. "Sorry," he told me. "I'm leaving on the first as planned, and I'm heading north to the finish line."

I smiled and paused. "I know you are, babe. And I'll be right there waiting for you!"

On February 1, 2018, the team set off. The first turn of the wheel started the fourteen-thousand-mile journey. I would monitor Dean's journey via various apps and trackers, the team would report back, and I would monitor timings. Once I worked out where they would stop for the day, I looked for accommodation as close to the road as I could.

The world record stood at 117 days, and Dean had aimed to come in at 110 days. I had other plans and was always trying to push him that little bit further each day. The problem on the ground was the team would be strict on where they stopped Dean. So, if he was slightly away from the hotel, they would stop him at a marker and drive to the hotel and then, in the morning, return to the marker. This was frustrating, as I knew Dean always had that extra push. But the team was always conservative and didn't understand Dean as I did. I would tell them to let him push to the hotel, as starting ever day going backwards was not good for the psychology of this challenge. They were not interested and would not adapt. I think they always thought they knew best, and I was just "the wife" at home. I was dealing with a lot of egos from the offset and had to navigate this as best I could.

Very early, within the first weeks, it wasn't just me the team were having issues with; the team itself had started to form cracks. One team member, the medic, was finding a lot of things difficult. It began with the flights and then the standard of accommodation. Next, it was driving conditions. He always wanted better. He wanted to enjoy the evenings, take in the destinations, and drink wine. But we had to remind him it was a fast-moving challenge. This wasn't a travel show we were filming; it was a record-breaking challenge, and focus was key. He was also very concerned about his weight, a problem I could fully empathize with. However, this wasn't the time for crazy diets and starving himself; he was having mood swings, and it was affecting the team.

Two other members of the team reached out to me and expressed their concern about his behavior. I was fine with them coming to me, as I wanted zero distractions for Dean. I knew this guy looked up to Dean a lot, and when he could see how in shape Dean was, he wanted the same; he wanted the quick fix. I couldn't be angry, as I knew this feeling all too well. But I hadn't known he had this issue. If I had, I would have chatted to him beforehand to establish whether this challenge was really right for him. That is all hindsight, though, and I can only learn from my errors in judgment.

The complaints didn't stop there. The production team was struggling, as the ground crew was not allowing them to film everything. They only wanted the positive stories captured and were blocking any filming of the issues they were having. Again, the production team came to me, and I had to talk to the team. It was a never-ending "he said, she said"; "they did this, they did that"; and "we don't want to ride with him." And it was exhausting.

Next came the bullying allegations, and this was when it got serious. One day, I was home with the baby and my dad, who was in recovery, when a member of the production company arrived at my house unannounced and angry. He told me the crew on the ground had been experiencing bullying from one of the support team, the medic again. He said they were finding it very difficult to work with him, and they were being treated terribly. He told me, if I didn't sort this, he would be pulling his guys off the ground and quitting.

I contacted one of the other team members and asked what he thought about the situation. He immediately got on a call to me and told me he'd witnessed things too and that I should address it with the medic. I contacted him, and he told me what the others were saying was 100 percent not true, and if they said anything like that, he would sue them.

I had no idea what to do. This was a mental health campaign, and we were dealing with a bullying allegation.

A few days later, the head guy came back to me and told me he was dropping the bullying complaint, after having received threats of legal action. I asked if it was still a concern, and he said it was just a misunderstanding, and everything was fine.

We were less than two weeks in, and every single day, I was getting calls, texts, or visits with some issue or another. The pressure was intense, and I could feel my body struggling. I had to discuss the situation with the team, as there was no way I could burden Dean with this. I had to get the team to start pulling together. The ground team and production were at constant odds. Team members on the ground were complaining about other team members but wanted to keep what they said anonymous. The same was true of any complaints from production. They were all having issues with each other and expected me to resolve the issues without telling anyone who had said what.

I spoke to the production team and explained that this was too high profile a campaign and too important an issue to just ignore the concerns raised. I needed to know if they wanted to make it a formal complaint. They told me no; they were happy for me just to have a word with him, and hopefully, that would be enough. I contacted him and explained the situation. I told him the production team was still feeling intimidated and asked if he could just be aware of this and show the team respect. I told the other team members they needed to speak with him. There was very little I could do from where I was, and communication between them would go a long way.

I went to bed and woke up the following morning in agony. My stomach was in incredible pain. I tried to brush it off. But as soon as I tried to move, I struggled to breathe; I couldn't move.

Mollie came into the room, and I could see the look of worry on her face. "What's wrong, Mummy?" she kept saying.

The poor thing was distraught, but I could hardly breathe. I got her to pass me my phone, and I called my dad. I didn't know what else to do. Dad came straight round, and as soon as he arrived, he called an ambulance. Each burst of pain made it impossible to breathe, and I was doubled over in pain. The paramedics arrived, and after a quick exam, they rushed me straight to hospital.

While in the ambulance my phone started to ring. It was the medic. I couldn't breathe, so I definitely couldn't talk. I messaged to say I couldn't talk, and I would call when I could. He replied saying that wasn't good enough; he wanted to talk *now*. I told him I was in the back of an ambulance, and I would call when I could. That wasn't enough for him. He demanded I call ASAP.

I arrived at the hospital, and the ER staff approached me. The pain was now unbearable, and I had begun to vomit as each wave of pain engulfed me. They took me straight in and began examining me. A number of doctors checked me over, and they were convinced it was appendicitis. That would make sense—only I'd had an appendectomy twenty-eight years ago! They were convinced I still had my appendix. It was all very confusing.

The phone continued to ring. Only now it was Dean ringing. I still couldn't speak, and the doctor was getting irritated by the phone. So, I messaged him and said I was busy and would call back as soon as I could. He replied saying the team had told him I was in hospital and that they had some issues too.

For the love of god! I was furious. Why did they have to tell Dean? He didn't need to be worrying about me, and they shouldn't be going to him with issues. As the doctor was inserting an IV into my arm, my phone was blowing up, so I answered the call. That was a bad idea, as I was met with an incredibly noisy voice shouting down the phone at me. I told him I was in the middle of getting an IV in my arm, but I was interrupted by the caller, the medic who just kept shouting. He was furious, saying the bullying allegations were continuing and that he was going to sue production, and he would spend hundreds of thousands destroying them. I told him to stay calm and explained I would talk to them again and that they just wanted to be treated fairly.

The other team members had also called and said they knew the behaviors were still happening and causing difficulties. But they also felt he was just having mood swings and various issues because of his yo-yo dieting and irritability about the accommodation not being to his standards.

As the phone calls proceeded, the pain got worse. The doctor now told me to hang up the phone, or he would take it away. He said they couldn't find the cause, and after observing me, he wondered if the whole thing might be stress related. He told me about how the body reacts to stress and that I needed to change my lifestyle. He then prescribed me some medication for the pain and let me rest for a while.

After a few hours, the pain subsided. The hospital let me out that evening, and I was ordered to go home and rest. I knew that would not be an easy task. Resting was not one of my strong suits at the best of times, and in this current climate, it was next to impossible.

As soon as I got home from the hospital I had to reply to the number of messages from all sides—Dean worrying about me, half the support team wondering what was going on, production wanting an update, and the medic wanting an apology from production. The team had arrived at their next stop point, and production had decided to get a separate hotel to stay away from the team members. The medic called me and said he wanted a face-to-face with the guys who were complaining. I said it wasn't a good idea and asked him to give them space, as they felt intimidated.

An hour or so later, I received a call from him saying he had spoken to them, and they said they hadn't said anything. I couldn't believe it. After all I had said, he'd still gone to them. Production called me. They were furious, saying he had come over shouting at them and threatening to sue them all.

Eventually, I managed to calm them down. But one of the production team decided he wanted to go home. I told them, if they wanted to make the complaint formal or have a team member removed, they had to say so. It was brand-new territory for me, and I was trying to work out the best way to deal with it.

My dad was messaging me telling me to rest, as were my friends. But if I rested, then what? Rest was not an option.

A few days later, Dean got into a bad accident. He was cycling along the hard shoulder and did not notice a low bar as he went under a sign. He was cycling along at thirty-eight miles an hour and went flying over the handlebars. His heart monitor banged into his chest with full force, his wrist was injured, and he had a slight head bang and cuts and bruises. The medic said Dean was to be monitored daily and advised he was concerned about his heart.

Two weeks passed, and I got more calls from production saying the team was not cooperating. I had had enough. I sent a stern email to the team and told them they needed to stop it; they had to allow production to do their job. I got an email back from the team telling me that they were there to support Dean's record-breaking challenge and not to make a documentary. They did not like production being there and had no plans to make it easy for them. It was unbelievably hard to manage all these egos.

As soon as Dean finished the ride, the medic approached him before he could even get his helmet off. He began ranting and raving at Dean and demanding all sorts. Dean told me later he felt his heart beating out of control and felt sick after that discussion. I contacted Dr. Google and found that Dean was in peak athlete condition, and during an endurance phase, stress could be very damaging to the heart. Combine that with the injury, and that was enough for me.

I spoke to Dean and the other team members and asked how they would cope without the medic. I asked about the daily checks, and Dean told me he hadn't been getting daily checks. After the injury, the medic had emailed me saying that Dean's heart needed to be monitored every twenty-four hours. This had been two weeks ago, and Dean hadn't been checked.

I spoke with the rest of the team, and they agreed they would be OK without the medic. Dean also agreed. Not only was he not a benefit, but he was also becoming destructive. For the sake of the challenge and for his own well-being, the medic had to go.

I tried to discuss it with him the best I could, but it was not easy. An air of petulance began to show. The attitude seemed to coincide with messages I'd begun to receive from the other team member who had resigned in December. I didn't know at the time, but there were things going on in the background—things operating in a sinister way to do us harm. At this point, though, I was completely unaware. I spoke to him and told him the situation; he wasn't happy but agreed it was best to leave.

I offered to book the flights, but he insisted he would book his own flights and he had other plans and places to go for his business. I asked if he was sure and thanked him for his work to date.

He was off the team, and the rest of the team carried on without him.

CHAPTER TWENTY-FOUR

MEET ME HALFWAY

Things quietened down for a few days, and I had a few moments of reflection. I looked back over the past eight years since Dean's parachuting accident and realized every move I had made was around making Dean happy, making sure he was OK, keeping him going, and doing all I could to please him. Somewhere along the way, I had lost sight of my own continued growth. I needed something that was just me that would be my own little challenge, something I could do when the current challenge, Dean cycling the Pan-American Highway (PAH), was complete.

I played on Google one evening and came across Mrs. World, a pageant about women empowerment, about wives, mothers, philanthropists, and entrepreneurs. *Perfect. Let's see if I can become Mrs. World.* I put together an application and sent it off. In all honesty, it was a joke aimed at myself. I wasn't a model, I hated getting pictures taken, and I certainly wasn't a beauty queen. But I knew our next challenge was going to be working with human trafficking, and I knew this would be a great way to spread awareness. I was never one who wanted to be the center of attention. Even selfies make me cringe. But anything that could bring attention to the charity work could only be a good thing. I sent off the application. Really, I didn't think I would hear anything and thought nothing more of it.

With the challenge, things were going a bit smoother. The team on the ground was making progress, and funds were starting to trickle in. However, the remaining two members of the ground team had begun to express concern about the lack of attention they were receiving in press and social media. This was a surprising turn, as, in general, they had been OK. This was not long after the medic had left and I'd received emails from the ops manager, but any connection between all this wasn't apparent to me at the time. What they said was they wanted more exposure and wanted media attention.

I explained that the attention would come eventually—once records started to break. They just needed to be patient. Their argument was that Dean was getting attention, but Dean couldn't do it without them. I was back to managing egos, and by now, I was getting a bit fed up with it.

The production team had also forgotten to factor in a couple of the countries. And the one remaining member of production's partner was pregnant; he had to go home to be with her. If he left, we would have no one filming. He was not willing to stay; therefore, they had to bring in someone new. Luckily, they had a partner producer in Colombia, so Frances and I had to arrange to fly him and his girlfriend down to Ecuador to meet the team. Around this time, we were due to have the vehicles loaded onto a ship in Florida to send down to Panama City.

Two weeks before the cars were due to arrive, as I sat down on a Friday evening ready to enjoy a glass of wine, the phone rang. My eyes rolled. Typical that it came in as soon as I had a moment to myself. I looked at the phone. It was Frances. I knew she would only call if it was important, and I was right. I answered, and she told me she was calling to inform me the paperwork for the vehicles was not correct for the shipping; they would have to send the titles off to be stamped for shipping, and it could take up to four weeks.

Holy shit, this was not good. Dean was due to arrive there in fourteen days, and without cars, there was no challenge. I told Frances I would call her back. I got out the map and mulled over our options.

The only realistic option was to drive the cars down to Panama. It was four thousand miles and seven countries—the United States of America, Mexico, Guatemala, Honduras, Nicaragua, Costa Rica, and Panama. I figured the drive would take about eight days if it was really pushed, so we had six days to get to America and get the cars out of the port.

My first thought was to call some of the guys I know. These were seven dangerous countries, so a security professional would be the safest bet. I began to call around. I was speaking to SF guys, Marines, SEALs and was met with complete resistance. I was told it was either too dangerous, or they wanted to charge extortionate amounts of money.

I began to get frustrated. I gulped down a few more sips of wine, and then I had an idea. I called Frances back. "The cars need to be driven down, and no one will do it," I told her.

"Why not?" she inquired.

I told her everyone said it was too dangerous, too difficult, or too expensive. Then I hit her with it. "Frances, would you be up for flying across to America with me and driving the cars down together?"

I paused, waiting for the normal answer—no, that's far too dangerous and so on. I waited. Then it came, "OK, sure. When do you want to leave?"

I couldn't believe it. I had contacted some of the toughest guys I knew, and they'd all said no. But my twenty-four-year-old PA recognized my desperation, believed in the challenge, and was willing to do whatever it took to make it happen.

We began to put plans in place, and I received a message from one of the guys asking what I was going to do. I told him the plan, and he was horrified. "You can't do it, Alana. It would be too dangerous, even for a guy."

It was this kind of rhetoric that spurred me on. The task could be taken on as dangerously or as safely as it needed to be. I planned the move with intelligence and research. I had no plans of driving unsafely, into unsafe territories, or overnight. I would give Frances full security training and check on her regularly. I know concerns circulated around the man's network, but there wasn't much I could do about their lack of faith, other than to get on with the task and prove them wrong.

I contacted the team member who had been dealing with shipping. He agreed to fly to Florida to meet us and take the third car. We informed the sponsor of our plans, and they insisted on sending one of their junior members of the team. I tried everything to change their mind, but they insisted. I gave him what training I could and did what I could to teach him safety, but it was just an extra burden on what was already a difficult mission.

I had one final job to do before I set off. Fundraising was still one of my major tasks, and the wonderful woman helping us with the charity work had managed to secure me a meeting with a woman who was responsible for grant giving for her company. I had a meeting with her, with the purpose of pitching the charity to be in line for receiving a grant of £75,000.

I flew down to London to meet with both of them, and we all went for lunch. The waiter seated us, and the usual question arose. "Will you be having wine with lunch?"

I looked at both of the women, and we all nodded together. It was International Women's Day 2018, and we were three strong, smart women who always deserved wine with lunch! After an amazing chat and a lot of feelings of female empowerment, we began to wrap up our lunch. The woman whose company I was pitched reached over to me and told me all the wonderful things she felt about me and the work we were doing. She was so impressed, she told me, she was recommending us for the top tier of grant award—£150,000. I couldn't believe it. This was amazing news and a huge step toward our target.

Two days later, my bags were packed, and I was ready to go. It was Mother's Day, and I had to kiss my babies goodbye, fly to Florida, and start this challenge. The other team member had arrived before us and checked into a hotel. He had been working with the port to get the cars released—with little success.

The following morning, I was up early and ready to speak to port authorities. It was becoming nearly impossible to get straight answers, and I was on the phone for most of the day getting pushed between departments. Finally, late on, I spoke to someone who said I would have to go to the port. We attempted this, but it was closed. We had to return the following day, and time was ticking.

The following morning, we arrived at the port and refused to leave without the cars. We sat outside in what you may call a semi-silent protest. We tried all the usual complaint tactics, including the age old "can-I-speak-to-your-manager" trick. Eventually, we got to speak to someone who could help.

By this time, though, the sponsor's guy had caught way too much sun in the protest; Frances was dying of hunger, her words not mine— for such a tiny girl, she always needed to eat—and my patience was wearing thin. Finally, as evening was setting in, they gave us our cars.

The RV, which would become Dean's bed in the next stage, was perfect and ran like a dream. The second car was good; it just needed a jump-start. But the third car, the one sourced for the production team, would not start. It had been sitting there and had just seized up. The frustration was real, but there was nothing we could do. We couldn't get a mechanic till the next day, and we were already a day behind. I made the decision to leave the car behind and go with the two vehicles. We hit the road and began the long drive ahead. The plan was to get to Panama, drop the vehicles at the hotel, and fly across to Cartagena, Colombia, to watch Dean break the first record. That was the ideal plan. But really, it was just to get the cars there.

We made a plan—we would rotate the driving as we got tired, and when you weren't driving, you were to sleep. We drove through most of the US part of our journey on the first day and had our first sleep at the border town from which we'd be crossing into Mexico.

The following morning, we met the manager of the motel at the Texas border; he was chatting with the other team member. I approached, and he asked me the plan. I told him we were driving south, and he called me "a naive girl." Well, could have been worse; he could have said old lady. But still, his words were incredibly rude and ignorant. Nonetheless, I had neither the time nor the inclination to educate him.

For the first border crossing, this one into Mexico, the plan was for the guys to travel in the RV and Frances and I to take the car. We headed first and made it across without any issues. We waited at the other end for ten and then twenty and then thirty minutes, and the boys were a no-show. A border town is not the ideal place for two women to be hanging around, so we called to chase them up. They had been detained and were struggling with the paperwork.

Frances, luckily, had printed copies of everything and was more than adequately prepared, but it meant we had to get back to them. We couldn't drive, as our car might get caught up at the border, so we locked up the car and walked across the border to meet them. We presented all the paperwork required, and the border guards issued us what was needed. However, we had now lost a few hours of daylight, so we needed to haul ass to make it past Mexico City before dark.

We arrived on the outskirts of Mexico City at sunset, and we still had thirty miles to go until our hotel. The guys wanted to carry on into the night, but I knew the difference between brave and reckless. We needed to stick to daylight hours. We made it to the hotel, and I made the plan to meet for breakfast at 6:00 a.m. and to be on the road by 6:30 a.m.

The guys got some food and got their heads down. Frances and I, however, still had work to do. Frances had to get all the data sent by the ground team uploaded to Guinness World Records; this had to be done every day with the data from all the tracking equipment. We also had to get the social media posts done, along with the work from the other business. This would take us into the early hours, leaving enough time for a few hours' sleep before our alarm went off at 5:30.

By 6:00 a.m. I was up, ready, and down for breakfast. I sat in the lounge and watched truckers come and go, all staring as I sat alone. This was uncomfortable, and I didn't want to be drawing any attention to us. At 6:15, Frances appeared just in time for some breakfast. But by 6:30, we were all checked out and packed up with no sign from the guys. I went up to their rooms and banged on the door. They were both still asleep, and we were now behind.

Timing is something Dean and I are very particular about; timing's everything, and every minute they were snoozing was another minute of daylight lost. The frustration was definitely real. At 7:10 a.m., they arrived, wanting breakfast. My anger was hard to hide, but we got on the road eventually at 7:30, and now we had to make up time.

Dean was still powering through South America and called me angry. He had become frustrated that the new production team hadn't arrived. He was traveling through amazing scenery, and things were being missed. He had emailed the team, and they'd returned with the frustrations of the earlier days. Dean was finding it extremely difficult—not the cycling but all the issues from the teams. He has since always joked that cycling the fourteen thousand miles was the easiest part. It wasn't really a joke; it was the reality for his mindset. I tried to keep him upbeat and promised I would be with him as soon as I could.

We continued to travel through Mexico and decided to stop at a truck stop for food. The guys had gone ahead and were searching around the shop. I went to the RV and found it unlocked; safety and security had just gone out the window. We were in Mexico, and truck stops are a breeding ground for opportunistic thieves. I kept my frustration to myself.

But then, as I entered the gas station store and went to grab a coffee, my anger brewed over. There on the coffee stand was the full set of keys for the RV, just sitting there for all to see. For fuck's sake guys! Can we just be slightly security aware? It was something I just saw as basic. I had to be aware that they were here voluntarily, and I had to use some sensitivity. But the woman in me was screaming for it to have been an all-woman crew!

As we drove across the mountains, my thoughts lay firmly with Dean. I knew the twenty-one kilometers of mountain I had just descended was the same mountain Dean would have to cycle up. That was a real eye-opener for me, showing me just how incredible his endurance and strength was.

Our next border crossing was into Guatemala. This was definitely one of the more beautiful borders. The sheer beauty of it—the landscape, the people, and even the livestock just roaming around the streets—was one of the first things that struck me about Guatemala. I watched and listened to the children playing in the streets, not an iPad or phone in sight. They were just using their imagination to create games and entertainment. Every part of the drive through Guatemala was like candy for the eyes, just beautiful and sweet.

We got through there pretty quickly, and arriving in Honduras, we immediately felt the shift in energy. There was still a lot of beauty around, but you definitely felt a sense of decline in safety—call it a sixth sense. The first city you come to is San Pedro Sula. This was an incredibly busy city, and getting through it wasn't easy. Again, my thoughts came back to Dean. The road was six to ten lanes wide, and the cars drove pretty erratically. How was he going to do it, navigating all this traffic? I was sure he had a plan, but seeing this challenge he'd be facing definitely gave me a bit of fear.

We got through Honduras in good time and still had four days to get to Dean. Looking at the miles, we felt like we could make it in time to cross over to Colombia and see him achieve his first world record. The sun was beginning to set just as we approached the Honduras to Nicaragua border.

As we drove up to the gates, we saw a group of young guys approaching us. They reached the guys' car first and tapped on their window. We could see the young men were telling them to get out of the car. Frances and I were in the car behind and could immediately see they had guns. I looked at Frances and could see the fear in her face. I had to remain calm and show her there was nothing to be scared of—no matter how I was feeling. I got out of the car and tried my best Spanglish to calm down the situation. They then pulled us all over to the side and were all speaking in Spanish, looking us up and down. None of us knew what they were saying, and the guns were definitely worrying us. They were not in uniform, and we had no idea what might happen. I looked at the guys and knew they were scared; I knew what happened next was all out of fear, but it didn't make it any easier at the time.

The team member who was with us was the only military person among us, and he looked the toughest. He didn't like the situation and retreated immediately back to the RV. Frances begged him not to leave us, but he went, and the boys were shouting at him in Spanish. I knew he was scared too, and that was his coping mechanism. What it meant was I had to step up and look tougher and work out how we get out of this situation.

Frances was terrified, and I was responsible for the sponsor's guy. I could see they were almost trembling, so I looked them both in the eye with the brightest mummy look I could give. I told them everything was cool, and I would handle this.

I puffed up my chest and walked toward the guys. I looked at the one who I guessed was in charge. He had a lot of tattoos, so I pointed them out and gave him the thumbs up. I told him, "Mi esposo mucho amor tattoos."

It was the best I could do. I got my phone out and showed them a picture.

"Rambo!" they shouted and laughed.

That was it. I had broken the ice. I told them I was heading south to see him (pointing south and saying *esposo*). I showed them our charity wristband and a picture with the kids we had been helping. They smiled when they saw them; these guys were just kids themselves.

I showed them the forms we needed to fill in to cross the border, and one said, "Ayuda" (Help).

"Yes!" I said. "Can you help us?"

I gave him ten dollars, and he helped me fill in the forms. He was delighted to help, and the rest of the guys just relaxed. I gave them an extra ten dollars and said, "Muchas gracias!"

They replied with a very sweet, "De nada," and sent us on our way.

The guys got in the RV and proceeded to the border, and I got Frances into the car. Once we started moving, I immediately saw the relief on her face, and I also felt that wave of adrenaline leaving my body. We were safe, and we were on our way. Surely that must be the worst of it over! Who was I kidding?

It was now getting pretty dark as we crossed over the border into Nicaragua. The big trucks had already started lining up to bed up for the night, and we needed to be sure we were safely into Nicaragua and find a hotel for the night before darkness was totally upon us. We approached the border patrol and handed over all the passports.

The customs officer did not say a word to us. He took the passports and walked away. Five, ten, twenty minutes passed, and he hadn't returned. We were getting impatient and a bit worried. The group was still a bit tense from what had just happened in Honduras, and no one was chatting to each other. I stood at the customs desk while the rest of my crew all sat around. It was getting late, and as it got darker, activity actually increased in the area. Over an hour passed, and no one spoke to us. I kept asking and was shrugged off.

The guys went to lie down in the RV, and as I stood waiting, I could see little things going on. Men were passing with two or three girls with them. I could see them exchanging things with the customs guards, while the girls headed into the Honduras side toward the truck drivers.

I was starting to get nervous; I could see people looking Frances up and down and decided to get her into the RV to be safe. When we got to the RV, it was unlocked with the guys fast asleep inside. It was like banging my head against a brick wall. I put her in and told her to lock the door. Hours passed, and finally the customs officer came out of his office. He started speaking to me in Spanish, and I told him my Spanish wasn't good. His English wasn't good, so we ended up starting a Google Translate conversation.

He told me our paperwork wasn't correct, and we would have to pay to get the right documents. I knew everything we had was correct and this was just a bribery attempt. I told him all the documents were correct, our passports were all correct, and nothing was wrong. He said they needed the original documents for the car. Every border wanted the same, and they would take it and not give it back. I had made a lot of copies, and they told me the copies would only be accepted at a cost. These things were incredibly frustrating; trying to stay within the laws in places where officials were making the laws up as they go along was incredibly difficult. Frances had some copies in the car, so I went over my signature with wet ink to show it was original. He accepted it but said I still needed to pay $100. I knew the money would go straight in the customs officers' pocket, but they still had our passports, and they were in control. I paid them, and they told me to wait.

Hours passed, and I stayed awake while everyone else slept. This place was active, lawless, and dangerous. I couldn't have slept even if I'd tried.

As the sun started to rise, the customs officer came back to continue our Google Translate conversation. He told me it was too dangerous to cross through Nicaragua on our own, and he must accompany us to the Costa Rica border. WTF? This guy who didn't speak a word of English wanted to sit in a car with us for an estimated seven-hour journey! That wasn't going to be awkward at all!

Back to Google Translate. I explained it was a kind offer, we were grateful, but it wasn't necessary. He explained it wasn't an option. Nicaragua was experiencing an uprising, and unrest was getting worse every day. The only way we could leave was with him coming with us. I was concerned, firstly thinking of Dean cycling back this way and then for us traveling with this stranger. I asked if he would go in the RV, but he insisted on coming in our car. This was a worry, but we agreed. What option did we have?

I later learned this was more frightening for him than us. The last border agent who helped foreigners cross from border to border went missing and was later found murdered; it was him who was taking the risk traveling with us.

After what was possibly the longest seven hours of my life, we arrived at the Costa Rican border; when we pulled into the huge parking lot, I'd never felt such relief. Our customs border exited the car and ushered us to the checking point. He looked nervous. I had this vision of Costa Rica being this amazing country full of beauty and hospitality. I had believed that, when we got here, a feeling of safety would return. But that wasn't to be.

As we approached the counter, it was instant hostility. The customs guards beckoned us toward the police. I walked up to the two uniformed officers. One of them reached out his hand, looking toward our documents.

I handed them to him, and he shook his head. "You're not passing the border tonight."

I couldn't believe it. We had two full days left to make it to Panama with enough time to fly to Colombia to see Dean break the record. But worst still, we had only three days left to make it on time to Panama for Dean to arrive and continue the world record. This wasn't romantic and sentimental anymore; the record now relied on our making it. Ahead of us was three days of driving, and nothing was stopping me getting across this border.

"No," I told him. "We need to cross tonight."

Immediately, he extended his hand.

Oh, here we go again, I thought to myself. It wasn't about whether or not we could cross the border. It was about how desperate we were to get across. This was the police. What hope did we have? I went to my emergency pocket, where I kept a small amount of cash, and indicated that was all I had because they will take all you have. When traveling, especially to places like these, always keep cash in separate places so if someone takes all of the first you always have a backup.

"I have twenty, maybe forty dollars," I said while showing him the cash.

"OK. OK." He accepted it, looking around to make sure nobody was watching.

He took our passports in to be stamped, returned them to us, and sent us on our way.

As we crossed the border into Costa Rica, my previous impressions of Costa Rica were reaffirmed. It was beautiful, lush greenery and a lovely sound of wildlife. But we had no time to take in the scenery. We had to get to the Panama border by sunrise. That meant a serious amount of hauling ass. We began the move, but it really wasn't long until dark descended upon us.

As we pulled our way through Costa Rica, my heart felt kind of low. I knew from the sounds and smells that what was outside was beautiful, but we had no time to wait or stop. We had to keep moving.

As we approached the next town, we stopped for a break. Frances and the guys went off to get food, and reality began to sink in for me. I knew we could never make the plane to get us to Cartagena now. My dream of watching Dean break his first record was gone, and I had to call Dean to tell him we would not make it.

I went into the call strong, but as I heard his voice, I could not hold back the tears. I couldn't let him hear me cry. He needed to know I was strong. I pulled away the phone and took a deep breath. "Don't worry, babe," I told him. "I will be waiting for you in Panama."

As I hung up the phone, and around the corner away from my three traveling partners, I broke down in tears. I was devastated. But I dried my eyes, went back round to the trio, and summoned them back to the vehicles.

As Frances and I drove on, we noticed the RV with the guys in it pull up ahead. We pulled into the parking lot alongside them. *What's up now?* I thought to myself.

I got out of the car. "Guys, you good?" I asked agitatedly.

They replied that they needed sleep. At this point, I had been awake since Guatemala. I'd stayed awake while they slept during the crime zone of Nicaragua and driven through to Costa Rica, but they were tired. OK. I looked around. There were lights ahead, a hotel. We pulled the car and RV over to the lights and spoke to the night manager at the hotel. I asked if we could borrow their Wi-Fi, so we get the final Guinness evidence uploaded. The guys could then sleep in the RV, and we would get back on the road in a few hours. They told us to wake them up, and they would drive while we got some shut-eye.

Frances and I went into the reception while the boys slept. We worked away to get the Guinness stuff uploaded. Frances looked exhausted. I encouraged her numerous times to go to sleep, but she was undeterred. This girl was on a mission. It was then I realized the true internal power of a woman. She wasn't military. She wasn't a mother. She had nothing vested in this except her own pride. She had determination, and I admired her very much. She was a twenty-four-year-old girl, and she had more grit than any man I had ever come across. I smiled as I agreed to continue working with her.

As we sat typing away a smell came over us—and grew and grew. What is that? We looked around, and outside, we could see an orange glow coming from near the RV. Oh my god, is the RV on fire?!

The night manager came over telling us not to worry; the fire service was on the way. Just then, the sirens sounded. We ran outside to find a wild bushfire burning, the RV not far from the site. Oh, shit. We needed to get the boys out of there.

We ran over past the firemen. We threw open the door, expecting panic from the boys. But instead, we were met by loud snores! Unfazed, undisturbed, and in full REMs, they slept on. We needed to move them out of the path of the fire. Frances took the car, and I jumped in the RV, and we got back on the road, the guys still fast asleep.

A few miles passed, and the hibernation started to end. I could hear the rumbles as the guys started to come to life.

"Be careful of the bump on this road," one said sleepily.

"Yeah, dude. We left there ten miles down the road. Go back to sleep."

We were on the move now, and we needed to get across the next border. As we approached the next town, my mind couldn't get away from Dean. I knew he would be crossing the finish line, a victory we had worked so hard on. I wouldn't be there with him, and that made me feel like I had failed. I knew that no one there could make him feel like he would if I was there. I would never miss another chance at watching his successes.

We pulled our way through the break of dawn. As I drove the RV behind the car, I could see the car swaying from side to side. I flashed Frances to pull over. She was pushing it too hard; she needed some sleep. I got one of the guys to take over the RV and took over the car for a while. Frances moved to the passenger side but refused to sleep. She couldn't drive any more, but she stayed firmly as my wing woman.

We entered the border town between Costa Rica and Panama. Finally, we were almost on the homestretch. I was super tired so asked one of the guys to go source a helper to get us across. He returned and said he needed $18. What? This was the most anyone had ever asked to be "bribed" with. No way. But he insisted this was a different country, and that was what was needed. I was exhausted and just wanted to cross, so I gave it to him.

We waited. And waited. Of course, the guy had done a runner. The team member had not checked the guy out, and only a bit of man trust was used.

I need to sort it, so I got out and grabbed a border patrol officer from the Panama side, got our paperwork sorted, and crossed. I should have done that in the first place. I was no longer in the mood for any shit and just wanted to get there now.

I was now on three days with no sleep but all I could see was my guy ahead of me, waiting and eager for the encouragement he so needed. Eventually, we were given passage across, and I drove; I drove like my life depended on it.

As we made our way across the lands of Panama, Frances sat next to me in somewhat of a daze. But it was when she started chatting to her auntie in the back seat that I knew she had surpassed just tiredness. "No one is there," I told her.

I was exhausted but now on autopilot. It had been days since I'd showered and was concentrating heavily on the white lines on the road.

Frances was also in a rush to make it to the airport. This trip was so last minute that she had forgotten to say prior that she was due in Dublin that weekend for her best friend's bachelorette; her flight from Panama was arranged for this day, and we were racing against time to get there not only for Dean but also for her flight. I flew down the road, ignoring her conversations with her family in the back seat and my inability to see the street lines.

I pulled into the departure area of Panama airport with minutes, literally minutes to spare for Frances's flight. She jumped out and ran. I waited for the message to say she was checked in. Then I headed to the hotel I'd booked Dean minutes from the airport.

I pulled into the parking lot and excitedly began to get out of the vehicle, ready to see my man. But then I looked down at myself and realized I had driven three days nonstop, with no sleep, wearing the same clothes, in heat and humidity, and with fluctuating adrenalin. I was a mess. And Dean, my husband who I hadn't seen for three months, was in that reception with a camera crew waiting for me.

I rummaged around the car, trying to find any way I could make myself look less like a vagrant and more like the woman he'd married. I grabbed a bra and attempted the click-and-turn motion. But between the sweat and weight gain from stationary bloating, the usual easy twist of the bra was at a halt. I had to admit defeat. I had to walk into this hotel reception looking and smelling the way I did and greet my husband. I took a deep breath and walked toward the door.

As I approached, I caught a glimpse of him. All my worries disintegrated. I now ran through the door. There he was—the guy who I had done all this for. I embraced him with all my heart. I had done it. I hadn't let him down. A rush of love flew over me, followed by, finally, a rush of tiredness.

I looked at Dean, and his voice slowed down. I couldn't recognize him. My exhaustion was in full throttle. He was so skinny and talked funny. He took me to the room. I had a quick shower and lay on the bed. Within seconds, I was asleep, and I slept deeper than I have ever slept. My job was done, and it was time to go home.

CHAPTER TWENTY-FIVE

❦❦❦❦❦❦❦❦

COMING HOME

I met everyone at the RV in the morning to talk them through the vehicles. I tried to explain the ins and outs of the RV, but two of the team could not have been more disinterested in what I had to say. They were dismissive and avoided all eye contact with me. I asked if all was OK and was ignored. I was still pretty tired and in a daze from the past eight days, so I didn't have the inclination to delve deeper into what the issue was, but it was clear they didn't want me there.

I was about to head onto the plane anyway, so I gave all my attention to Dean. Dean took me to the airport, and I held him tightly in my arms, like we were the only two people in the world. "You're on the homestretch now. You've got this. Go and keep making us all proud!"

We kissed and said goodbye. I hated walking away from him, but I took a deep breath and kept moving through to the terminal. I got onto the plane and just sat and stared straight ahead. I was in a complete daze.

Eleven hours later, I landed. I hadn't moved from the seat, hadn't eaten, hadn't put on the airplane TV. I'd just sat there.

I got off the plane so excited to see my babies. My dad was there waiting for me. We collected my baggage and got into the car. My dad did not stop talking the whole way home. He told me everything that had happened since I'd left. I sat in silence while he downloaded the last ten days onto me without asking once about my trip.

It was the first time I realized what life was like for Dean, for soldiers coming home from war, and for the oil guys coming home from offshore. Every time Dean had come back, I had downloaded just as Dad was doing to me. But actually, all I wanted was a hug with my babies, a warm bath, and to sit in silence for a while. Some guys like to go to the pub and blow off steam; others like to get straight into home life. Whatever the decompression process was, I now understood it, having stood on both sides. The phrase, "walk in another man's shoes" had never resonated so much. Dad kept talking, and all I could do was smile.

A few weeks following our return, the woman I had met for lunch on International Women's Day called me. She told me that, following our meeting, she'd spoken with the board of directors. The board had agreed to make us their preferred charity and had decided to donate the top amount. However, they had also decided to increase the original offer to £200,000.

I was blown away! This was so amazing and just the news I needed. Things had been heating up on the road and back home. The support team had become more and more demanding, the whole Pan-American Highway 2018 (PAH18) challenge had become so big, my own work was overpowering, and I felt under pressure from every part of my life. I didn't have my husband to talk to, and I was too proud to reach out to anyone. My stress levels were through the roof, and between production and the ground team, I was ready to break.

One Sunday, I was trying to clean the house and fend off calls and complaints from all angles. My kids were playing up and demanding my time, and I felt like my head was going to burst. I was juggling everything and felt I wasn't doing any of it right. I hit a wall and then hit the deck. I just collapsed. I never blacked out, but I was shaking uncontrollably and just began to cry. I was crying so hard I was hyperventilating. Mollie tried to hug me, but she was just a little girl with no idea what was wrong with Mummy.

Just at the point where I felt I would lose my mind, Frances called. I told her I couldn't talk, and I hung up.

Thirty minutes later, I was still curled up in a ball in the hallway. Suddenly there was a knock at the door. Frances and her sister, Una, had arrived, one with a huge bar of chocolate in her hands and the other with a bottle of red wine. Instantly, I felt better and less alone, and I felt like I mattered. We spent the evening chatting about everything that didn't involve PAH, Dean, support teams, businesses, or documentaries. We talked about Una's husband's socks, their parents' decorative skills, the most mundane of subjects. And it felt amazing. It was exactly what I needed, right when I needed it. Meaningless chatter had never been so meaningful.

That evening had given me a recharge. And little did I know how much I would need it going forward. The team on the ground's demands had now become uncontrollable. They were demanding a new title and a change in the name of the challenge, along with a number of other demands. They were making Dean's life hell on the road, as well as creating a nightmare for us back home. Every day without fail, there was an issue. Dean was now stressed from the moment he woke at the start of the day, until the end of the day, when he dreaded coming off the bike.

One day, Dean completed his day's ride. I had booked the team into a hotel in Mexico, and when he arrived, the team was nowhere to be found. Dean had just completed over 150 miles; he was extremely hungry and shaky. They had all the money and the bank cards; and they had disappeared. They later turned up saying they had needed a break and had gone out for dinner.

That was the final straw for me. They were playing with Dean's health—on top of their completely unreasonable demands. I later discovered that the member of the team who had left in December had flown out to Mexico and had met them, I believe with the sole intention of harming Dean and disrupting the challenge. Then I received their email.

I made a call to Dean. We spoke briefly, and once I made sure he was fed and safe, I asked him a question. "Dean, can you do this without them?"

The email I'd received had told me I would either comply with all their demands, or they would walk and leave Dean without any support. This was an ultimatum. They thought we would have no choice but to comply with their threats. I wanted to know if Dean was willing to give into them or if he could, indeed, do it without them. I knew he could, but I needed to hear it from him.

He told me the bike ride every day was the easy part. On the other hand, he was struggling to cope with the constant stress, the agitated state of the team, and the need to walk on eggshells. He told me he would make it work and that was all I needed to hear.

I emailed the team back and told them we would not be giving into their demands. If they insisted on leaving, I would accept that and get them home.

They told me they were done and that they would sort themselves out. They did not need me to book flights or anything else, for that matter. They were rude and dismissive. But I could not take it to heart. I was, however, devastated for Dean, as he had tried so hard to keep them happy.

I didn't know if it had always been their intention to do this or if the other guys who had left previously had gotten in their heads. I later discovered the depth of the involvement and intentions of the previous members of the team. This included me seeing all the emails and texts between the whole of the original team and people who were meant to be supporting us. To see in writing a plan to disrupt and destroy the challenge truly floored me. Dean was a forty-one-year-old guy proving to the world that it was never too late—that anything is possible. A sixteen-year veteran had battled so much to get here. That, along with all the money we had raised for people who so desperately needed it, and, well, we couldn't believe people wanted to harm that, to harm our family.

I couldn't let this get in the way of our ultimate goals and what truly mattered. We had to keep our eye on the end game, and I had to keep juggling the plates. I continued to try to keep everything away from Dean. But I had at least one less thing to worry about and wasn't getting the daily complaints and abuse from the team. I would do all I could from back home, and Dean would get up every day and plan his day. He had his military pal left with him, and he would google "how to change a puncture" and use YouTube as his bible. I booked massages for Dean along the route, and I would just pray I picked the right kind of massage place.

As Dean pedaled through Mexico, we began preparations for him to enter the United States. This was a huge milestone in many ways. There was a friend driving down from the north to help Dean, his friend, and the production team. We were now in a country that spoke Dean's language; sourcing assistance would be easier. And we only had Canada to pass through before we were on the homestretch.

Back home, I was still playing the juggling game, and sleep was now a precious and rare luxury. The kids were super excited to soon be seeing Daddy, although they still found it confusing why he was away. At work, my old business partners had become more difficult and were causing me a lot of issues. Our personal finances were not great, given what we had spent on the challenge, and we were surviving on one income. This was all stressful but manageable. I had no idea the toughest part was only just beginning.

The support team had begun a campaign of abuse and humiliation against me. Members of their staff were messaging me; they would tell me all I was doing wrong and were acting very strangely. I had no idea of the level of depravity this would eventually reach; at this point, it had only just begun.

Often, the struggle for me throughout this challenge was no one—and to an extent, not even Dean—considered that I was just a young mum raising two young children. I was a mother trying to do my best for my family, looking after my husband, and trying to keep my businesses afloat—all while running a huge campaign to raise a huge amount of money for charity. This wasn't personal gain. This wasn't for my glory. This was to help others. This was for Dean, and I was taking a beating for it daily. At best, I would describe it as exhausting. But when I added the stress of the support team, my ex-business partners, and the production team, it was soul destroying.

I would think back to my mum, when she would remind me that I had to focus on what mattered. She would say, "Alana, when you have greater things to concern yourself with, the opinions of ignorant people can't phase you." I had to keep remembering why I was doing this, all the people I was helping, how much Dean needed this, and how proud the kids would be of their daddy. I had to push all my other thoughts and feelings to the back of my mind and stay focused on the goal.

As Dean was getting closer to the finish line, we were beginning the preparation for the final celebration, the final fundraising event; and this one was going to be big. It was time to start the planning for the Wheels Down Ball. And making the list for it came first. I am a huge fan of lists; I always operate on a to-do list, and it is always done with pen and paper. I've attempted in the past to use apps and e-tools. However, I've always reverted to old-school pen and paper. To this day, this is still the way I do it. Writing down goals or tasks keeps you focused; you don't score an item out until it's done. Even if you move it to a new page, it still doesn't get scored out until the task is complete. As for the goal and dreams of life, they too are written and checked on regularly. It's incredibly important to keep the subconscious as engaged as the conscious. This is as true for business as it is for personal and family life. Set a goal, make a plan, and write it down.

Just as I was at the stage when I thought I couldn't fit anything more into the tank, I received a letter to say I had been crowned Mrs. Aberdeen and was in the final for Mrs. Scotland 2018. So, here I was, a pageant girl. I looked in the mirror, and all I could say was, "They have got to be kidding!"

I guess this should have been a moment to celebrate and be excited about. But yet again, there was no time and too much going on. It was time to start preparing for the flights over to the finish line. Dean was powering through, and there was no doubt in my mind, he was breaking this next record. But there was a new goalpost thrown our way.

With a few weeks to go until we set off, we received an invitation in the post inviting Dean and I to Harry and Meghan's wedding. This was just the news I needed. I had known from day one that Dean would do this in under a hundred days, and I had been pushing him little by little ever since. Now I had a great reason to push him that bit harder. I dropped him a few messages telling him to get in touch.

When he finally returned my call, it was the middle of the night with me and evening with him. He was worried as he had had so many missed calls. I told him we had been invited to Harry and Meghan's wedding, and in order for us to attend, he had to be cycling into Prudhoe Bay on no later than day 101.

He paused for a while.

Then I interrupted his silence. "You can manage that no problem, right?"

Again, a small pause. "Yeah, I guess I can do that," he said with the same passion he had for everything—like, yeah of course I'll break two world records, of course I'll pass Special Forces selection, of course I'll marry you. It was just a very blasé yeah.

It didn't bother me; I had not doubted since that day I started working out the trip and planning the daily miles. It was never a doubt in my mind that he would be cycling in under a hundred days.

The thought of mentioning on that call that I was in the running for Mrs. Scotland never even crossed my mind, that sort of thing really wouldn't interest Dean, and it didn't feel right to tell him about it. I pretty much kept it to myself. But there was that part of me who was the little girl with her burn scars, the girl who was abused, the girl who never felt quite good enough—well, she was doing a secret little happy dance and was dying to tell everyone. That was definitely a thought I would keep to myself; my world was definitely not a world in which beauty played any part. That wasn't necessarily a bad thing. I had children now, and I had to teach them about the importance of concerning yourself with bigger things, seeing what really mattered in the world, and ignoring material and superficial life consumers.

Dean now had his focus; he was pedaling hard toward that finish line and the second world record of his trip. We had a feeling that the United States would be the easy leg of the trip. We couldn't have been more wrong. The wind, the roads, the car break-ins, the delays, and the permanent battle with Mother Nature was soon testing us to our very limits. Frances and I were busy preparing the next stage of our move while still making sure Dean was safe on the road.

Heading to the finish line was Frances, the kids, my dad, the sponsor, and me. We had to make it to Anchorage in Alaska, where we would hole up for a few days in order to get all the data sent to Guinness headquarters. We then had to meet with the Guinness adjudicator and make our way north to Prudhoe Bay.

I was incredibly grateful my dad was there, although I probably didn't show it as well as I should have. It's very true that you take your stresses and anger out on those who you love the most. I am always striving for excellence and pushing myself to achieve the very best, and I automatically assume everyone else wants the same. I want it for them and expect them to keep up with my pace, and that can be very unfair on people at times, especially my dad. He has never understood or kept up with my pace, but he has always been there to help when asked.

That is often the problem. I don't ask; I expect everyone should just know. This is definitely an area I am constantly trying to improve on. Sometimes, we think everyone understands what we're going through and should know exactly what is needed to fix it. More often than not, people need the facts stated to them. I was struggling, and I had been for a long time. But I told very few people. I either waited for the offer or did it myself.

We set off from Aberdeen on our journey to meet Dean at the finish line one cold crisp April morning. All these years of planning, and it was almost there—the time we had been working toward. We all hopped on the plane with great excitement and anticipation. Tommy was almost two now, and Mollie was soon to turn six. They had spent a very long time without seeing Daddy and were bursting with excitement.

We arrived in Anchorage and checked into our hotel. The kids had pizza for breakfast, while Frances and I sent off all the final evidence to Guinness World Records. The data gathering process throughout was intense, but it definitely made it easier for us when it came to supplying Guinness what was needed. Every day, Dean would upload videos and pictures to the WhatsApp group. Photos would be used for social media and photo book material and videos, for socials and evidence. Logbooks were required for evidence, as well as the information the ground team would send to us and the data from the devices. We were also still actively pushing the fundraising and managing the sponsors' involvement.

We waited until the last minute to get the hour and thirty-minute flight to Prudhoe Bay. Prudhoe Bay is certainly not a place you want to stay too long, especially with kids. We jumped on the plane when Dean was about five hundred miles out. As we flew across the mountains, we were hit by how white it was below. It was blinding. The plane was heading to an oilfield, so it was full of riggers and workers. When they saw us and the kids getting on, I think they were in total shock. Prudhoe was a place for oil workers and staff. It wasn't a tourist place, wasn't a place for kids. There was no alcohol allowed, and the coldness was almost unbearable.

We left the plane and entered the terminal through a tunnel. When the truck turned up to pick us up, they pulled right up to the terminal door, and we were all ushered into the cabin of the truck. When we arrived at our accommodation, they opened the doors before letting us out, and we had to head straight into the building through the door. The brief moment you felt the outside was like stepping into a cryogenic freezer. It gave us a moment of wonder, thinking what Dean would be going through. We were at the end of the earth and the edge of nowhere, and he was cycling right into this abyss.

Frances and I decided the next morning to take the truck out to the end of the Dalton Highway, a road made famous by the show *Ice Road Truckers*, the same road Dean was currently cycling up toward us. The plan was to take in the road and see how Dean would feel as he approached. We were keen to get some handheld footage and use it as B-roll. I was the first to step out of the car, and despite the three layers of thermal clothing, snow boots, winter coat, hat, scarf, and gloves, I could barely last thirty seconds on that road. Frances tried the same and lasted slightly less than thirty seconds.

That was when it hit us. How on earth was this one man, on a bike, in this weather, meant to cycle all this way and through this wall of ice? I hated the word *impossible*. But was this it? How was he going to do it?

The following morning, the weather report was dire. Day 99 had arrived, and I can't lie; nerves had gone full throttle. Dean was only forty miles away, but what he had to travel through was horrendous at best, life-threatening at worst.

One of the camera crew arrived in a truck. He asked to speak with me privately. "Alana," he said, "he's not going to make it."

I took myself off for a moment and returned.

Now was not the time for pleasantries, and it wasn't the time for pussyfooting around Dean. I looked him in the eye, and I told him to deliver a message for me. I told him he needed to take Dean aside and look him in the eye just like I was looking at him now. I told him to tell him that his family was waiting for him. Mollie, Tommy, and Alana were here waiting for him. He had been gone long enough, and it was time for him to come home. We were here, waiting, ready with the biggest hugs for him, but we would not accept him not doing his absolute best—his absolute best—and the only option was crossing this finish line today. I told him to tell him I was angry, and I was waiting for him; the longer I waited, the angrier I got.

The cameraman looked at me in shock. I think he expected more compassion and warmth. But this was not the time for this. I needed him to use the last bit of strength and adrenaline he had to get to this finish line. I knew he could do it, and the strength in my words were for him.

The cameraman went off to deliver the message, but my own mind was full of doubt, not about the record but about what was yet to come.

CHAPTER TWENTY-SIX

❧❧❧❧❧❧❧❧❧❧

A NEW CHALLENGE
AND A ROYAL
WEDDING

How much can one person take? It was a question that had circled my mind since Dean set off on his Pan-American Highway challenge. The only answer I could think of was that the universe never gives you more than you can take; the stronger and tougher you are, the more it will give you. If you use it correctly, that power and knowledge can do amazing things does that mean it hurts any less? Definitely not. But having the inside scoop that it's all for a greater good definitely helps.

I was now at the stage where I was ready to go and meet Dean at the finish line, but I was plagued with nerves. I knew it was almost time to tell him everything that had been going on. The abuse from the support team was now in full swing, the charities were pushing really hard to fundraise, and my business partners were now relentless in their pressure on me. That and all the other issues I was facing—I hadn't shared any of it with Dean. I was a young mum who had sacrificed a great deal of time with the children to do the work I was doing, which largely centered on helping the most vulnerable people in society. Yet much of the time, I felt like one of those people myself.

There was no more time to think. It was time. I gathered all the kids up, prepared the data for Guinness, met the adjudicator in the lobby, threw on all our warm clothes, and headed toward the finish line. The finish line was right on the road of the oil company's base. The only other things on that road were oil tankers and polar bears. A couple of little blond kids and a load of young women must have been a pretty strange sight to anyone who was working there. The adjudicator, Sarah, a lovely young girl, had maybe underestimated the temperature and climate. She was wearing some cute heels and a pencil skirt. I could see the chill in her already, and we were still in the truck.

As we sat waiting, suddenly we saw a small black dot appear on the horizon. As I watched the dot get bigger and bigger, I was filled with a sense of pride.

I had to ignore all the other feelings about the bad things that had been happening and even the email I'd received just as we were about to leave for the finish line. It was an email from a solicitor claiming to act on behalf of the support team. They had decided to withdraw their support for the challenge and withdrew any permission for their logos to be used by the charity. Dean was just about to cross the finish line covered in Lycra with their details on it.

They knew exactly what they were doing. They had failed to stop Dean completing the challenge. And now they wanted to stop him being able to advertise his big moment. It was beyond disgusting, and I couldn't bear the thought of telling Dean. Dean had been so lovely to the team; even when they'd treated him so terribly, he was always good with them. This latest move was despicable.

We later checked all their social media and websites, and they were still actively advertising their support and connections with the challenge. It was nothing to do with not wanting to be associated with it but purely about wanting to hurt Dean and ruin the moment for Dean and myself. I wouldn't let them take this from him, and I decided I wouldn't tell him anything yet. I wanted him to at least have a small moment of enjoying his victory.

Dean crossed the finish line on May 11, 2018, coming in at 99 days, 12 hours, and 56 minutes. We were all there to greet him, and the moment was magical. It was bloody cold, though, so we got inside as quickly as we possibly could. As we got him into the canteen, ready to feed and thaw, I looked at him for a long time. He had lost so much weight; he looked so vulnerable. He had pushed his mind and body to the absolute limits, and he had done it.

I got him his food and drinks, and he sat down and ate. The rest of the crew came in and joined him. I left, as they seemed uncomfortable with me there. They had been so used to the isolation; I had to play everything very carefully with them.

Once Dean had fully refueled and chatted to everyone. It was time to head up to our room and catch up one-on-one. As we got into the room, we had the biggest cuddle. He had done it, and we knew at that moment we had done it. The fundraising was going well, and we now just had to get back in time for Harry and Meghan's wedding.

"One question?" Dean turned, an inquisitive look on his face. "Today I opened the last letter. You only wrote a hundred. How did you know?"

I smiled and looked at him. "Dean, from the day we started planning this and you did your first training ride, I never doubted you would come in under a hundred days." I couldn't tell him back at the beginning that I knew this, as it would have put too much pressure on him, but there wasn't a moment I doubted it.

He smiled and nodded his head. He knew exactly what I had done.

I tried my best to keep everything that had been happening from him. But before long, he looked in my eyes and asked what was wrong. I could never hide anything from him. He always knew when something was wrong face-to-face. I couldn't lie to him and couldn't hide it anymore. I told him everything.

He sat in shock for a second before giving me a hug. He asked me why I had been dealing with it all myself. He told me I should have called and spoken to him. I explained that wouldn't have been fair on him or the challenge, and I did not want that on my conscience. He told me he was home now, and we would take it on together.

We had twenty-four hours to spend in this oilfield. The kids enjoyed playing, while Dean took call after call from friends and spon-sors. We worked on all post-ride interviews with the camera guys and talked through our plan for when we went home. We now had to plan to get back to Anchorage and then onto London in time for the wed-ding. The PR team had been busy booking interviews and post-ride appearances on most of the UK networks.

We landed back in Heathrow on Thursday morning, and Dean had to leave us at the airport while he headed straight into London to begin meetings. Frances, the kids, and I were left to deal with the mountains of baggage. We had the baby push-chair, two big bike boxes, countless amounts of suitcases, and not one single offer of help. We formed a mini train and managed to get through the airport relatively unscathed.

We jumped in a couple of taxis and headed to our hotel. We had the evening to get ready for the wedding. I was still living in hope that Dean would fit into the morning suit I'd had to quickly purchase with the measurements Dean had sent me from the road. Dean got home late that evening after several interviews and was exhausted.

However, the following day, the press team had arranged a whole load of new interviews. It was incredibly hard for Dean, as the ques-tions he was being asked were all around the wedding and how excited he should be for the wedding. Truth was, he wasn't excited; he was in a daze, a big cloud he was trying to come down from but without being given the chance to do so. I knew all he wanted to do was lie in bed with me and the kids and watch some brain-numbing movies.

But he persevered like the true soldier he is. The morning of the wedding arrived, and I woke now with a bit of excitement, excitement to spend the day with Dean, excitement to be in the presence of this union, and excitement that the whole world would be celebrating too.

My excitement, however, was short-lived, and that brief moment of joy was soon crushed. I reached over to check the time on my phone, and there was a message from a number I didn't have saved. It told me to enjoy the day but to ask Dean about a girl he had been having an affair with before he left. It was cold and cruel, and I felt like I had been punched in the guts. I immediately tried to call the number, but the line was dead and has been dead ever since. Someone had actually gone out of their way to buy a phone, send a message, and then destroy the phone. This was how much they wanted to hurt us. They absolutely hated our successes and happiness and wanted to make sure they got in the way of every possible moment that we may be happy.

My eyes immediately filled up. It wasn't that I believed the message; it was more that someone out there was actually plotting and scheming to hurt us in such cruel ways. I handed the phone to Dean, and he looked at me and asked who it was from. I told him it was a burner phone and asked if he knew anything about it. He told me he had no idea what it was about and asked who would send something like this. I told him this was the tip of the iceberg compared to all the other emails, messages, and now Twitter campaigns that had begun.

He was angry, and I was angry. But we had to get ready and go celebrate the day. When I look back now, I see this was the start of us bottling up our feelings again. Neither of us had any idea how to deal with this; this was brand-new territory for us both. We could not understand the level of hate and nastiness, and more so, we couldn't understand why it was being directed toward us.

I had started this campaign to get Dean out of a dark place. I'd sacrificed time with him and time with my babies. We'd suffered financially. And our own health had suffered. Yet we'd continued doing it, knowing how many people we were helping and the lives we were changing. Dean had proved anything was possible by breaking the records, and we were now home to celebrate a friend's wedding. These people took all these things as reasons to hate us and were actively spending their time trying to cause us harm. How could we possibly understand this?

It was a hard lesson and one that took a while to really sink in. I still don't think I fully understand it. Instead of lashing out at strangers, why don't these types of people use other people's successes as inspiration and drive to go achieve their own dreams? Why do they, instead, spend their time trying to bring down a person who's had success? Does this really make them feel better? The hatred boils inside them like a cancer, sometimes crossing boundaries and becoming obsessive. I was recently told one of them has an alert set up so that, each time our name is mentioned, he'll get an alert and will immediately reply to the comment on social media. I can't imagine a life where you deliberately set up a reminder to feel hatred, bitterness, resentment, and jealousy.

As we got ready that morning, the kids hovered around, still super excited to have Daddy home. I knew they were going to be highly disappointed when it came to us leaving them. But they had Frances there, and she was definitely up there as one of their favorite people.

My lovely friend arrived in the morning to do my hair and makeup, while Dean tried on clothing that wasn't skintight and made for absorbing sweat. He had gone from four months of perma Lycra to a rigid morning suit. Dean had lost almost thirty pounds during his ride, and I had to purchase his suit based on measurements he'd sent me using a motel receptionist's tape measure. Although very skinny, the suit I had bought fit perfectly, and he was still very handsome. I was very proud to be accompanying him on this special day.

We both took deep breaths and got ready to paint on the smiles and hide the pain we were feeling. Dean messaged Harry, sending all the best before the crazy day ahead, completely unaware of the pain he too was feeling at the moment. I guess Dean and I had lived with the royal family on our TVs, newspapers, and now as friends for the whole of our lives. Dean knew a great deal about Harry as a man and as an Army buddy, but as typical men, their inner feelings were rarely discussed. The crap written about Harry on a daily basis all his life had become a norm for us and most of Britain to see, so we almost naturally assumed it was water off a duck's back to him. When you've lived with abuse all your life, you learn to normalize it surely?

But to look back now and know the pain that both Meghan and he were feeling on this day, how the press had gone so far to ruin things for them, how they had to walk up that aisle with smiles and joy, it made me realize that it doesn't matter who you are, how rich or poor, famous, or unknown, whatever walk of life you are from, nothing can shield you from the pain of bullying and abuse. I think for people such as Meghan, Harry, and even myself and Dean, the pain is amplified because it's so far from our nature. If we were one of those people who thought with purely selfish intentions and no desire to help anyone, then maybe it wouldn't hurt so much. But when your reason for getting out of bed every day, and your natural serotonin release comes from helping other people and then you're attacked for doing just that, it hurts; oh, god, it hurts so much.

And the more good things you do, the more they try to find "dirt" on you. For every good thing you do, they feel that extra bit shit about themselves. But instead of using that as motivation to go out and do something good in the world, the easier option for them is to find something negative about you. And if they can't find it, they make it up. I'm sure this is the case with one of our trolls, who has tweeted literally thousands of times about us, each time with complete lies and obviously under an anonymous account (don't worry, we know who they are). But I sometimes believe they actually believe what they say. The obsession and jealousy has overtaken reality. This also rings true with many of Meghan's most famous media stalkers. They have developed their own convenient logic and narrative and immersed themselves in it so deeply that they can't allow the truth to derail their campaign of hatred.

Giving the kids big hugs, we jumped into the taxi and headed to Windsor. We arrived at the castle, the sun beating down from the bright blue sky, the streets lined with decorations and well-wishers, everyone in their best dressed. It was simply picture-perfect. We arrived at the Farmhouse at Windsor Castle to be greeted by an already busy reception. Dean was still in a daze from his last few months in relative isolation. I was jet-lagged, exhausted, and extremely dehydrated. The first place we headed for was the water fountain.

I excused myself past a number of extremely well-dressed individuals to make it to the water fountain. One gentleman was standing right in the way of me getting my hydration on, so I politely asked for him to excuse me. As I raised my head from the fountain, Dean was already in conversation with him. I chuckled to myself, as I knew Dean had no idea who he was. As usual Dean had no idea about celebrities and couldn't pick most out in a lineup. To me, however, Idris Elba was unmistakable. As we stood and chatted, two other woman approached Idris and hugged him.

Within minutes, we were all called to the coach. We hopped on the same coach as them, and as they took their positions at the front, we headed to the back. Typical security people, we needed to have full range of vision and be in the background. Dean whispered to me as we sat down, "That guy must be really close to H!"

I looked at Dean inquisitively. "Why's that?" I asked.

"Well, his friends are here on their own. And people who know Harry through charities and people close to the couple seem to have husband and wife invites, whereas that guy got to bring his wife and mum!"

I looked at Dean in complete disbelief. "What makes you think that's his mum?" I asked.

He told me that the other woman was obviously his wife, given the affection he was showing, and his closeness to the older woman made him think she must be his mum, as they were all together.

"Dean," I said in a sympathetic and educational tone. "That is Idris Elba with his partner, and the 'older' lady is not his mum. It's Oprah Winfrey!"

This was, without a doubt, one of Dean's most endearing qualities. He has absolutely no clue who anyone is. And even if he did, he would still treat everyone exactly the same.

As we got off the coach, the gentleman up front told us to be prepared—that the cameras would be there as soon as we departed. I was so naive as to what this meant. The private, introverted security professional in me had me walking fast, stone-faced, with my head down and aiming to get into the chapel as quickly as possible, avoiding the cameras as much as possible. The only picture they caught of Dean and I had us looking more like we were walking into a funeral, rather than a wedding!

Once again, as everyone headed down to get seats near the front, we followed true to form and hung back. Dean spotted two friends we knew, and we made a beeline for them. Things became a bit more natural for us then, and my little mind thought, as we were safely in the chapel, we were safely out of reach of the cameras—that was until my dad texted to say he could see me on TV. I looked up and realized there were cameras everywhere. I immediately went back to feeling uncomfortable.

Any woman knows the feeling of feeling watched and having to look perfect for a prolonged period of time—tummy pulled in, back straight, smile, stand on both feet, and don't slouch. Let me tell you, if you haven't experienced it, it's excruciating, especially when it goes on for hours.

I can't really complain, though. Our friend was just fourteen weeks after giving birth, and any mom knows the complications of breastfeeding and socializing, especially with no access to a bathroom or rest area to express. Add that to the hours of waiting (100 percent for security reasons and totally understandable). However, if it had been me, I don't think the cameras would have stopped me. I would have been getting the pump out! She did very well.

As time went by, we'd been unaware of how enormous the crowd was that had now formed outside—that was until the first VIP guest arrived and the chapel doors opened. You could hear the roars and excitement outside. It wasn't surprising. Harry has always been a massively loved member of the royal family, as Diana's son, as a war hero, for his amazing charity work, and now as he had met the love of his life, who was everything he had ever wanted and needed. Who wouldn't be happy and excited for this day?

The moment the bride entered the chapel was a moment I will never forget. To step into that chapel on her own, no father by her side; I can't even begin to imagine how that must have felt. My dad and I have had our ups and downs, but for all the things I could say about him, I could never imagine him not being by my side at such a special moment. Watching Meghan walk down on her own and knowing how her heart must have been torn between pure joy and pure heartbreak was very hard to watch. Prince Charles meeting her halfway, well, I thought it was so lovely and so needed in that moment. Even the strongest women need support now and then.

When Harry saw her walk in, I think that was it for me; the room got pretty steamy. I'm not crying, you are! So, between the immense dehydration, holding myself stiff as a board for three hours, and the room making my eyes water, my head began to pound. As Harry walked his new bride out of the chapel to their adoring crowd, the guests all headed off to the reception.

The reception was exquisite, and the room was incredibly intimate.

It really was a fairy tale. The only disappointment, we couldn't enjoy ourselves. With everything that was going on, along with how we were both feeling physically, we struggled just to keep the smiles on our faces. As the security couple, we did our usual and headed to the corner of the room. We watched as everyone chatted, hugged, and enjoyed the food.

There were a few people who really stood out to me. James Corden was one. He really knew how to work a room; Dean and I were huge *Gavin & Stacey* fans and watching him that day gave me a newfound respect for him. I always find it incredibly difficult to work a networking room. I either stay my introverted self in a corner somewhere or end up in deep conversation with one person and really get to know them. Often, during events I've hosted, I have to get my guys to drag me away in order to get to everyone. James seemed to have the perfect mix of showing interest and excusing himself at the right time. It really was skillful.

Some of the ladies stood out with their amazing beauty and poise, among them Amal Clooney. Dressed in a gorgeous mustard dress, she caught my eye more than once that day. She is an amazing woman and works in areas I am incredibly passionate about too. If I had been in any other mindset, I most definitely would have introduced myself.

That was our biggest regret of the day—that we both felt so poorly, physically and mentally, that we just didn't enjoy it like we should have. Following the amazing speeches and the performance by Elton John, we quietly decided to slope off. It was an amazing day, but in the end, all Dean wanted to do was get back to his babies and spend some real time with them. We said our goodbyes and sneaked away before the bubbles really got flowing.

As we left the castle grounds, Dean called an Uber. Once again totally naive and thinking nothing of it, we just walked off past the police cordon in order to meet our ride. Suddenly, we were met by a swarm of reporters and paparazzi. We smiled politely and ignored most of their questions. But as we got into the taxi, they got closer and closer. As I tried to get into the cab, one of them knocked the hat off of my head, and suddenly, I felt very uncomfortable. This lasted all of about three minutes, but I couldn't wait to get out of there and felt a slight feeling of violation. I said to Dean later that evening that I could never imagine being in the spotlight like that, having these guys chase you about day in, day out. The damage to your psyche must be horrendous.

I think about people like Britney Spears, who literally had adult men paying a hound of pap rats to follow her around and make her super anxious, with the sole purpose of getting her to have a breakdown. I mean, you really have to take a long, hard look inside yourself if you think that's an honest earned living.

We returned that evening to two super wide-awake and excited kids and one babysitter fast asleep!

The following, day the four of us headed to Legoland and had an amazing day as a family. It was time to head home. Our mission wasn't complete. We still had money to raise, and there was no time for rest. I had two big fundraisers to plan, and we still had much work to do. For Dean, the bike ride was over. But for me, the road ahead was still long.

CHAPTER TWENTY-SEVEN

❧❧❧❧❧❧❧

PAH: THE AFTERMATH

The thought lay firmly in the forefront of my mind that, any day, I could just give up. We had set our goal firmly on raising £1,000,000 for the cause. But what was it really worth? I'd given birth during this process; time had been taken away from my family, from time with my babies and with my husband. We'd lost out financially, personally, and professionally. The pain and suffering had been very real and intense. Yet, to everyone else, the narrative was different. Their words—"you guys are amazing; you guys are so lucky; you guys are the best"—continued to ring in my ears. It would drive me crazy. And despite those who loved me the most begging for me to give up, I knew I couldn't. I couldn't be me if I gave in. I wouldn't be ending it because I wanted to. I would be giving up because of the pressure from others, from people with the sole intention of seeing us fail. How could I ever give into that?

Dean returned home to enjoy his newfound brush with fame. As the Special Forces war hero who had just broken two world records and had already raised over half a million for mental health charities, he was a hero. He was a legend, and I made sure he enjoyed every moment. As much as I could, I kept all the bad stuff away from him.

Luckily, I had Frances with me in the office, and she was pretty much my daily sounding board. The previous support team had upped the ante with a mixture of solicitors' letters, anonymous poison pen letters, and the start of a heavy and prolonged campaign of abuse on social media. Barely a day went by when something wasn't written about me, Dean, the campaign, or even the kids.

I was also preparing for the Mrs. Scotland competition; it was something very new for me, but it was exciting. For the first time in my life, I was being a girl, being feminine. My coach was even teaching me how to walk, something I thought I'd been doing perfectly well for the past thirty-six year. However, apparently, I'd been doing it wrong all this time. I'd been walking to get where I wanted to go. Yet, according to the world of pageantry, I should have been walking with purpose, stance, and poise—with shoulders-back, head-up, hip-swinging confidence. Who knew?!

I do mock. However, this element of the training has actually never left me. Before this experience, I most definitely walked with concealment as my intent; I wanted to get places with as few people noticing me as possible. I wanted to hide my height at every opportunity and would slouch, crouch, and do everything I could to not be noticed. Following the pageant training, I realized this was insane. I had spent my life embracing my burns and my intellect but had totally ignored my God-given physical advantages. My height was one; I had forever tried to be "shorter," not such a tall poppy. This was part of my upbringing. You stay in your lane. You don't try to rise above. You get down and stay down. This was why I always found it so hard to stand out. It wasn't me. I wasn't meant for that. I had a purpose in life, and it took a beauty pageant to start opening that mindset in me.

There was a lot to do to prepare for the pageant. The other girls were experts at this. They knew how to walk and how to talk, knew the world of pageantry inside out. Then there was me. I was the one who took the photographs, not the one being snapped. I was the clever friend, sometimes the funny one, not the beauty. And I knew nothing whatsoever about hair and makeup. Don't get me wrong; I was confident. When it came to business or intellectual attributes, I had all the confidence in the world. However, this world was alien.

But that was exactly why I'd done it. I believed in seizing every opportunity to get out of your comfort zone—never a place a person should sit comfortably in. If you find yourself stationary and comfortable, unless you're preparing your last will and testament, you should be checking out of that situation and pushing your boundaries somewhere. For me, this was the place I was at my most uncomfortable. Being beautiful was so far from me, I had to learn the art of acting to make it work.

In July 2018, I attended the Dorchester Hotel in London with the pageant group. I was incredibly nervous. I'd spent the previous year in the presence of some of the wealthiest people in Britain, including celebrities and royalty. Yet this situation, with this beautiful, well-turned-out group of women, was my nemesis. Nevertheless, I painted on the face, curled my hair, and joined the group.

The first lady to greet me was this raven-haired beauty Jordana, Mrs. Bournemouth, who was competing for Mrs. England. She was simply stunning—her posture, her outfit, her hair, her makeup, and her confidence. I was blown away, and it would be fair to say I had a bit of a girl crush. When I entered the room, she came straight to me. I immediately did that look-over-your-shoulder thing. Was it me she was approaching or was there someone behind me?

"Can I get you some champagne?" she said.

That were the words I needed to hear. I nervously sat and spoke with her. Years later, I learned that my nerves and anxiety meeting her had nothing on how she was feeling. Everything I saw in her, she equally saw in me. Where I saw her stunning beauty, she knew my inner self. She had already taken time to learn about what I'd done in life, and this scared her deeply. To me, I felt lesser than her, not realizing she felt exactly the same way about me. It made me realize that this is likely how every person goes through life—what intimidates one person will be another person's gifts, and another person's gifts will be the other's nemesis. If we could actually all realize that, we could probably fight through much of the self-doubt we have. We could focus on our own strengths if we could see ourselves as others do.

As the pageant approached, I was gaining in confidence in the areas I'd previously lacked. I was still actively working on the fundraising, and Dean was preparing for the road ahead after the challenge. There wasn't a day that went by that I wasn't reminded of the hate campaign against us, but I particularly remember one trip to London.

We had just secured another £100,000 donation, and my Mrs. Scotland pageant was approaching. Dean and I had had very little time together, and this particular evening, we had no meetings. We were in London and decided to head out for dinner together. We treated ourselves to a wine-tasting menu at a lovely French restaurant, and as the courses started to arrive, I began to relax. Finally, some time together just me and him.

My enjoyment was short-lived. I received a message from the pageant director asking me to call her urgently. She'd received a letter to her home address. It was anonymous but, at the same time, frightening. How had the letter sender obtained her home address? How much energy had it taken for them to find this detail?

The letter told of how horrible a person I was, how I was a fraud, how I'd stole from charity, how I didn't deserve the title, and how I was pretty much Lucifer reincarnated. She sent me a screenshot of the letter. And just like that, our lovely evening crumbled.

I burst into tears; I couldn't understand it. The hate being directed at me was now becoming obsessive and frightening. She assured me the letter had no effect on her or my chances in the competition, but how could it not? She didn't know who I was. She didn't know me really, and like everyone else who had received this type of poison pen about us, she most certainly didn't need the hassle.

It was evident at the Mrs. Scotland pageant. I went on to win every award that was independently awarded—Best Marriage, Best Interview. But as I got to the final two, I was given runner-up. I was told later that the girl who had won was a safer bet. A number of the judges said they had voted for me, but the final say was the owner, and I guess the fear of more repercussions for backing me was too much for them.

A few days later, however, I got a call to say that the winner had not passed the application stage and that I would be crowned Mrs. Scotland 2018. This was amazing, if not bittersweet. I wish I'd been awarded the crown fairly, without judgment, but this was how these people trying to hurt us operated. They posted letters with the sole intention of hurting us, and they didn't care how deep that hurt went.

There have been many well-known faces over the years who

couldn't handle the pressure of constant criticism and abuse and, unfortunately, decided to take the only way out they could think of—by ending their life. Was this their aim for me? Did one of us have to physically die before they would stop?

The list of people who received letters was endless and scary. Our sponsors, clients, family, and friends were targeted. Even the girl who waxed my eyebrows received a letter at her home address. On top of that, they focused on my daughter, sending things to her school and to her modelling coach. I think that was the most frightening; it basically went, "Don't coach this seven-year-old girl, as her mum is an evil, fraudulent monster!" This one was definitely up there with the most insane.

No, there was no reason behind the campaign against us. It was just pure vindictive evil, jealousy, and obsession. The majority knew to ignore it, yet some would still ask questions. We found ourselves on the permanent defense. Even among those who knew we had done nothing wrong, there was still an excuse to ask us questions. And of course, no matter how uncomfortable it was, we felt we needed to respond and defend.

Dean struggled the most. He was a person who did not like his integrity questioned and would vigorously defend it no matter who it was doing the questioning. For me, I only responded to the people I really cared about. I wouldn't deal with idle gossip or naysayers. I had no time for that, and this would frequently cause arguments between Dean and me. He couldn't understand why I didn't want to be on permanently defending myself. And I couldn't see why he needed to justify or defend himself to every Tom, Dick, or Harry.

It really hit the fan and came to a major head in November 2018. Dean and I were ambassadors for the SBSA (the Special Boat Service Association), an association for injured Special Forces soldiers and their families. Dean was the Scottish representative for the organization, and every year, I would organize a luncheon or event for the members, such as the Gleneagles event.

This year was special. I had arranged it on Remembrance Day weekend, which also fell on a rugby weekend. I had arranged for a number of the older soldiers, a few legendary rugby players, and current members to all attend in Edinburgh. I was excited for every-one involved and for Dean to have a great evening with his buddies. That Saturday morning, I had also booked my Mensa exam. I became a member of Mensa when I was eight years old but wanted to retake the exam as an adult.

As I entered the hall in Edinburgh, I received an alert on my phone. At this stage, I still received incoming email notifications. I no longer practice this and wish, at this time, I'd learned to switch off notifications. A message popped up from a journalist. He was a name I knew, as he'd previously actively attempted to get Dean to sell stories on Prince Harry, as well as his fellow soldiers—something we always politely declined. His email stated he was due to run a story the following day about Dean cheating on the bike ride.

I was in total shock. Say anything you want to about Dean, but he would never cheat on a physical feat. I immediately emailed our PR girl, and I was quite calm about it. It was obvious nonsense. We had all the evidence from Guinness World Records, all the data, and anything a person would need to show this accusation was bullshit.

She quickly invited me to the world of the British Press; she told me the truth played very little part in what was about to unfold. I was completely floored, yet I still believed people were inherently good. Presented with facts and truth, surely a person would never actively go out to ruin a person's integrity, reputation, and life just to sell a paper?

How wrong was I! Despite all the evidence presented to him, the reporter still went ahead and printed the article—"Prince Harry's Special Forces Friend Cheated on Bike Ride." It was a headline I would never forget.

That evening, I ran a successful event for the soldiers, sportsmen, and veterans and, afterward, settled with them for a night cap. I told a couple of the older gents about the article coming out the next day. They told me to ignore the rags and that everyone who knew Dean knew it was nonsense.

The next morning, I woke in the hotel room. Dean was already awake, dressed, and ready to go to the newsagent for a paper. I told him to ignore it and not to let this ruin our day. We were there with the kids and had planned a family day in Edinburgh. We immediately argued. He told me it was easy for me to say and that it was his integrity in question. This really drove me crazy. It was awful for him, but it had been me that had been dealing with this for months. The article took a swing at both of us. Yet we knew it was bullshit. We knew it was easily proven bullshit. So why was he letting this get to him?

The abuse I had been receiving over the past however many months never came close to bothering him as much as this did. This was incredibly hard. For me, we were in this together, but it only seemed to get to him when it was a direct attack on him. I think this was when I realized the difference between men and women. Women actively protect the tribe and will do all they can to make sure they are all safe with full absence of ego and pride. A man, on the other hand, will always protect his own pride and ego; primitively, it is an integral part of men's existence.

I know he cared about us but none of the previous abuse had touched him, as I'd kept it well away from him; I couldn't keep this away. He assumed that, because I'd dealt with it to this point, it didn't hurt me as much as this article hurt him.

That afternoon, we visited the natural history museum in Edinburgh as planned with the kids, and he would have been better off not being there. The whole time he was on calls, and the kids asked questions that were ignored. He was letting these people destroy our happy family life, and I wasn't happy with that. This was their aim, and this reaction was letting them win.

Dean became very active in defending his world record. A number of people told him to say nothing, but it was incredibly hard for both of us to sit in silence. Dean instructed a second examination of evidence from Guinness World Records and told them not to approve it unless they were 100 percent satisfied. He spent hours on calls with friends, colleagues, and sponsors defending himself and proving he had done nothing wrong.

I wanted to approach this differently. I told him he'd done nothing wrong and had nothing to prove; the truth would eventually come out, and patience was the key. Allow Guinness to do its job, and eventually we would have our vindication. I know this was nearly impossible for Dean. His career of sixteen years in the Army and in the Special

Forces had been based on his integrity, and he was an incredibly highly regarded former Special Forces solider. His integrity being in question was killing him. I told him the paper was nothing; the journalist was nothing; the support team member quoted in the article saying, "He wasn't getting enough media attention," was nothing. No one with any level of intellect would read that article and believe it; nor would they care about it. At the time, I hadn't yet realized the full power of the British tabloid press.

We'd already begun planning our next challenge. Dean wanted to become the first person to kayak the River Nile, and this time we would do it for the cause closest to my heart—human trafficking. We had donors and sponsors lined up, yet one by one, they began to pull out. They were all big players in the London scene, and I found it hard to believe people would be pulling out because of this one article. I sat with a prominent figure, who I will not name. It was not that they, in any way shape or form believed what was being said, this person told me, but most people in the industry were terrified of the power of the UK press. The press had the ability to literally destroy people and companies, and it wouldn't be the first time the press had yielded that power simply because someone went against them. This person was terrified to even consider going up against such a force. Associating with us could make anyone who did so a target, and no one was willing to take that risk.

We had many good people around us who cared for us deeply, and they all said the same thing. Keep your head down. Don't rile the press. Just move on and try to forget about it. But how could we? We'd done nothing wrong. Why were they attacking us like this?

We hadn't realized at the time, but the timing of the attack on us coincided with the press upping their attacks on Harry and Meghan. We were just part of this game of abuse. The press would grab onto anything to which Harry or Meghan's name could be attached as headline—or they would just make it up, usually the latter.

Of course, now armed with this article, the trolls on social media went into overdrive. They set up alerts so anytime our name was mentioned on Twitter they immediately responded, sharing the article, calling us frauds and cheats, and warning people to stay away.

At one point, we counted over seven hundred tweets by one person in one week!

The pressure was now intense. I would wake to messages and comments and was feeling sick on a daily basis. I deleted all my social media accounts from my phone. But that didn't stall the sickness. It turned out, that was due to more than just stress. We were expecting our third child.

There were some very intense feelings—excitement and nervousness were mixed together. I was still having issues with my businesses. This coupled with planning Dean's next challenge, the trafficking campaign, and defending this hate campaign, along with everything else we had going on, and I knew it would be hard. Dean was taking the whole thing very personally, and he wasn't able to see the effect it was all having on me. I knew my eating issues had been creeping back in over the past few months, and I was worried about the entire situation.

I was struggling to sleep—a mixture of anxiety, stress, workload, and children. I was having palpitations daily and just never feeling quite right. I would go and visit my great-auntie Molly for tea and digestives. That was always a great way to make me feel better. She would tell war stories, and we talked about mum and everyone else who was no longer with us. I was slowly creeping up to the age at which my mum had died, and that had always played on my mind. Every part of me at this point was fighting to stay positive—telling myself daily to fight, don't let them win, be the Alana you know is in there. Molly gave me that strength. She only knew me as the little girl she'd looked after all those years ago. I never shared my pain with her, and I kind of like that. It was innocent.

One evening, I went to bed while Dean was still awake with the kids. My head was banging, and I just needed to sleep. I went to bed, and in the middle of the night I woke. I knew immediately. I made my way to the bathroom, a trail of blood behind me. I called for Dean. He eventually woke and came in. I just bowed my head. I couldn't say any words. I just cried.

Dean, well, Dean was angry. He was furious. His anger wasn't directed at me; I knew that. But I also just wanted him to sit there quietly with me. I didn't say anything. I just cleaned up and waited for him to come back down to my level.

It wasn't long. His sadness kicked in, and he helped with the cleaning and got me back into bed.

Another layer of hardness had formed in me. Pain was both physical and emotional at this point, and I did think about all those people who had written the articles, posted the tweets, and written the letters. I thought about every stroke of a key typed with hate and distain, with prayers that something bad would happen to me. Could the power of hateful energy be strong enough to cause something like this?

I couldn't think like that. I had to believe the power of kindness, love, and forgiveness was stronger. The world can't heal with hate and constant thoughts of revenge. I could never bring myself to their level. I was going to go out and carry on with the work I was meant to be doing. They were not going to take any more from me. I had work to do.

CHAPTER TWENTY-EIGHT

※☙⁘✿⁙❦⁘✿ॐ

TAKING ON
THE WORLD

I needed to move on with my next campaign. Human trafficking was my passion, and I needed to close the mental health chapter. We had given the first £500,000 very publicly. But the remaining money for mental health we decided to hand over privately and move on. We ended with our closing statement:

> It is with mixed emotions that today we draw to a close the Pan American Highway Challenge 2018. As a husband-and-wife team we set off on this challenge with 3 goals:
>
> - Raise one million pounds for mental health charities.
> - Break a world record.
> - Raise awareness of the issue surrounding mental health.
>
> We close today with a final amount raised of £900k ($1.3 million). While this is just under our

target this is a net amount with every single penny going to the mental health charities. This amount includes a pound-for-pound match donation of £265k that was donated at the annual company dinner for St James's Place and donated directly to the mental health charities.

We are extremely proud of what we've been able to achieve especially given we have never undertaken anything like this before and were starting from the very beginning.

What did we achieve:

- We have seen the opening of a new Family school with The Anna Freud National Centre for children and families
- We have connected the charities to a number of new High Net Worth individuals and companies
- The Mix were able to answer over 2,000 calls from desperate young people as well as provide over 300 counselling sessions because of our donation
- Young Minds used the funds for their Parent Helpline and digital services providing much-needed support to parents in crisis
- Our donation supported the training of 8,000 allied mental health professionals with the Anna Freud National Centre for Children and Families
- Our support has enabled Help4Heroes to care for veterans with significant mental health and physical challenges resulting from their service
- The funds from PAH have provided further support to veterans and their families through the Walking with the Wounded program

- The British Legion have described their involvement with the PAH campaign as "the highlight of 2018 for The Royal British Legion"
- The funds received by The Royal British Legion have helped deliver high-quality care for veterans with dementia and supported younger veterans on their "Battle Back" programme
- We have seen the appointment of a new Suicide Prevention Minister
- A huge reform happened in children's mental health management
- A new 24-hour veterans helpline opened with Combat Stress
- Dean, new to cycling, brought home 2 Guinness World Records to the UK as the first man in history to cycling the Pan American Highway in under 100 days
  - The fastest man to cycle the Pan American Highway (99 days)
  - The fastest man to cycle the length of South America (48 days)

We have witnessed firsthand how the money has helped change the conversation and the impact it has had on so many lives. We knew it wouldn't be easy but had no ideas of the hurdles and barriers we would face. As a family we made huge sacrifices, suffered losses, dealt with illnesses, gained new family members, and had amazing ups and downs along the way. This campaign took over our lives, but we never wavered from our goals, even when things like having a baby got in our way! We faced many challenges and learned a lot of important lessons.

Today however we have a new cause that is begging for our help, and now is the time to move on and help them. We must say goodnight to the PAH, draw from all the many lessons we have learned along the way, and put them into practice for the next challenge. We firmly believe our challenges along the way were all in preparation for what we have coming up, and this challenge requires strength, resilience, thick skin, and a strong heart. Every single moment will be worth it in order to save even one person.

Finally, and most importantly, we want to say a huge heartfelt thank you to everyone who has supported us along the way. To our sponsors, donors, and supporters, this would not have been possible without any of them. We have witnessed such an incredible amount of support from so many companies and individuals, and each and every one of you contributed to the success of this challenge. From the guy who donated a pound a day, every day without fail throughout the challenge right through to our incredible main sponsor St James Place from the bottom of our hearts ...

Thank you,
Dean and Alana Stott

As we raised a glass to welcome in 2019, for the first time in a while, I was feeling myself again. We were working on a new challenge, and I was excited to begin tackling it. This was the area in which I was really ready to kick ass. Having witnessed what Harry had done with the Heads Together campaign and being directly involved in the power of collaboration, we wanted to replicate this in the world of trafficking. In the past few years, I had been given a major crash course in fundraising, but to be fair, I had been practicing my whole life. Whether it was debt collecting, involvement in charity funding, working in banking, or raising investments for projects, asking for money was never something that came that difficult to me. Planning and understanding the market were some of the key elements. But over the years, I had developed the perfect formula. And one of the components over recent years that had ensured success was collaboration. So many charities clamber for the same pot of gold, without realizing, if they would all just work together, not only would there be more funding but the goals and objectives they needed the funds for would be achieved much more quickly.

I set to work on planning the campaign I would go on to call Breaking Chains. I would take the model of Heads Together, but this time, I would run it; and in order to be part of it, anyone involved would need to be active in collaboration. I wanted large and small players alike. Researchers, people on the ground, extensions of the work, I wanted them all. We set off contacting as many people in the industry as we could.

Of course, we were sometimes met with a questioning response: "Who are you and what do you know?" However, I wasn't deterred. I was way past the "I'll-prove-you-wrong" stage. I had no time for that. We would quickly get past that insecurity and get down to business. I personally visited every charity and presented the opportunity to join.

I was also busy preparing for the Mrs. World contest that was rapidly approaching. May 2019 would see me heading to Las Vegas with all the women who'd take part in the contest from around the world, forty in total. I was incredibly excited but equally super nervous. There was pushing out of your comfort zone, and then there was sailing so far out of even the slightest bit of comfort you can't remember what comfortable feels like. It was so far away from "me," I struggled to even fake it.

However, I knew I had the opportunity to reach forty countries, to put a spotlight on human trafficking, and to show the world what Scotland had to offer. I was excited to meet the women and, let's be honest, just have some kid-free Vegas time!

A major stumbling block for me was hair and makeup. These women were unbelievably glamorous and well turned out. Me, well I spent most of my time in sweats with a scrunchie in my hair. Makeup was never my favorite thing, and fake smiles came even lower than that.

One day, like a fairy godmother coming down from above, my

amazing friend Nicola said to me, casual as you like, "Alana, I'm coming with you!" Nicola is one of if not the top makeup artists there is. What she cannot do to a woman's face to enhance her beauty is not worth knowing. But what about hair? Well, the absolute babe spent her evenings learning about hairstyling. She spent much of her free time with her hairdresser friends learning everything she could. She ran raffles and competitions in order to raise the funds to travel there and spent hours and hours with me predeparture practicing makeup looks. I don't think she fully understood what it meant to me that she did this. She put her life on hold to help me out, and I will always be eternally grateful for that.

My nerves were rapidly creeping up. Not only was I leaving for ten days for a competition like nothing I'd ever done before, I was also leaving Dean with both children for ten days. This was something he'd never done before and was way out of his comfort zone! I was working out harder than I'd ever done before, and I was firmly focused on this opportunity. The outside noise was still very loud, but I was doing my best to ignore it. The competition was giving me a reason to be very controlled with my exercise and eating, and this control was giving me the strength to deal with all the other issues circulating us.

Our diary was booking up with speaking events and appearances. I was attending sporting events, parliament, and government meetings, where I was able to spread the message about tackling human trafficking. Working alongside the Scottish rugby team, I was delighted when they told me all their contractors now needed to have an active modern slavery statement. It was these small steps that were making what we did worthwhile.

We were still being asked quite regularly about the *Daily Mail* article. But by the time Guinness had conducted its own thorough investigation and had concluded, without doubt, that there was no issues with Dean's record, strangely enough, no newspaper was interested in printing that. Defending ourselves from the lies had now become part of our day-to-day life.

But over the years, we've learned how the majority of people know and actually accept that these tabloids actively share untruths and have no accountability. I once had a lesson in how they made money, learning the headline was the essential part. The tabloid could pretty much put anything it wanted in that headline, with carefully placed punctuation marks and wording; the aim was to get the click. The article itself could be in direct opposition to the headline, or more falsehoods could be printed. Neither truth nor consistency were the aim. All that mattered was the click. I was soon to learn more.

Soon, April 2019 had arrived, and it was time to take flight and head to Vegas. My bags were packed (all four of them!), and I was as ready as I'd ever be. I had final meetings with Dean and Frances to be sure they were completely comfortable with everything that needed to be done with the charity, business, and kids. I had to release control and trust them.

I know Dean had my back, but he struggled to show it. I was in group chats with all the other ladies, who were sending all these lovely pictures of parties their husbands had arranged, the flowers and gifts they had been given, and the cute letters that had been written. And I can't lie, I had a hint of jealousy. The funny thing is, we all have this. The grass is greener; they have it better than me. We all have these feelings. However, it's important to remember you can't have it all. If you opt for the tough guy, the stoic guy who's able to evacuate countries and single-handedly rescue embassies, then he's probably not going to be the party-throwing, chino-and-sweater-wearing type. It looked great on social media. However, I thought I would last five minutes; it wouldn't take long until I was in full control, and I needed a challenge. I needed someone who could push me as much as I pushed him, who would be honest with me when I was being lesser than myself and vice versa. I had looked after Dean all these year, and to expect him to suddenly become the attentive one would have been unrealistic.

We headed off to Vegas, Nicola and me. I vowed to give it my all, but I also promised I would always be 100 percent myself. We arrived in Vegas to a wonderful reception and headed to the hotel. I was informed very early on about the anonymous poison pen letters the pageant directors had received about me. It put me on the back foot. However, I was beyond caring. I had no energy left to deal with them. I told them it was bullshit, to bin it, and then moved on.

I met with my roommate Jordana, Mrs. England, who had arrived the day before. She gave me a brief lowdown of what it was all like—the other contestants, the organizers, the hotel—and we were ready to take them on.

The next morning, we headed down for breakfast. All the ladies were there and picking away at their little plates of food. Everyone looked amazing; it was more like a wedding breakfast than a morning in Vegas. Every lady was definitely bringing her A game.

As the small talk and niceties progressed, more ladies were arriving. A small woman with slicked-back hair and glasses who spoke in a thick eastern European accent was giving everyone instructions. And at one moment, this beautiful girl entered the room. She was tall, with flowing dark hair and legs that went on for miles. The short woman immediately got out of her seat and approached the girl. She beckoned her over to the table and stood her in front of us all. "OK, ladies, please take a look at this." The woman motioned her hands up and down the length of this beautiful woman. "This, ladies, this is what we don't want."

I was stunned. What did she mean? I looked around the room, and all the ladies were nodding. Had I missed something? Was there a joke coming? The girl just stood there saying nothing. The small woman then motioned to her skirt—a cute little miniskirt she'd paired with a cute T that complemented her whole body. "We are meant to be elegant ladies, the elite of the world. Ladies don't wear this; this is for strippers."

Holy shit, I actually was lost for words. What the hell had I just heard? The girl looked utterly embarrassed and then quickly moved away toward the buffet. I got up immediately and went after her. I told her she was beautiful, and she looked amazing. That moment right there, I realized this competition was nothing like what I'd thought it was. Every single stereotype of beauty pageants was confirmed there and then. I lost all interest at that moment. Instead, I decided I would spend the time having fun with the girls and trying to spread the word and educate as many as I could about human trafficking.

It was painful to see the plentitude of forced smile, fakeness, and causes clearly being promoted only due to being in the pageant; part of a pageant is that you do charity work. A lot of the women weren't active in the charity world but got involved in order to compete. I could only hope their brush with this work would encourage them to continue.

The funny thing was the ladies were all interesting when they were being themselves. Their own stories and rich lives were interesting, and when people relaxed, you could see who they were. But with so many of them just wanting to win, they weren't being authentic. It really was uncomfortable and sad at the same time. Imagine if none of them had cared and were just true to themselves. So much more could have come out of these pageants other than just a crown.

One evening, we were all invited to an amazing Japanese restaurant. It was a beautiful setting, and the head of the pageant, who was a much older man, was guiding us all into the restaurant. He wanted a group photo outside, and this was my next major red flag. Every time he wanted some attention or wanted someone to do something (including passing tourists), he would click his fingers or whistle. The first time this happened, I thought maybe he'd made a mistake. But soon I realized he was doing this as his way of communicating.

As we entered the restaurant and all took our seats, the lovely waitress and waiters were coming and going; he started whistling at them too. I could not believe it; this was not how you treated people. He then said, "Ladies, I am whistle and clicking my fingers. Is this offensive in anyone's culture? Raise your hand if so."

I immediately stretched my arm high into the sky. I looked around the room expecting to see forty hands raised in protest of the rudeness and misogyny. I looked around again. Not one other hand had been raised. The disappointment engulfed me. How were we meant to be strong, empowered women when we didn't call out these things for what they were? For far too long, men in positions of power have felt they can get away with behaving in certain ways by dangling the carrot—a job, a crown, money, whatever it may be. This situation was exactly that. One hand in the air was not enough—forty women and one hand in the air.

As we began dinner, I spoke to the other women. "Did you honestly not find it offensive?" I asked.

They all told me they had but didn't want to offend or piss him off. They didn't want to be in the minority and single themselves out. "Well," I said, "it is a good thing not everyone thinks like that."

It had taken one woman to be strong and stand up in some incredibly high-profile events over the past few years. One woman calling out someone's unacceptable behavior encouraged countless numbers of other women to stand up and tell their stories. One woman can start a movement, but it takes all of us to make the changes the world needs. I knew then I would always be that one woman. I saw that the majority were scared, worried, and anxious. They needed that one woman to be the first so they could follow. I would take that on; I would be that one if it stopped abuse of power.

The final stage before the big event was a four-minute interview with the judges—four minutes. You are on the stage in swimwear and sparkly dresses for two hours, but your voice is heard for four minutes. That, in itself, should tell you everything. But, I thought, let's make the most of it and use those four minutes to encourage these people to learn about modern slavery and let them know what they can do to change it.

As we sat waiting to enter the room, I could see the nerves on the ladies faces. They were terrified. I turned to one and asked what was wrong.

She said to me, "Are you not scared of talking to these people? It's terrifying."

What? You have no fear going on that stage in a swimsuit but talking about yourself and your cause is giving you palpitations? No, I had no fear. They should have nerves and excitement about meeting me and hearing my story! Not one part of me was nervous to speak and tell my story.

This is what's different about finding your purpose. When you truly know yourself and know what you're doing is for the greater good, what you have to tell is so important you have to take every chance you can to educate people on it. Then truly nerves can't enter the picture.

My nerves do come as I walk onto a stage; it's like jumping out of a plane. But there's no point to it for me unless it's elevating my purpose.

I entered that room, and out of the six judges, I would say one, possibly two, actually cared about what I had to say. The other four showed no interest, except one old guy telling me I was beautiful. Cheers, mate. But can you please listen to what I'm saying? He wasn't listening. He had zero interest in what I had to say.

As the week drew to a close, I was so excited for the final show—not just for the show but because I knew, once it was done, Nicola, the ladies, and I were going to hit Vegas, grab some steak and red wine, and finally have some real Vegas time! I had decided I would enjoy the night. It wasn't every day you got to perform on the same stage Elvis used to perform on. We'd spent the previous evening in the Elvis suite, which was very cool. The evening began with all the ladies on stage dancing to Barry Manilow, who was resident at this hotel at the time. We had a choreographed number to perform, and then it was the contest.

It was so interesting to see who made the finals. Backstage, along-side all the women who hadn't been selected, as the finalists were on stage, I looked around the room. I really believed that the winner was among these women who had not made the cut. They all had amazing stories, and the work they'd done was out of this world. I remember, in particular, Mrs. Belarus. She had the most amazing career, family, and story, and she was stunning. She was also a powerful woman and was one of the more outspoken among the contestants. Ah, that was it! The judges didn't like the ones who were vocal. They needed people who could be pretty and look good but didn't speak too much. These women were all better than this, and I think many of them had now realized that.

I have since been introduced to many other pageant systems, and I have to say there are ones out there that do have standards. These systems have removed the outdated eye candy side of the awards and are creditable. I will also say that there were people who worked at Mrs. World who were lovely, kind, and looked after you. But a pageant to promote the strong, powerful, successful women of the world it was most definitely not.

I heard many stories after the event from the women. For exam-ple, one woman told me the owner had spoken with her afterward;

she'd spoken about her husband and his job (a very prominent and lucrative job) and had been told she should have mentioned it before, as she would have had a better chance. The judges seem to have been told who to vote for. I was told by one that they knew who the winner would be from the start. It was all very much lacking in integrity.

I ended my time in the pageant world there and then. I had no regrets. I had stayed true to myself. I had made some impacts, met some lovely people, and stepped well out of my comfort zone. That, in itself, will never do a person any harm. Failure only exists when you don't try. The only failure to me is allowing the fear of failure to stop you from even beginning. You cannot fail if you try. And to succeed, you just have to keep wanting it, keep learning, and keep trying. Never give into fear.

CHAPTER TWENTY-NINE

FACING DEMONS

Competing in Mrs. World opened me up to a number of things good and bad. But as I returned home from Las Vegas, I knew I had something to fix. Being aware of a demon is the first step to tackling it. If we don't acknowledge the problem and continue to deny its existence, how can we ever take steps toward fixing it? The whole process had brought something to the surface that was never far from me, and I knew it was time to tackle it. I was chatting with major companies about podcasts and speaking engagements, as I was "inspirational" or "motivational." I was writing daily Instagram posts about anything being possible. However, like many things on the internet, it felt fake. The one thing we rarely see online are people's vulnerabilities and pain. We see the smiles; the filters; the happy families; and the straight-out-of-a-magazine picture-perfect moments. But I promise, that is never ever the case.

My positive mindset and anything-is-possible attitude had brought me to achieve everything I'd ever set my sights on. But—and I would say, in a subconscious, deliberate way—I never set my sights on anything extraordinary or anything that required extreme physical effort (like cycling fourteen thousand miles!). I often blamed my burns. Then other times, it was my workload that was holding me back. But a lot of the truth of the matter was, for the large period of my life, I lacked energy. And most importantly, for the better part of almost twenty years, ever since my first experiment with them at eight years old, I'd taken laxatives on and off and often on a daily basis, sometimes as much as twenty a day.

I decided it was time. This was my one Achilles heel, my secret shame so to speak. And I had to put an end to it in order to move to the next stage of my life. So, in my typical logical way, I googled, "How do I stop taking laxatives?"

All of a sudden, all these sites popped up about eating disorders. I never quite believed I fell into this category. I felt that was a label for super skinny people and I felt I was also able to control my laxative use. The truth was I'd tried many times to stop. But every time I tried, I felt pain, bloating, swelling, and mental trauma. I would get bigger and uncomfortable in my skin. I wouldn't leave the house. The only thing that would bring me relief was to take some more of them. And once they kicked in, I felt better again. I had convinced myself that my issues were more digestive than anything to do with a mental illness. But as I googled, I couldn't get past the sites without reading more about eating disorders.

It was incredibly hard to read. I had always been the type who helped others fix their problems. I was a dream, believe, achieve type of person. I believed in the law of attraction. I motivated people. I surrounded myself with the 1 percent of the 1 percent. I was in control. Did any of this sound like a person with an eating disorder? But then as I read, I saw the same questions on all the sites:

- Have you ever made yourself sick?
- Have you starved yourself to achieve your perfect weight?
- Do you weigh yourself daily?
- Do you thinking being thin will solve your problems?
- Do you feel guilty after eating?
- Do you secretly eat or secretly starve?
- Do you use vomiting or laxatives to remove food once eaten?
- Do thoughts of food and weight consume your life?

I answered yes to every single question. It was beginning to sink in that I may actually have an issue. It was strange, after having worked on a mental health campaign for so long, that I hadn't quite identified it.

As I learned more, I read about how no one knew the cause for eating disorders, but triggers such as loss, grief, sexual assault or abuse, trauma, stress, and PTSD were common. I began to trace every stage of life that my issues had been particularly bad, and it wasn't hard to calculate. I was plagued with insecurities and issues from a young age. As a teenager I was dealing with so much no child should have to deal with. At school, the other girls were slim, cool, and attractive. They watched *Grease*; I was still watching *Annie*. They wore Adidas and Nike I wore hand-me-downs from my sixty-plus-year-old aunt's wardrobe. They kissed boys. I looked after my baby brother and changed burns dressings. So many of them had no responsibility, and I was working two jobs. I desperately wanted to fit in and be more like them, and my weight was the one thing I could control.

I remember the first time I purged by vomiting. I was twelve years old and spending the summer at my grandma's in Inverness. I was working in a café and hanging with older and, as usual, much cooler people than me. Once again, I was back to the need for control. So, I just banned food completely. That day, however, I craved food! I just had to have it. So I went to the shop and bought everything. I came home and methodically prepared a picnic party. I lay all the food out in front of me—cake, biscuits, chocolate, you name it. And I ate it. I ate it all! It felt amazing until I didn't. Guilt hit me, and I needed to get it out straight away. So I vomited. It was very hard the first time, but over the years, I learned what foods were easier to vomit and had less back taste.

You learn how to conceal it, the many tricks of the trade. After Mum died, I hit the ultimate low. The amphetamines given to me by my coworker killed all appetite, so I never had to purge. I just didn't eat. Despite being pregnant, my weight plummeted. Following the termination, I continued to lose weight. When I was arrested at fifteen, I remember sitting on the bench inside the cell; it was a tiny little bench, and you could have fit another me next to me and still had room. I could see I was thin, but I still had it in my head that I wasn't.

Over the years, I achieved, I overachieved, I found new methods of control, and I often got past it. But I carried the demon with me—the laxatives, the diet pills, the mad diets, the low blood pressure, and the dizzy spells. I was always looking for a bathroom. I engaged in binge-purge cycles and starving cycles. All of this had been in and out of my life for twenty years.

One of my particularly low points was trying to get weight-loss pills from a clinic. A person needed to be a specific BMI before the clinic would give the pills out. I was nowhere near the overweight category, so I drank about three liters of water, wore every piece of heavy clothing I had, and loaded my pockets with coins. For such a logical person, all of my good sense had gone out the window.

But with all I knew, now it was time to take control the right way. I had my own children now. I had to be a positive influence for them. They were smart kids and would notice that I never sat at the table with them for dinner. I had to make this change for us all.

This was my Pan-American Highway challenge; it was my Everest, and I was going to defeat it. This was not going to be easy, but the one thing I am good at is solving a problem once it's been identified. I had identified the problem. Now it was time to solve it.

The first step was being aware of the problem. That was done. I admitted I had an eating disorder. The next stage was to talk to Dean. Telling others is usually harder than admitting it to yourself. How will they react? Will they believe you? Will they understand? But you just have to rip the Band-Aid off.

I told Dean I had something to speak to him about. At first, his reaction was, "OK, so you're going to stop taking those tablets now? Does that mean no more diets? I've seen you being sick, but I didn't want to ask."

The biggest thing that confused him, he said, was that I had so much knowledge about food, health, and nutrition. I was his own personal nutritionist. I created meal plans and recipes. I knew food and the industry inside out. He couldn't understand how I could risk my health with all that I knew.

This may take a bit of work, I thought.

The next day, I made the call. I called the doctor and booked an appointment. I told Dean the appointment was booked, and he said, "I'm coming."

This was going to be hard enough without him being there too, but I guess it would save me repeating myself. I spoke to the doctor and told her everything. She was lovely and referred me to the eating disorder clinic. I cried a lot, and when we left, Dean gave me a huge hug and said, "We will do this together."

Today, I stand here as a fully qualified, advanced sports nutritionists. My meal plans and coaching have powered Dean through everything he does. I have forgotten more about weight control and nutrition than most people will ever learn in a lifetime. I have coached people through weight loss, muscle gain, and improving their health. And now, and most importantly, I help people with their own eating disorders.

Having an eating disorder is nothing to be ashamed of. I spoke with a great friend, who is one of the smartest women I know. Once I discussed my issues with her, she also admitted hers to me. Funny thing was, I knew; I had seen the signs in her for many years but never really asked. She said she was the same with me. The one thing we both discussed was, why us? We were both high-powered, successful women. We looked after everyone around us, yet we did this to ourselves.

The truth is, eating disorders can affect anyone and everyone, and I truly mean anyone. I have met people from all walks of life who suffer from this illness—teachers, doctors, fitness instructors, and even Tier 1 Special Forces operators. It doesn't discriminate. It's cruel and relentless. But I'm pretty relentless myself. And I've built knowledge over the last thirty years about every form of extreme dieting. I've learned everything that shouldn't be done and everything that should be done. Now, it's about helping others.

CHAPTER THIRTY

COMING TO AMERICA

Returning home from Vegas, I was ready for the next chapter;
I was powered up to prepare for the Breaking Chains campaign and the launch of Dean's book. With the online abuse
still continuing, I had now deleted much of my social media, as had
Dean. We understood that our mental health was more important. In
hindsight, it may have been a bit drastic to delete accounts altogether,
but at the time, it felt right in order to protect our family.

We were very busy preparing for the Nile challenge and the slavery collaboration. Things were looking good, and I was starting to
understand the impact this campaign could have. Would it be overly
optimistic to say we could end slavery, stop profit from the abuse and
sale of human life? Why not? It had to start somewhere.

I met with a great friend who was a big supporter of the Heads
Together campaign. She ran her late father's trust and had agreed to
fund the setup and development of the collaboration. This was huge.
It would help us reach our goals so much more quickly, and we could
really get moving on this undertaking.

As summer approached, we decided to take our first family holiday since the challenge had finished—some time for just the four of
us with no work, just fun and relaxation. We were incredibly excited
and packed our bags ready to go. The plan was to have seven days to

switch off before getting back to it and full steam ahead for the next charity challenge and the book launch. The car was packed, kids all strapped in, and off to the airport we went.

As we drove to the airport, I received a phone call. It was our manager. She'd received a call from our contacts at the MOD, who had been approached by the newspaper, the same journalist who had written the previous article. I checked my emails as we chatted, and I had received an email from the Office of the Scottish Charity Regulator (OSCR). OSCR had also been the subject of a targeted campaign by the "anonymous" trolls over the previous year and had received hundreds if not thousands of tweets demanding they investigate us. I believe the campaign had gotten so intense OSCR decided to conduct an inquiry. It was very clear in the email it was a general inquiry and not an investigation of any wrongdoing.

The strangest thing was it was a private and confidential email with the letter attached. The letter was also posted but not received until days later. Yet the journalist had all the information that was in my email—before I had even read it.

Years earlier, many members of the British press had come under scrutiny, resulting in the Levison inquiry. This was a dark stain on the history of journalism, revealing that practices such as phone hacking were widely in use. It is believed by many that this practice has continued unchecked. Whether this is true or not, I don't know. What I do know, however, is that no one else had access to my emails, and OSCR confirmed that this letter was only issued to us.

The journalist claimed the "investigation" was regarding £400,000 of funds that were unaccounted for and that we were being investigated for misappropriation of funds. This was a complete fabrication; nothing in the inquiry said anything of the sort. Digging to imagine where the threads of this story had come from, we could only conclude that it was connected to the fact we'd donated the final amount privately, rather than via the press. However, all the paper had to do was check the publicly available accounts of all the charities and ours to confirm the donations had been made. Each one of the charities could also have confirmed this if the journalist had bothered to ask. Along with our accounts, and following targeted harassment and numerous poison pen letters, our main sponsor had conducted an audit of our accounts and the Royal Foundation had audited our accounts twice. Each audit had concluded there were zero issues, our accounts were perfect, and every penny was accounted for.

Obviously, this did not matter to the journalist or the tabloid. The following day produced the headline "Special Forces Friend of Prince Harry Is Probed over Claims of Financial Irregularities after World Record Breaking Bike Ride that raised £500,000 for Charity." It followed with, "The probe comes after Mr. Stott was accused of cheating on the 99-day bike ride."

Yes, accused by *him*, the same journalist who had written the previous story. Once again, despite full evidence contradicting the tabloid's claims and utterly without facts, the paper had fabricated just one more made-up story in order to attach "Prince Harry" to a headline.

I could not believe this was happening again. All I'd ever wanted to do was, firstly, protect Dean and keep him active, focused, and with purpose and, secondly, raise a lot of money to help as many people as we could. Those months upon months of traveling between charities; learning all we could; and finding the motivation to help them—the knowledge of what the money would do for children, veterans, and mothers who were struggling to cope—that was why I did this. I knew I would sacrifice a lot and that we would miss out on work and time with the children, with our family. I knew I would sacrifice my own goals. I signed up for all of that; that was my choice. But this, I never expected this. I'd never thought there were people out there who actively spent their time trying to ruin other people's lives. It just didn't compute with me. I spent my life trying to help people. I could never go out of my way to deliberately hurt anyone. I once had to put a mouse out of its misery after it had been caught in a trap, and it broke me (clearly, it still upsets me). So I just couldn't register their actions. My excitement for our family holiday disappeared as the knowledge sank in that I would have to deal with the fallout of this article over the coming days.

Arriving on holiday, I felt like I, once again, had the weight of the world on my shoulders. The following morning, I was receiving calls from other newspapers, even my local paper, asking for comments. At this point, the PR team advised us just to say we looked forward to the outcome of the inquiry. I know we both wanted to say more, but we couldn't. Our wonderful, relaxing family holiday we had all so been looking forward to turned into me being on and off the phone and answering emails.

The article was riddled with lies and falsehoods, and this time, it was targeting not only Dean's integrity but also our charity work— one of the most important things to me. It was truly devastating. The online attacks increased. We were back under the spotlight, and I struggled to keep my mental health intact. The eating disorder slowly started to creep back in, and I had to work very hard to keep it under control. Dean and I argued regularly, deciding what was the best way to handle things. The pressure was intense.

Even my wonderful assistant had begun to suffer. The previous support team, disguised as anonymous trolls, began posting personal details about her, including her full address and passport details, all over the internet. She was a pretty private person in general, and she began suffering from anxiety and panic attacks. When her hair began to fall out, I knew this couldn't go on. I told her it would be best for her to find another job. But she refused; she wouldn't abandon us. I completely insisted, but she stood strong and told me she was standing by what was right. I will truly always be grateful to her for that; her strength gave me the strength I needed. She did, however, remove herself from social media and privatized everything.

The sponsor who had signed up for financing the trafficking collaboration told us that, until the inquiry was cleared up, their board of directors had decided to put a hold on the donation. OSCR had said it would take twenty-eight days for the report to be returned, so we were not overly concerned; it would just be a short delay. But days turned into weeks, and weeks turned into months. In October 2019, four months after the department had begun the inquiry, we still had no results. And to top it off, Dean's book was due for release.

We had a number of media agencies and promoters lined up for the book tour. However, one by one, they started to drop out. They didn't want to do it while the inquiry was ongoing. I called OSCR every week and got the same update. We were told that our case was not a priority. The department had no major concerns about us, and OSCR had bigger fish to fry. They were a small team, and we just had to be patient. They didn't care that the charity was suffering, and the great momentum we'd built was slowly disappearing. The fight to end slavery never seemed so distant.

As 2019 came to a close, we were no closer to a resolution. I still worked on the campaign, but we were still always being questioned about the newspaper claims. I was no longer working in the properties. Our other businesses had slowed down due to the work we'd been doing with the charities, and I had lost all sense of purpose. All these years of hard work, and I didn't know where I was or where I was going. I thought things couldn't get any worse. I was wrong.

At the end of 2019, I turned thirty-seven—nothing special to most people, but to me it was huge. It had been my scary age. This was the age Mum had passed away. I never knew what came after thirty-seven. I loved life, and being on this planet was a privilege. Even with all the background noise, I still expressed gratitude every day for being alive and healthy, and I just prayed I would always be around for my children. I remember as a child thinking Mum was old, but here I was her age, and I still felt so young. I was now thinking about how she must have felt knowing she was leaving us; that pain must have been horrendous. I spent my birthday in the bar with my dad. We drank, cheered, probably belted out a few tunes, and most definitely cried a lot.

I'd kept in regular contact with Mrs. England, and we'd decided she and her family would come to stay with us for Christmas. This was a great way to end the year—lots of kids together and fun times.

Auntie Molly had not long returned home from hospital after suffering a fall a few months previously. She had fallen over outside and, during her time in hospital, had developed sepsis. She was ninety-five years old and a tiny little thing; many didn't expect her to pull through. But we watched her get strong and stronger, and she was able to get home for Christmas. She was nervous on her feet since the fall however, and sadly, she fell again just after Christmas. She was an incredibly independent woman and hated having people running around after her.

It's such a difficult process to get someone of that age home after falls, but she was determined she was going home. Nevertheless, the weeks past, and she was still struggling to get about. Every day, we would visit and chat, tell stories, and complain about the other residents—loudly. Her hearing never allowed her the privilege of discretion when she was gossiping, and it really would make me chuckle. I watched residents come and go, and I could see her getting sadder.

One Sunday in February 2020, I was sat chatting with her. She seemed distant but completely with it at the same time. She dropped a pill, and as I bent over to get it, I noticed other pills on the floor. I asked if she had been taking all her medication, and she shrugged.

I had taken her in some new clothes, and as I was folding them away, she took my arm and looked at me. She said, "Alana, thank you."

I told her she had nothing at all to thank me for. I, however, knew I had so much to thank her for. Every core principle, every moral and ethical bone in me was installed by her in one way or another. She was the basis for my life and the person who was incredibly important to me.

She once again repeated, "No, I want to thank you. I don't say it to you much, but I appreciate everything you do."

I shrugged it off once again; she was a legend and deserved everything.

Just then, the woman in the bed across from Molly's dropped her phone. She was in with a broken hip, so I went over to help her. As I bent over to pick up the phone, I looked back at Molly. She was sat on the chair chatting to the left of her and nodding her head. She looked round and saw me looking and stopped talking. People may say she had an infection and was seeing things, but I had seen that before. If she was in that state, she wouldn't have stopped chatting. I'd seen her many times trying to include me in chats with the random people she would say were in the room. But this was different; she was fully aware of her surroundings.

I hugged her and gave her a kiss, telling her I would see her soon. I waved goodbye, and that was the last time I saw her alive. She passed away that evening. On February 16, 2020, at ninety-five years old, Mary Duthie, my Auntie Molly, was gone.

Dean still tells me to this day that I have never cried about Molly. This is obviously not true, but I save it for private moments. My family, my mum's family, went ahead with the planning of the funeral. During the service a number of the congregation were surprised I wasn't in the family procession. But I just smiled. I didn't need them to accept me or include me, as much as I didn't need to help them with the words spoken by the minister. They told the story of the Molly they knew, and I held in my heart the Molly I knew—all the things they had missed, her love of travel and her amazing wit and sharp tongue. I didn't need to prove anything; I was at peace, and I had spent her final days with her. I had known so much loss in my life. But this was a goodbye to a wonderful, amazing woman who was ready to go. There was no room for bitterness or regrets. She was free and at peace, and so was I.

The day following the funeral, we all met at Molly's house to help clear it out and to pick up anything Molly wanted us to have. All I really wanted were the photos and a couple of little things that reminded me of her. As I cleaned out the top cabinet, I came across her Parker pen. She'd had this pen forever, and I used to love seeing it. I asked if anyone wanted it, and they looked at me like I was crazy. It's a pen, Alana. No, nobody wants it. I was delighted I would get to keep it. I still loved writing; I had from the time I was a little girl. I'd stopped for many years when life had made me lose my creative mind; I'd even convinced myself I didn't have one. I popped the pen in my bag, picked up the photo albums, and said my final goodbyes.

The following week, I saw an ad for MasterClass, an app with training and courses for anyone involved in writing, screenplays, film, or television. For a while now, I'd been thinking of my long-forgotten dream of writing and making movies, and I slowly doodled poems just like my mother and grandfather before me. I thought about buying the course, but it was expensive—£170 was a lot of money at this time, as we were struggling. We were no longer able to keep Frances working and had to let her go that month. Money was very tight, and no matter how much I wanted to, I said, No, I'll have to put it aside for now.

The very next day, the post arrived. I opened it, expecting the usual bills and junk mail. Those were, indeed, there. And then I opened an envelope that contained a check from Auntie Molly. I cried. I don't even want to look at it. I hated these things. But then I saw the amount—£167 payable to Alana Stott. *Wow,* I thought. *A day after I'd turned down something I wanted for £170, I get this? Is it a coincidence?*

I went to put the check in my pocket to take it to the bank. As I put my hand in my pocket, I felt coins. I pulled them out, and there in the pocket were three golden pound coins. I had in my hand the equivalent of £170. I looked up into the sky and smiled. I was listening. I had forgotten about this stage, when the angels leave earth. But this angel was one of the best, and she was now on the other side. She was guiding me, and I was taking that guidance all the way. That was the very moment I started writing this book, and my 3:00 a.m. thoughts returned to me. But now, instead of falling back to sleep, I was writing them down. My creative juices were flowing, and once I had opened the tap, there was no stopping me.

Very soon after this came March 2020, otherwise known as the beginning of lockdown. For many, this was a crazy time, a terrifying time, a time of anxiousness, and a time that began the pandemic of COVID-19. For Dean and me, the world had stopped. So, finally, after all these years, we did too; and it made us think, a lot. Auntie Molly had always been on at us to slow down and take more time to stop and smell the roses. I don't think it was a coincidence that she passed away weeks before the world was forced to stop.

We thought about our life, how we lived it, our children, and what we wanted for them. We spent more time just being in the moment with the kids and having real time together as a family. That hour a day we were allowed outside was everything to us. We took them to the park, and Mollie and I learned to ride a bike together. Yes, at thirty-seven, I still couldn't ride a bike, despite my double world record-holding husband. But at thirty-seven, I finally did it. That's when I stopped panicking about thirty-seven and knew, it was going to be a good year. I was going to make life good. I had to remember the law of attraction. All the signs were there; I just had to ask for it.

Harry and Meghan had not long moved to California, and we had been hearing how amazing it was there. Following a chat, I turned to Dean and said, "What are we doing?" Since the day we met, Dean and I had said we wanted to live in the United States. Our first few months of dating, we'd talked about it every day. Then life hit us—accidents, injuries, babies, marriage, businesses, charities, and challenges. We'd forgotten our real dreams and desires. The first few weeks of lockdown we'd gone back to talking about it every day.

Dean joked that it was a shame we only realized this now, as there was a pandemic in the world, and the borders were all closed. I looked at Dean. I was more serious than I had ever been. "I don't care what the world is doing. Do you still want the American dream?" I asked.

He looked back at me. Now he was serious. "Yes, I do. But—"

"Stop," I said. "If this is a yes, then I promise I will make this happen. Trust me and leave this to me."

Dean nodded his head, giving me the go-ahead. My mind was made up. We were moving to America.

That night, I started the research. I stayed up all night. I worked out the visas, the entry route, the costs, schooling, everything. This wasn't going to be easy, but nothing worth it ever is.

The next day, we contacted an immigration lawyer and got the process moving. I didn't stop there, though; I went ahead and booked the flights, in the hope the United States would open the borders and allow UK citizens to travel to the United States.

I told my dad, but he didn't believe me. "Alana, we are in a pandemic. The USA is mid election. And the world is screwed," he said doubtfully.

I told him, "Dad, please know it is happening. You need to start preparing."

It took a lot of planning, many sleepless nights, and a lot of work. I said goodbye to the people I needed to and sold much of our possessions. I made sure Dad was safe, and in a house, and that he was looked after and happy. We spoke with the kids and explained it all.

Mollie looked to me for reassurance. And when she saw on my face full excitement and realized I was fully on board, naturally, she was too. "Let's do it!" she said eagerly.

Tommy told me he would only come if Grandad, Auntie Molly,

and Frances were coming with us too. I'd told him Auntie Molly was in heaven up in the sky, and now I was telling him we were going on a plane, which is in the sky. I really hadn't thought it through, had I!

Dad was now slowly coming round to the idea, especially when I gave notice on our lease, handed back our office, and sold off most of our possessions.

I found a property in California that was within my search perimeters. I knew we were going to California, but that was the limits. I searched everywhere and eventually found a fully furnished former model home that was perfect, as we now had no possessions. The area looked good, and the school had a good rating, so that was perfect too.

Our leaving date was fast approaching, and the governments were no further forward with opening the UK-to-US border, but I wouldn't let this stop us. I discovered that we could get into the United States via Mexico if we stayed there for fourteen days before entering the United States. I spoke to Dean and the kids and told them our adventure to America was now going to involve a fourteen-day stay in Mexico.

Dean laughed. "Of course, it is. We are the Stotts, after all!"

The final goodbyes were not what we may have hoped, but they were still pretty special. Lockdown rules were now pretty heavy, so a big going away party was out of the question. In a way, this made it a bit more special. I got to see the people who truly mattered, and we said goodbye our way. I met with my girls, my friends, the ones who had supported me through thick and thin, and they each gave me something very special to take away. It wasn't goodbye; it was see you later.

The final goodbye was to my dad. I knew this would be tough for him, but deep down, he knew that this was the right thing for us and the kids. We stood at the airport. I said goodbye to him, to Aberdeen, and to that giant chapter of my life.

We flew off to Mexico and had a two-week road trip. We had a little beach holiday in Veracruz and a city break in Mexico City. We loved Mexico; the people, the scenery, the food were all amazing. But we were truly excited about getting on that plane to the United States of America.

As we drove from LAX airport, we plugged the address of our new home into the satnav. We drove along the interstate. And then it happened; we passed the sign for "Orange County." Eleven years ago, sitting at home with baby Mollie, no money, no idea what the future held, I'd sat watching a new series, *The Real Housewives of Orange County*. I'd said to myself there and then that, one day, I would live there. I would have a family. I would be happy. And I would live in a typical American detached home in Orange County.

As we drove through the streets of Orange County, passing all the sights I'd previously seen watching the show, I had to catch my breath. Had I done it? Had I manifested this all those years ago? We were here, and I had made it happen.

We turned a corner and pulled through the gates of our new community, soon arriving outside our beautiful new home. It was exactly as I had pictured it—the palm trees, the sun beaming down on the glistening pool. I looked at my family. I took in the expressions on each one of their faces. I saw their delight as they headed toward the pool. And as the golden glow of the Californian sun shone down on Dean, he looked at me and smiled. "You did it, babe."

"Yes, we did. We made it."

In December 2020, eighteen months after the initial inquiry was opened, OSCR issued the conclusion of its findings. There had been no misappropriation of funds, no financial irregularities, and no misconduct. We had been fully vindicated. To this date, none of the tabloids have removed their damaging articles. None of them have apologized for the damage done to my family or to the charity. And none of them have printed a story about our vindication.

Our story was not unique. What had happened was not unusual. I wrote my own article about this, and it was published by the Hacked Off inquiry in the United Kingdom, an organization dedicated to holding the press accountable for what it prints. The number of letters I've received since publishing the article is incredible. Many lives ruined by tabloid lies. I now work with the group to help bring an end to this abuse of power.

I have since opened my own production and publishing company, and I am living my dream of filmmaking and storytelling. So many times along the way, I could have given up. I could have said it was too hard and quit. But nothing worth having is ever easy, and if it's worth having, then it's worth starting on that journey, one step at a time. Remember, the only failure in life is never trying in the first place.

Our journey is far from over, in fact it's only just begun.

Where are you on your journey?

Do you know what you really want?

Are you working toward it with a plan written down?

Are you attracting it and making it happen?

Nothing is impossible. With the right mindset and belief, you can be, do, and have everything you desire. Be determined, believe, stay humble, work hard, give back, and never give up.

One life, make it count.

ACKNOWLEDGEMENTS

A lot of time and thought went into even the decision-making process of writing this book. Sharing the details of your life is never an easy choice to make. My decision was made when I began to speak to other people about their thoughts on the subject. When they asked me what the book was about, I explained it was about my life, the struggles I've faced and how I overcome them, how I live my life, and how I want to help others who have been through similar struggles.

One friend told me, "Alana, that is a story that needs to be shared."

Another shared their own story with me and told me they were able to do that because I spoke first. The one that touched me the most was a dear friend who told me she had begun to seek treatment for a secret trauma she had experienced; hearing me talk previously had encouraged her to open up. I realized there and then—this was not about me but about using my experiences to help all those at the start of their journeys. I am living proof that where you begin does not define where you end; that anything is possible; that you will survive and, of course, thrive.

So, that being said, I firstly dedicate this book to everyone out there going through struggles. You are not alone, and we will walk through it together.

Secondly, to all my friends—when it comes to you guys, its quality not quantity. Thank you for always being by my side and for always making me laugh and giving me an equal mix of grounding and star reaching. I can't possibly name you all, as I am sure you need plausible deniability. But if you have ever gotten lost in Australia with me, been responsible for the child who bust my head open with too many tickles, drank wine with the smallest bachelorettes ever in Italy, drove a car at speed across Central American countries, lived with me in homes with no doors to the bathrooms, made me look amazing in Vegas, or hugged me and then kicked my ass when I felt like giving up—if that is you—then this is for you.

Next, to my family, my brothers, my dad, and to all the angels in heaven—without you guys, I wouldn't be where I am today. Through good times and bad, you will always be family.

Finally, to my team, Dean, Mollie, and Tommy—words can never describe the love I have for you all. You give me the reason every day. I am so incredibly proud of you all, and my heart is full every day watching you grow. Dean, you are an amazing man; anyone lucky enough to have you in their life is truly blessed. Tommy, you are a rock star. I can't wait to watch you grow and become the man who changes the world.

But Mollie, this book is mainly for you. No matter what life throws at you, be kind; show compassion; stay strong; and always remember, *she who dares* wins!

Made in the USA
Las Vegas, NV
13 November 2023

80785355R00152